TREATING THE EATING DISORDER SELF

A COMPREHENSIVE MODEL FOR THE SOCIAL WORK THERAPIST

MARY ANNE COHEN

NASW PRESS

National Association of Social Workers
Washington, DC

Kathryn Conley Wehrmann, PhD, LCSW, *President*
Angelo McClain, PhD, LICSW, *Chief Executive Officer*

Cheryl Y. Bradley, *Publisher*
Rachel Meyers, *Acquisitions Editor*
Julie Gutin, *Project Manager*
Julie Palmer-Hoffman, *Copyeditor*
Sue Harris, *Proofreader*
Lori Holtzinger, Zinger Indexing, *Indexer*

Cover by Jen Huppert
Interior design, composition, and eBook conversion by Xcel Graphic Services
Printed and bound by Sheridan

First impression: April 2020

Library of Congress Cataloging-in-Publication Data

Names: Cohen, Mary Anne, author.
Title: Treating the eating disorder self : a comprehensive model for the social work therapist / Mary Anne Cohen.
Description: Washington, DC : NASW Press, 2020. | Includes bibliographical references and index. | Summary: "This book explores how to achieve multicultural, diversity, and gender competency in the treatment of eating disorders. The author's guiding principle is that every person's eating disorder is as unique as their fingerprint, and the goal of the social work therapist is to collaborate with clients to arrive at an individualized treatment approach that works for them. Treating the eating disorder self contains the latest findings about best practices in the field of eating disorders, including extensive coverage of medications, trauma, and attachment theory. Written with modern challenges in mind, the author also explores the impact of the Internet and social media on the eating disorder client. Readers are guided through the causes of eating disorders, how to conduct an eating disorder assessment, how to formulate an individualized and comprehensive treatment plan for each client, and how to integrate psychodynamic and cognitive–behavioral techniques. Written in a personal and self-reflective tone, and using case studies extensively throughout, the author demonstrates the healing impact of the therapeutic relationship, moving through issues of transference, countertransference, and resistance, and ultimately finding hope"—Provided by publisher.
Identifiers: LCCN 2019055267 (print) | LCCN 2019055268 (ebook) | ISBN 9780871015501 (paperback) | ISBN 9780871015518 (ebook)
Subjects: LCSH: Eating disorders—Treatment. | Eating disorders—Psychological aspects. | Eating disorders—Patients—Rehabilitation. | Eating disorders—Social aspects. | Therapist and patient. | Eating disorders—Case studies.
Classification: LCC RC552.E18 C634 2020 (print) | LCC RC552.E18 (ebook) | DDC 616.85/26—dc23
LC record available at https://lccn.loc.gov/2019055267
LC ebook record available at https://lccn.loc.gov/2019055268

Printed in the United States of America

This book is for Mike Scanlon:
Loving you is livin' in the heart of Saturday night

In loving memory of
Leon and Lily Lifshutz and Aaron Cohen

Contents

Contents

Introduction

For many people, trusting food is safer than trusting people. For many, loving food is safer than loving people. Food never leaves you, never rejects you, never abuses you, never dies. It is the only relationship in which we get to say where, when, and how much. No other relationship complies with our needs so absolutely.

This book will explore the two worlds of the binge eater, bulimic, anorexic, and chronic dieter: the inner world of emotions and the outer world of cultural pressures. These two worlds collide together to cause the development of an eating disorder.

Every person's eating problem is as unique as a fingerprint. This is not a book that advocates a "one size fits all" approach to heal an eating disorder. The goal for the social work therapist is to create an individualized and comprehensive treatment approach in collaboration with our clients that will help them break the chains of emotional eating and body image distress.

Finding the freedom to live a life unburdened by obsessive thoughts about weight and size and compulsive behaviors about food and eating is a tremendous relief, freeing the person to embrace life with more curiosity, zest, passion, imagination, and love. The role of the clinician is to help people sink their teeth into life, not into their relationship with food.

What the Social Work Clinician Needs to Know

Social work clinicians increasingly see clients with eating disorders in their agencies or their practices. Sometimes the client directly seeks help with binge eating, bulimia, anorexia, chronic dieting, or body image struggles. Other times, a client does not discuss their eating problems until therapy is well under way, and the person has come to trust the therapist with the shameful "confession" of having an eating disorder. And sometimes eating disorders are not full blown but "subclinical," and a client has not fully realized the impact of their eating disorder behaviors on their self-esteem.

Given that at least 30 million people of all ages and genders in the United States are diagnosed with an eating disorder at some point in their lives and given that clinical social workers are one of the nation's largest providers of mental health services, we need to be aware of the latest diagnostic and treatment information on eating disorders (National Association of Anorexia Nervosa and Associated Disorders [ANAD], n.d.-a).*

What We Know for Sure: The Perfect Storm

We know the perfect storm for the development of an eating disorder includes six interrelated factors. Identifying and understanding how these factors express themselves uniquely in each client will help us create effective interventions.

1. Media and Social Pressure

Our culture fosters the relentless pursuit of thinness. Through advertising and the media's coverage of fashion models and celebrities, we get the message that young, skinny, and white is the ideal image. Many other cultures also define success according to weight and appearance. A poignant and heartbreaking documentary, *The Illusionists*, notes that women in Africa and Asia spend vast amounts of money on skin-lightening products with sometimes detrimental effects to their health (Rossini, 2015). In America and Western Europe, in contrast, white people are invested in tanning sprays and tanning salons that also can negatively affect their health. Some people even become obsessed with tanning, which has given rise to the label "tanorexia." The media breeds within us perpetual dissatisfaction. If you are a woman of color,

*That eating disorders are usually a shameful and solitary behavior complicates accurately calculating statistics on eating disorders. Men often consider this a female disease, which leads statisticians to conclude that the number of men with eating disorders is probably much higher than the statistics claim. And many sufferers may be on the spectrum of eating disorder behaviors without having a bona fide diagnosis from the fifth edition of the *Diagnostic and Statistical Manual of Mental Disorders* (American Psychiatric Association, 2013).

you want lighter skin. If you are a white woman, you want darker skin. We can never get it right. The poet William Butler Yeats writes,

To be born woman is to know
Although they do not talk of it at school
That we must labor to be beautiful.

And labor and angst we do. And men do, too.

2. Genetic Predisposition

Eating disorders are biological as well as psychological illnesses. To date, scientists have identified more than 400 different genes that are implicated in overweight or obesity, although only a handful appear to be major players. Genes contribute to weight by affecting appetite, satiety, metabolism, food cravings, body-fat distribution, and even the tendency to use eating as a way to cope with stress. Research suggests that for some people, genes account for just 25 percent of their predisposition to be overweight, whereas for others the genetic influence is as high as 70 percent to 80 percent (Harvard Health Publishing, 2019).

A family history of anxiety, depression, or addiction can predispose a person to eating disorders. Therapists in the field of addictions have applied the metaphor of a gun to describe the multifaceted reasons that people turn to drugs and alcohol. This is applicable as well to illustrate the development of eating disorders.

Sandra, a 19-year-old bulimic girl, came from a family where her father was a binge eater and alcoholic. This genetic background predisposed Sandra to an addictive relationship with food, and so the threatening "gun" got created. The gun got loaded when Sandra was 10 and her parents divorced, and her dad remarried and moved to another state. She started turning to overeating for comfort and companionship. But it was only after she left home to go to an out-of-town college that her sense of isolation, anxiety, and depression mounted. This emotional upheaval triggered the gun. Sandra began to binge and purge and developed a full-blown eating disorder.*

An empathic and nurturing relationship with a therapist can help soften and hopefully avert the impact of that bullet.

---

*All case examples in this book are true and based on hundreds of actual persons. All names and identifying details have been changed for confidentiality. These cases are presented in the hope of illustrating the heartbeat of what it means to connect with the inner, authentic core of eating disorder clients.

3. A Traumatic Life Event

Physical or sexual abuse, the early loss of a parent, or other traumatic events set the stage for people developing an eating disorder as a coping mechanism for pain and a way to dissociate from their anguish. When the boundaries of a child are violated through abuse, a child concludes that adults cannot be trusted. The child may learn that trusting food is safer than trusting people.

When Dave was nine, his beloved uncle sexually abused him and directed Dave not to tell anyone because he would not be believed. Dave began having insomnia and turned to overeating to quell his anxiety and confusion. Although he continued to be a good student, his insides were in turmoil, only relieved by the "sweet" comfort of food. This coping mechanism persisted through adulthood until his work in therapy helped him grieve the abuse he suffered and find other ways of soothing himself beyond the food.

4. An Obsessive–Compulsive Personality

People with obsessive–compulsive disorder (OCD) are driven to perfection. OCD is a biological illness, and we see this especially in anorexics, compulsive exercisers, and orthorexics who strive to eat only "clean" food. But no amount of exercise, weight loss, or "clean" eating is ever good enough to quell the anxiety of the person with OCD who can never get it perfect enough. Therapy, and sometimes medication, can help dial down the unrelenting quest for that elusive perfection.

Ashley came from a family devoted to sports where the children were pushed to choose a sport and devote their free time to practicing and staying as lean as possible. Ashley developed bulimia in college when she became drawn to creative writing and wanted to leave her life of sports behind. Her family's disapproval locked her into a cycle of guilt, overeating, undereating, and purging until she came to therapy to sort out this conflict.

5. Weight Loss Diet

Diets have been called the gateway to eating disorders. When people experience emotional distress, they often turn to the "solution" of dieting to make themselves feel better and more in control. Although diets initially can lead to weight loss, they invariably set up cravings and rebellion and then breakout bingeing. The restriction of dieting will eventually lead to overeating, which may lead to purging and then even stricter dieting. A vicious cycle is created, and the person may become trapped in a lifetime struggle of chronic dieting and bingeing.

6. Family Attachment and Communication Problems

The seeds of eating disorders usually begin in childhood. From the very first moment of our lives, a connection exists between eating and deep emotions. The vital emotions of trust, dependency, security, generosity, and the acceptability of our needs begin at birth in the feeding experience with our parents. Love has its origins in the satisfying feeling of being well nourished. Family is where we learn to love and where we learn to be loved.

Learning Self-Care

How we feed ourselves, how we take care of ourselves, and how we tend to our own needs are based on these early patterns of how our parents cared or did not care for us as children. When we are taught that our needs and our hungers are acceptable and approved of, we, in turn, learn to care for our needs and our hungers in loving and self-protective ways. With that secure foundation, we do not need to resort to eating disorders to fortify ourselves. This capacity to soothe one's self may be the key ingredient in preventing an eating disorder.

However, when we are shamed, neglected, or made to feel inadequate, we come to treat ourselves in a similar manner. Eating disorders are attachment disorders. When early attachments fail to nourish, addiction to food or substances becomes an attempt to repair the hurt self—to provide comfort, consolation, and to fill up the vacuum within. Emotional eating takes the edge off anxiety and is easier to control than the uncertainty of human connection.

Developing healthy attachments through friendships, love relationships, support groups, and psychotherapy provides good medicine for the body, heart, and soul.

Who Gets Eating Disorders?

Teenagers and young adults—both girls and boys—are vulnerable to self-consciousness and the messages that appearance is everything, weight is an accurate measure of one's worth, and thinner is always better. Adolescents' vulnerability comes from the fact that they are developing their identity and trying on for size the various cultural definitions of what will make them popular and attractive.*

Adults—both men and women—also struggle with eating issues and body image dissatisfaction, and these may appear at different stages of their life. For adults, eating disorders can emerge in the following ways:

- A person may develop an eating disorder as a teenager and never resolve it, and it persists through their older years.
- An adult may develop an eating disorder as a teenager, succeed in resolving it for a period of time, but relapse as an older adult.
- People begin suffering from an eating disorder or body image dissatisfaction for the first time in adulthood usually when loss or grief rears its head—such as through a divorce, the death of a parent, the loss of a job or financial security, empty nest syndrome (when children move out), or illness.

What's New in the Field of Eating Disorders?

Over the past 10 years, much has remained constant. Food is still the most commonly abused anxiety "pain killer" on the market. It is, after all, the cheapest, most available, socially sanctioned mood-altering drug. Bingeing, purging, starving, and dieting are behaviors clients can easily resort to as self-medication for anxiety, depression, anger, sexual fears, and a myriad of other emotions not related to hunger.

In recent years, significant strides have been made in research and clinical observation that have deepened our knowledge and treatment of eating disorders. In 2013, the fifth edition of the *Diagnostic and Statistical Manual of Mental Disorders* (DSM-5) for the first time included binge-eating disorder as a valid and bona fide diagnosis. This has helped reduce the shame and stigma about seeking help as more people are realizing that their inability to heal their eating disorder is not a matter of moral failing or insufficient willpower but due to a legitimate psychological disorder.

The latest scientific research has increasingly demonstrated the biological complexity of weight gain and weight loss. The simplistic

* The earlier in life that children become self-conscious about their eating and exercise, the more likely they will develop anxiety about their weight and develop restrictive eating habits. Childhood should be a sacred and carefree time to explore the enjoyment of moving one's body for pure pleasure (Smolar, n.d.).

equation is no longer valid that weight is solely dependent on calories consumed and the amount of exercise generated to burn them. Rather, more than 20 variables have been researched regarding weight:

- **Fetal programming:** Babies of mothers who smoked during pregnancy are more likely to become overweight.
- **Sleep deprivation:** Lack of sleep increases production of ghrelin, the hunger hormone, and decreases production of leptin, the satiation hormone.
- **Neurotransmitters:** Deficits in serotonin and other biochemicals underlying depression and anxiety may trigger cravings for high-sugar and high-fat food.
- **Brown fat:** Brown fat burns calories faster than white fat, and researchers are trying to harness this for weight loss.
- **Microbiome:** Differences in our gut's bacterial mix may have an impact on what we weigh.
- **Synthetic chemicals:** Artificial chemicals found in toys, plastics, cookware, and cosmetics have been implicated in weight gain.

This information is reassuring to many of our clients who are always quite ready to blame themselves for their inability to lose weight. Knowing these factors may help clients reduce their self-blame and better appreciate that weight struggles are complicated and multifaceted (Gunnars, 2018; Koenig, 2019; Peeke, 2014).

The burgeoning of social media in the past decade has affected—for better and for worse—the lives of those with eating disorders. I will explore what social workers need to know about this double-edged sword.

Over the course of time, our society has also come to recognize that eating disorders are not just the domain of skinny white girls. In fact, more men, African Americans, Latinos, and gender-fluid clients are now seeking treatment. The good news is that there is more racial and size diversity in advertising, including plus-size models. I will explore what social workers need to know about multicultural and gender competency in eating disorders.

The body positivity movement is helping people focus more on health and self-acceptance than the number on the scale. People are practicing conscious eating by listening and responding to their stomach's hunger, not to an external diet. This is a bold and courageous decision in a world where restriction and anxiety about calories have ruled the day. I will explore what social workers need to know about the vicious cycle of bingeing, purging, and starving that dieting promotes and how to teach our clients to get off this destructive roller coaster.

New medications to alleviate the depression, anxiety, and obsessive-compulsive and bipolar disorders that so often afflict emotional eaters have become more effective; this demonstrates how an eating disorder is as much a biological problem as an emotional one. This book presents information that social workers need to know about the latest medication updates.

From my perspective, the most heartening evolution over the past decade is that psychotherapists are less constricted by a posture of reserved detachment in which the therapist is the all-knowing expert and the patient is the passive recipient of the therapist's wisdom. Psychotherapists have become more interactive and more "real" and not afraid to have a deeply human connection with their patients.

In my own psychotherapy practice and supervision of social work therapists, I encourage the collaborative partnership that clients and therapist create. When tears and laughter abound in sessions, eating disorder clients are enlivened to become more vibrant and genuine with their thoughts, feelings, and imaginations. Our authenticity helps undo the pain of early attachments that led many of our clients to learn that trusting food is safer than trusting people.

In Part 1 of this book, I will explore the inner world of the emotional eater: attachment theory, how to conduct an eating disorder evaluation, how to blend psychotherapy and behavioral–cognitive strategies, the role of medications, and the ingredients needed for a healing therapeutic relationship.

In Part 2, I will discuss how the clinician can develop multicultural, gender, and social media competence. Literacy in these three areas will bring us a deeper understanding of the impact that this outer world has on the eating disorder patient and how to intervene to modify the harmful effects.

This is a book about hope: hope that as we clinicians become more empathically attuned to our clients, they will come to trust the nourishment of human relationships as a way to blossom and heal their inner selves. May our clients come to appreciate and claim their hunger for connection and their hunger for life!

Part 1

The Inner World of the Emotional Eater

1

When Trusting Food Is Safer than Trusting People

In 1982, I coined the term "emotional eating" to describe the varied, conflicted, fluctuating, and frustrating relationship many people have with food. Emotional eating is when you are hungry from the heart, not the stomach. Emotional eating falls on a continuum from mild to moderate to severe. There is a large spectrum of problematic eating behavior: overeating, compulsive overeating, binge eating, bulimia, self-starvation, laxative abuse, orthorexia, compulsive exercise, and chronic dieting.

Sometimes clients oscillate between bingeing and purging, bingeing and starving, or starving and purging. No matter where people fall on the spectrum—from an 80-pound anorexic to a 450-pound binge eater—their relationship with food and their bodies is fueled and driven by emotions too hard to digest: sadness, fear, depression, anxiety, grief, trauma, betrayal, anger, sexual problems, feelings of abandonment, and rejection. I view eating as a relationship that a person has with one's self and, like all relationships, it can be either nurturing or abusive, supportive or neglectful, nourishing or punishing.

We can think of an eating disorder as a "needing" disorder. When clients express shame and guilt about their eating behaviors, I often say, "Your eating problem is your attempt to make yourself feel better. This is a healthy and creative intention and that is a good thing! But let's see if we can expand your ways of taking care of yourself so that eating is not the only game in town to comfort yourself." People recruit overeating, purging, starving, chronic dieting, and weight obsession as a way to "solve" their emotional problems by detouring, distracting, or denying their inner feelings. In the end, of course, they find eating disorders do not provide a lasting solution to resolve inner turmoil.

The overeater, anorexic, and bulimic keep trying to come to terms with the emotional hungers and conflicts in their lives. Many emotional eaters were taught a deprivation model of life in which they were seen as "good children" if they could get by with less than they really needed. And emotional eaters have lost faith in the reliability of human relationships to comfort and solve their anxiety.

The compulsive overeater greedily downs her food, trying to capture a feeling of fullness and abundance, only to be left emotionally hungry and empty in the end.

The anorexic struggles to deprive herself of the need for food and tries to force herself to live in a deprived and hungry state in an attempt to control and conquer her fears of deep neediness. She craves the sensation of emptiness to prove she has conquered her neediness.

The bulimic hungrily embraces an abundance of food only to then deprive herself of keeping it inside by purging. She is unable to feel entitled to hold on to the nourishment because of guilt, shame, or anxiety and feels compelled to give the food back.

Life for all of us is confusing, exuberant, contradictory, hopeful, messy, joyful, hurtful, and disappointing. Sometimes it is hard to be a human! We all search for ways to manage life on a daily basis. For the anorexic, bulimic, and compulsive overeater, the ultimate coping mechanism for all of life's uncertainties and frustrations revolves around attempts to control eating and weight loss.

Emotional eaters simplify their inner confusing feelings by focusing on fat/thin, good/bad, black/white, either/or. Life then becomes structured, organized, and purposeful. Emotional eaters shift their pain from their heart to their stomach and crystallize inner emotional anguish into feeling fat.

Jacqueline's Story

Jacqueline was a pretty woman in her early 30s, with curly blond hair.

"Tell me what brings you here," I asked, "and how I can help."

"I had a baby two years ago," she began, "and then my husband, Peter, was diagnosed with colon cancer. He died when our daughter, Beth, was six months old. And Beth was recently diagnosed with autism."

"And do you have family?" I asked.

"Both my parents are dead. While I was pregnant, my mother died of breast cancer and my father of a heart attack. I'm alone in the world outside of my sister who lives in London."

She stared straight ahead, lost in reverie. The image of her husband's and parents' deaths and Beth's diagnosis was overwhelming.

"Jacqueline," I said, "you've been through so much. How would you like me to help you?"

She straightened up suddenly and said with determination, "I'm here because I'm fat and I need to lose weight!"

The language of pain comes in many dialects. Emotional eating problems and the fear of being fat is one such dialect in which we recruit our bodies to express what we cannot utter in words. Our eating problems become a vehicle to communicate matters of the heart that have no other channel. The language of food and fat is a symbolic one, a way to express our inner emotional battles over feelings of emptiness and fullness, vulnerability and protection, urge and restraint, desire and despair.

When we cannot express the depth of pain we carry inside, we transform our emotional suffering into physical suffering. This obsession with food and fat is often a shorthand way of expressing much deeper layers of yearning and anguish.

Jacqueline had been assaulted by so many massive losses in her life that she could not bear to face her grief, rage, and abandonment. Her wish to lose weight was a safe, clear way to express her pain—a language so many people speak.

The inner world of every emotional eater crystallizes all conflict and problems of life into one single obsession: "I'm fat. I'm ugly. I need to lose weight."

The goal of Jacqueline's therapy—as with all emotional eaters—is to investigate, explore, and discover a richer, nuanced, and more expansive experience of oneself rather than just "my food and body are my only problems in life."

Deprivation and Abundance: Feast or Famine

The themes of abundance and deprivation, feast or famine, are constantly played out in the struggles of the eating disorder patient. And not just with food.

All of us experience life on a continuum through the lens of deprivation or fullness. Julie was a wealthy "trust fund baby" who never had to work. Her financial and material life was filled with abundance, yet inwardly she felt emotionally starved. Raised by alcoholic parents and a parade of changing nannies, Julie developed anorexia in an attempt to train herself to make do with as little as possible. Trying to overcome and deny her inner hunger for love and connection, Julie turned to self-starvation to help her "triumph" over her inner sense of emptiness and neediness. Through her anorexia, she was the one creating her emptiness, which gave her, paradoxically, a feeling of control.

Deprivation also played a role with Elisheva's relationship with food as she oscillated between overeating and undereating. "My parents went through the Holocaust," she explained. "They were literally starving to death, and their desperate fear of hunger never left them even decades later. As a child, whenever we had to take the New York City subway train, my mother would always pack a bag of food. Mama explained, 'You just never know.' I realize this instilled in me an anxiety about whether I had enough or whether it would be taken away. And that also translated to my worries about food, love, money, safety!"

My own life has also been played out with the fear of deprivation. Although I was raised in a loving family, the trauma of my mother's early life affected my relationship with food. She was separated from her mother at age five and grew up in many foster homes, constantly trying to deny her needs for mothering, security, and food. Learning to do without became her self-protection against anxiety and uncertainty. My mother equated having needs with being hurt and vulnerable. She wanted me to grow up to become self-sufficient and strong. She monitored my food, my weight, and even hid food from me. This turned me from a carefree child to a girl who worried whether I would get enough to eat.

At times I now have to laugh at myself at how the theme of worrying about "not getting enough" weaves its way into my life and not just about food. My vacation—I fear it won't be long enough. A massage—I fear it won't be long enough. A warm day—I fear the temperature will drop, and I will get cold at night. The redeeming factor is that I am aware of how my past casts a shadow on my present, and I can now observe it with some detachment and humor. We help our clients by instilling awareness about how deprivation from their past can persist in the present. We encourage them to observe how bingeing, purging, starving, and body hatred are attempts to deal with emotions about fear, not having enough, shame, guilt, and anxiety about their needs.

Attachment Theory

From the very first moment of our lives, a connection exists between eating and deep emotions. The vital emotions of trust, dependency, security, generosity, and the acceptability of our needs begin at birth in the feeding experience with our parents. Anna Freud coined the term "stomach love" to describe the baby's early bond to the parents who feed him. Love has its origins in the satisfying feeling of being well nourished. Family is where we learn to love and where we learn how to be loved. These early relationships create a pattern of how we care for ourselves and how we expect others will care for us.

When we are born, we latch onto our parents and then, in time, through our ongoing relationship with them, we begin to emotionally hatch and develop, continuing to evolve into our unique selves throughout the rest of our lives.

Early childhood experiences clearly affect and set the stage for our future emotional growth. Most laypeople believe that eating disorders just emerge out of the blue in someone's life. Nikki turns age 15 and becomes anorexic. Richard becomes bulimic at 17. Heather starts compulsive bingeing and laxative abuse when she's 23. The truth is the seeds of anorexia, bulimia, or compulsive overeating are planted long before the actual symptoms take root. Recovered bulimic Callie Bowld (2018) explains,

> An eating disorder starts with a tiny seed. Packed lightly just beneath the soil . . . it just sits dormant. Then there is some culmination of stressors, changes in your life that find you stretched thin, overly stressed and worried . . . until you start to build a coping mechanism in your mind. And that mechanism may be food—either a perverse deprivation or an over-indulgence. (p. 42)

Attachment theory helps us understand how early life experiences contribute to a person's affliction with emotional eating disorders.* John Bowlby (1988), the British psychiatrist and "father" of attachment theory, believed that attachment represents a lasting psychological connectedness that affects human beings from the cradle to the grave. The love style between parent and child will color all our close relationships—from friendships to romantic relationships as adults. These patterns, learned in childhood, persist throughout our life.

Most important, secure and loving bonds in our early childhood shape even our developing relationship with our own selves. Picture the intricate process of a parent teaching us to tie our shoes. With patience and repetition, our parent demonstrates over and over again how to crisscross the laces, make loops, pull the loop through, and form a bow. And then one day, by dint of much trial and error and loving guidance, voilà! We learn how to tie our shoes. Discovering how to respond to our own emotions is a similar learning process. With patience and repetition, our parents work to understand our needs and distress, identify what may make us feel better, and then try to comfort us. By dint of this repetition—like learning to tie our shoes—we internalize the lessons of

*Authors who have pioneered attachment theory include John Bowlby (1988), Mary D. Salter Ainsworth, Mary C. Blehar, Everett Waters, and Sally N. Wall (1978), and Philip Flores (2004).

how to identify our own needs and comfort ourselves. We absorb our parents' compassionate and empathic relating and make it our own. Over time, by internalizing their caring, we eventually learn to become independent and provide emotional nourishment to our very own self. With that secure foundation, we do not need to resort to eating disorders to fortify ourselves.

As little children, we also learn ways to calm ourselves without our parent's presence: sucking our thumb, cuddling our teddy bear, having a special security "blankie"—all help bridge the gap between needing our mothers to comfort us and doing it by ourselves. As our hatching continues, we become more separate and independent from mother. Learning to comfort and console one's self deepens one's ability for self-care without hurtful eating behaviors.

When Early Attachments Fail to Nourish

Eating disorders are considered attachment disorders. People with eating disorders have higher levels of attachment insecurity, which causes them difficulty in managing their feelings and emotions. When early attachments fail to nourish, addiction to food or substances becomes an attempt to repair the hurt self—to offer comfort and consolation and to fill up the vacuum within. Substances like food "take the edge off" and are easier to control than the uncertainty of human connection.

Those who have not experienced ongoing caring relationships will search outside themselves for an alternative form of safe haven. Food—starving, bingeing, purging, obsessive dieting—can become such a consuming passion. But searching for a refuge in the pseudo-security of emotional eating ultimately fails because comfort, intimacy, and love cannot be found through food.

A news story profiled a woman with 1,200 pairs of shoes worth $1 million. She acknowledged she could not tame her compulsion to buy shoes, which she felt was due to "a lack of emotion and love" in her life. Evidently, she could not extract sufficient nourishment and satisfaction from human relationships, so she became hostage to accumulating shoes instead. She searched for something "out there" to substitute for what was missing "in here." She became attached to a sole mate, not a soul mate.

Attachment theory helps us better understand the lure of emotional eating. If a person has not developed sufficient internal resources to draw on in times of stress, then bingeing, purging, and starving will seem like a helpful method to alleviate distress. And because insecure attachments early in life leave people wounded and mistrustful, they are not likely to turn to others for emotional support. This explains, in part, the prevalence of relapse in eating disorders. If the inner core self has not been strengthened through therapy, support groups, or a spiritual program, the person eventually falls back to emotional eating.

What Are the Different Attachment Styles?

The bonding between child and parent is a complex dance of emotions. The attachment style that develops ranges on a continuum from secure to insecure, with shades and nuances in between. The need for loving maternal attachment for a baby to feel vitalized was brought home to me in an unexpected way one summer on a backcountry road in Virginia. A young calf stood alone in a large green field, dejected and morose, its head down. From far on the other side of the pasture, his mother sauntered over and started to vigorously lick him up and down. The calf became animated and began to frolic and jump around, happy and enlivened by his mother's love.

Secure Attachment

Secure babies have parents who are tuned in to their children's unspoken needs and allow their children freedom to be curious and to safely explore their surroundings. When the time is right, they strive to teach their children to put feelings into words. Secure parents respond consistently and provide a foundation for their children to develop intimacy and autonomy, roots and wings.

Studies show that securely attached children learn to be empathic, beginning in childhood. As their parents have been attentive to them, so they learn to be attentive both to others and to their own selves. Ravenna, age 18 months, watches her mother stretched out on the rug with an ice pack under her. Jenny is in pain from having sprained her back. Ravenna watches when her mother finally struggles to get off the floor and stand up. The baby extends her tiny hand to her mother, offering to help her up from the floor. After Jenny scrambles to get up, Ravenna reaches down for the ice pack and hands it to her mother to comfort her. Her seeds of empathy and connection are developing.

Nourished by their intimate relationships with others, secure people have less need for emotional eating. For the most part, they can cope with difficult feelings, find ways to self-soothe, tolerate frustration, and ask for help. Adults with a secure attachment history find it easy to make an alliance with the therapist based on trust. They have already experienced that in their early relationships.

Insecure Attachments

Insecure attachments between parents and children are caused by emotional ruptures and separations. Pauline was hospitalized for an extended time with polio as a young child, frightened and separated from her family. Her keenest memory of loss from that time was that her dolls were taken away from her in the hospital. Her physical and emotional scars lasted a lifetime, contributing to depression and anorexia. Jack witnessed his mother's repeated drug overdoses throughout his childhood, resulting in his severe anxiety and bulimia.

Clinicians and researchers have identified a strong connection between these early insecure patterns of relationships and the later development of addictions. Because those with insecure attachments have so many unmet developmental needs, they feel hungry and insatiable for love and attention but, at the same time, shamed by their neediness. They believe their hunger makes them bad. Pauline and Jack experienced insecurity in their early lives, eventually abusing food as their go-to coping mechanism for depression and anxiety.

All insecurely attached children are vulnerable to eating behaviors or substance abuse because they find people too threatening or inconsistent. Relying on people all too often has led to pain and hurt. Stephanie, a binge eater, described the death of her mother when she was 10: "I have a mother-sized hole in my heart," she cried.

Researchers have investigated the variations of insecure attachments in children, and these early experiences can set the patterns for the adult's relationship to food, love, money, sex, and the ability to respond well to one's own needs:

- **Anxious-Ambivalent Attachment:** When parents respond inconsistently to their child's needs, the child will develop a mixed reaction, becoming clingy and dependent but then alternately rejecting the overtures of the parent. The child fails to develop a sense of security from the caretaker and is not easily soothed when distressed. People with this attachment style may develop bulimia in which they move toward food for comfort but then, feeling dismayed at "giving in" to their neediness, they purge and get rid of it.
- **Anxious-Avoidant Attachment:** Anxious-avoidant children do not turn to their parent when distressed. They experience the parent as rejecting and withdrawing support when they need help. These children learn that relying on others leads to disappointment and frustration. They may develop anorexia—the

ultimate declaration of independence: "I don't need food and I don't need anyone."

- **Disorganized Attachment:** When parents suffer significant depression or other mental illness or the child is subjected to physical or sexual abuse, the attachment between caregiver and child suffers extreme rupture. The child endures emotional abandonment when in need of comfort and has no way to cope with anxiety. Severe eating disorders and substance abuse can be the result of this impaired attachment style.

Children who are neglected or abused perpetuate that pattern by neglecting or abusing themselves and their bodies. They treat themselves as they were treated. After all, that treatment is all they know, and it is familiar (the root of "familiar" is "family").

Acting out with food is an attempt to compensate for unmet emotional nourishment. But, as Dr. Louis Cozolino (2014) has stated, "When you depend on a substitute for love, you can never get enough" (p. 126).

Along the Attachment Continuum

Although researchers claim that secure and insecure approaches are two distinct attachment styles, I observe that most people fall on a continuum between secure and insecure. Perhaps we all have aspects within us of security and insecurity, because parents rarely raise us with only one way of relating.

Many people describe enjoying a secure childhood, but when they hit adolescence, their parents became anxious, controlling, critical, and, at times, abusive. The emerging independence and sexuality of their child may threaten some parents. "I used to have a fun relationship with my father, until I started developing as a young teenager," said Nina, a recovering bulimic woman. "Then he became a totally different person—monitoring me and being paranoid about who I went out with. He slapped me across the face once when he thought my sweater was too tight." Parents who received abusive treatment during their own teenage years often repeat the same abusive pattern with their own teenagers.

Others describe having parents who were overwhelmed themselves and who paid little attention to them, ignoring their needs. But as time went by, when they grew up and moved out, these parents had more emotional resources and sometimes became more devoted and loving, especially when grandchildren came along. "My parents are the greatest grandparents in the world to my kids," described Mitchell, a recovering compulsive overeater. "But growing up, my brother and I basically had to raise ourselves. Our parents worked all the time and fought all the time. There was nothing left over for us."

Conversely, sometimes a traumatic event destabilizes even a secure family, and devoted parents get ground down by the suffering. "We were a great, fun-loving family until my sister died in a car accident," Jason related. "Then we all closed down from the pain, everyone in their own world. We all developed eating disorders or pill problems and never came out of our shared family depression. I'm trying to find my way back to my life and to my parents through my own personal therapy."

In other instances, when parents go through their own psychotherapy, they may grow and evolve into more loving parents and become more sensitive and attentive. They learn to better empathize with their child as their therapist empathizes with them. "Through my therapist's compassionate listening to me, I have learned to become a better mother," explained Loretta. "She really wanted to understand everything about why I hate my body and why I abuse laxatives rather than lecturing me not to do it, like everyone else does. From that experience, I learned to be more curious and more tolerant in wanting to understand my son, rather than just yelling at him all the time to behave."

Although the attachment style we are originally raised with may lay the foundation for our future relationships, people are also very adaptable and can change over time. A great deal of time elapses between infancy and adulthood, so intervening experiences can play a large role in adult attachment styles. Those who grew up with ambivalent or anxious bonding can become securely attached as adults with nurturing and loving relationships. Healthy attachments provide good medicine for the body, heart, and soul.

Attachment Styles: Food and Other Relationships

The eating styles of the compulsive overeater, bulimic, and anorexic extend beyond their relationship with food and are reflected in other aspects of their lives as well. Internal questions—What do I deserve? What am I worth? What am I entitled to have? How much am I allowed to keep? How greedy am I? What will other people think?—play out in realms other than food.

When we clinicians detect these patterns, it deepens our understanding of the attachment style of the client. We realize it is not just the food issues that need healing but tensions around taking, giving, keeping, deserving, and rejection. This provides fertile understanding and ground to enter into our patients' conflicts in a deeper, more fruitful way. It is not just about their eating.

Janet. Janet was a bulimic retired woman. Not only did she binge and purge on food, she binged and purged on clothes. Janet would go clothes shopping, take home everything she loved from the department store, try the clothes on, and return them by the weekend. Just like she "gave back" her food, so she gave back her binge of clothes. Growing up in her family, her father gambled, and the family was either rich or poor at any given moment. Her father had money and then "gave it back" by gambling. Janet unknowingly had incorporated the same dynamic.

Sandy L. Sandy L. was a secretive binge eater. She was told by her mother that when her mother was pregnant with her, Sandy leached too much calcium from her, causing her mother to lose teeth. Anxiety about taking too much became a theme in Sandy's life. Fearful of being greedy, she tried to restrict her hunger but would have breakout binge episodes. The following interaction with me illuminated her attempt to undo her "greed." Sandy came to session asking for a Band-Aid because she had cut her finger. After the following week's session, I discovered she had left me a full box of Band-Aids in the bathroom to replace the single one I had given her. Worried that she had taken more than her share, she overcompensated for "leaching" from me.

Mark. Mark grew up in an impoverished family with food insecurity. He alternated between bingeing and starving, and this style paralleled his relationships with others as well. He would hire multiple business coaches and then fire them for being "lame." He pursued many women and then dropped them for not being good enough. And he came to therapy with me, dropped out, came back, dropped out. This gave me the opportunity to point out how he was repeating his early life: When he had something nourishing, he couldn't trust it to stay. Whether it was a coach, a girlfriend, or a therapist, he had to get rid of them before he was abandoned, just like food had abandoned him chronically in his childhood.

Gregory. Gregory, a wealthy businessman, was always hungry—hungry for attention, approval, more money, and the need to binge on endless food. He could never get enough in any realm of life. He reported having gone to a prostitute over the weekend, and when he discovered she had an orgasm during their sexual encounter, he asked her for a discount. Because he had given her pleasure, he felt he shouldn't have to pay as much.

I felt compelled to ask, "At the beginning of today's session, you told me a story that made me laugh heartily. Do you want to ask me for a discount too because I was enjoying myself?" Gregory was taken aback by my brazen question, but it opened our conversation to a deeper level about his feeling chronically deprived and how he tried to make it up to himself especially through food and money.

"Everybody's got a hungry heart," as the song goes, and Gregory was open to exploring how his early life had left him with unfulfilled cravings. His food problem was part of a larger attachment deficiency that caused him to experience everything as feast or famine.

How Can We Repair a Damaged Attachment?

Eating disorders are ailments of isolation, secrecy, and shame. The eating disordered person is "locked in the past, paralyzed in the present, and fearful of the future" (Boskind-White & White, 1991, p. 74). The healing work is to unlock the past, revitalize the present, and create hope for the future.

"The vulnerable individual's attachment to chemicals [and eating disorders] serves both as an obstacle and as a substitute for interpersonal relationships" (Flores, 2004, p. 4). These behaviors are misguided attempts at self-repair for a person's inner sense of boredom, emptiness, and loneliness.

Psychotherapy can help a person move beyond insecure attachment patterns of the past toward restoring one's capacity for intimacy and self-care. As we will see, the relationship with the therapist can provide the nurturing and resilience building that our clients need. Isolation with pastry needs to be replaced by intimacy with people.

Attachment-oriented therapy includes empathic listening and emotional attunement to the patient's needs as the primary way to connect and repair damaged attachment.

"When I find myself bingeing after work, you suggested I ask myself, 'What do I want that bag of candy to do for me?' So yesterday I asked myself how I wanted the candy to help me. And my inner self said, 'Back off! It's none of your business!' Boy, I really failed at that," exclaims Olivia with frustration.

"Why are you frustrated? You asked yourself the question we discussed. Good for you!"

"Yeah, but the door was slammed in my face."

"Well," I remind her, "we only wanted you to ask the question. We didn't say there had to be an immediate answer!"

Unlike Olivia's parents, who always wanted quick and easy results, I applauded her efforts. We don't need the answer right now; we just want her to ask herself the question. She sees I am not frustrated with her, and she accepts with some pleasure that she did well simply by her spirit of self-inquiry. This may seem like just a tiny step forward, but it paves the way for Olivia to begin a conversation with her inner self. This helps repair the harsh inner parental voice that mocks her when she tries something and does not immediately succeed.

Even small steps forward by our clients deserve our appreciation, like creating a new tapestry one stitch at a time.

2

Conducting an Eating Disorder Assessment: Who, What, When, Where, Why, How?

Even before clients arrive for their first session, they are often uneasy about revealing their embarrassing eating behaviors. Social work clinicians will quickly observe and appreciate how fearful clients are for several reasons:

- Clients may project onto us the negative judgment of a family member or their own critical self-judgment. Maybe we will think they are too fat and should just exert more willpower and self-control. Maybe we will humiliate them like their parents did. Maybe we will chalk up their preoccupations to mere vanity.
- Bingeing, purging, or starving has comforted them, helped them soothe "undigested" and difficult emotions, and been a good friend in time of need. They are ambivalent about giving up the solace that eating or not eating has provided.
- Clients fear the therapist is going to take away their dieting, restricting, purging, or anorexic behaviors and therefore wind up making them fat. This worry can make us seem like the enemy at times.
- Shame and guilt also arise when clients begin opening up about their secrets and the extreme lengths they have gone to with their eating behaviors. Eating disorders are called "diseases of isolation," so to invite a therapist to meet the skeletons in one's closet is fearful and takes courage.*

*Gabriel Garcia Marquez, the Colombian Nobel Laureate, was quoted as saying, "All human beings have three lives: public, private, and secret." When our clients entrust us with their secret selves, the healing work deepens.

- The client may unconsciously fear that if they lose the numbing protection of their eating disorder, they will endure a resurgence of the very anxieties and depression that led them to recruit the anesthesia of food in the first place.

Some patients are more candid about sharing their struggles and are ready to "spill their guts." Let's listen to what patients tell me.

- **Amanda:** "I throw up in my bedroom into plastic bags which I store in my closet, so my parents don't catch me. In the morning I throw them out on the way to school."
- **Keisha:** "I have this trick at the dining room table. I cough into a napkin to cover up that I'm secretly not swallowing my food. That way no one knows I'm not really eating my dinner."
- **Paul:** "I'm ashamed to say how much I shoplift food. I'm like a drug addict stealing my stash. I have my favorite grocery stores and my knapsack."
- **Sharon:** "My mother and I have this ritual we enjoy together because we're always on diets. We chew chocolate chip cookies and then spit them out so as not to absorb the calories. I know this is weird, and I really do want to get clean with my food."
- **Gina:** "I really believe my middle name should be Shame 'n' Blame. What's wrong with me that I can't control my eating like a normal person?"

Clinicians need to communicate to all their clients like those above that eating disorders are biological and psychological illnesses and not moral failings. Nobody asks to get an eating disorder. Channeling the spirit of Walt Whitman, we say, "Be curious, not judgmental." And we help clients move from their eating cure to the talking cure with us.

We also want to communicate our compassion and understanding that eating problems do not make you a bad person but are coping mechanisms for anxiety, depression, fear, and anger. You cannot give up a coping mechanism that has served you until you replace it with something equally nurturing and less harmful.

Interview Questions

To fashion an individualized and comprehensive treatment plan, begin by referring to the DSM-5 to help ground your interview with the latest diagnostic descriptions of eating disorders (see Appendix A for a list of

DSM-5 eating disorder diagnoses). From there, the social work therapist will want to complete a thorough assessment with each client.*

The interview questions are a guideline for therapists to gather information about the depth and breadth of the person's struggle. Obviously, no one single session can cram in all this information without becoming an inquisition. We weave these questions into an extended consultation over several sessions.

The nine topics of inquiry are

1. Your present situation
2. Weight history
3. Diet history
4. Binge history
5. Purge history
6. Family history
7. Rounding out the picture
8. Concluding the first interview
9. Special treatment issues

To each of these topics, I have added my interpretation and commentary. In many instances, I have also included client responses, which reveal a wide range of emotions—fear, anxiety, mistrust, and hope.

1. Your Present Situation

"Tell me what brings you here and how I can help."

> Samuel: "I want to lose weight to win a bet with my mother-in-law. She said I couldn't do it."

Is Samuel motivated to change from some outside family pressure, or is he genuinely motivated to change from the inside? My hunch is he would have gone to a diet organization if his only motivation was to win this bet. I will try to engage him by asking whether he himself ever felt he wanted to get his eating under control before his mother-in-law's challenge.

> Deidre: "My husband and I are trying to get pregnant. I've been bulimic since age 18, but I really want to get it together for my baby."

*Thanks to Craig Johnson (1985) for the formulation of some of these questions in *The Handbook of Psychotherapy of Anorexia and Bulimia*.

Like Samuel, Deirdre is also putting her wish to get better on an external object (her unborn baby), but her wish to be a healthy mother has taken root within her. I feel the sincerity behind Deirdre's explanation and her desire to move forward.

"How did you feel about coming for this consultation?"

> Lily: "My mother told me to ask you if I'm going to get fat if I get my anorexia under control and start eating again."

Lily presents her mother's anxiety. Why is her mother invested in her daughter being so skinny? Is Lily putting her own anxiety in her mother's words? Or do both mother and daughter share a fear of food and weight? I don't know, so I ask, "What would be your worst fear if you weren't anorexic anymore?" I am trying to refocus Lily on her own thoughts and feelings.

"Why are you coming for help now? What events in your life are leading you to seek help at this time?"

> John: "My wife died three years ago, and I've gained 80 pounds. I realize I'm getting ready to move on with my life and want to start focusing on my overeating."

The death of a loved one, an illness, a move, or a separation can make a person more vulnerable and susceptible to an eating problem or can worsen an already existing struggle with food.

I am intrigued by John's words of "getting ready to move on with his life." He is telling me that he is not yet fully ready but in the process of getting there. I am reminded of Prochaska's stages of psychological change: precontemplation, contemplation, preparation, action, and maintenance. I would say that John is somewhere between contemplation and preparation. These stages of change help us appreciate that the decision to get better is not a straight line but a process that may ebb and flow (Prochaska, Norcross, & DiClemente, 1994).

"What is a typical day like for you with food?"

> Noah: "I'm good during the day. I don't really eat much, but when I come home from work all hell breaks out. I stuff down everything in the refrigerator and then wind up taking laxatives."

Noah reveals the most common eating pattern that the majority of people describe: undereating during the day and overcompensating at night. We will explore why he deprives himself during the day and why he resorts to laxatives after bingeing at night and eventually help him moderate his food intake during the day.

2. Weight History

"What is your current weight? What do you want to weigh?"

Asking people what they want to weigh reveals whether they have a realistic view of their bodies. When an emaciated woman tells me she needs to lose 20 pounds, I know she is struggling with a body image distortion, which we will need to address in therapy.

> **"What is the highest weight you have been as an adult? What was the lowest?"**
>
> Caryn: "I realize in order to stop bingeing, I will have to eat meals on a more consistent basis. I hate the idea that this may lead to my gaining weight. But I'm hoping eating more, rather than restricting, will break my yo-yo dieting cycle."

Though she did not answer the question directly, I want to learn how Caryn reached her lowest weight and whether it was stressful. This will help me get a realistic idea of her "natural weight." We want to help all our patients achieve their natural weight—the weight range where they are not restricting, bingeing, or purging. Often, someone's natural weight will be higher than they hoped. A period of disappointment and sadness may emerge as they struggle for self-acceptance.

> Dina: "I no longer weigh 85 pounds and, to be honest, I miss my anorexia. Although I feel better and have more energy, I wish I didn't have to eat so much."

Dina had a difficult time with self-acceptance. She continues to speak of "my anorexia," revealing how much her illness is still a strong part of her identity and difficult to give up. Her slow process of self-acceptance feels similar to the grief stages described by Kubler-Ross (1969): denial, bargaining, anger, depression, acceptance.

"What was your highest and lowest weight as a teenager?"

For many people, eating problems began during adolescence. I try to determine what might have been the trigger, such as a fear of one's developing sexuality or fears about leaving home.

"Did you have eating problems as a child?"

If a person struggled with rapid weight gain or weight loss as a child, it may indicate the problem has its roots in trauma such as sexual or physical abuse. This is quite distinct from the widow, for example, who only developed a binge problem while grieving her husband's death.

"Were you ever teased about your weight? By whom?"

> Leila: "My brothers constantly teased me about my weight, calling me Fat Fanny and Thunder Thighs. My father thought this was funny and joined in laughing. I became self-conscious about every morsel of food I put in my mouth. And I still am."

Getting weighed at school in front of the whole class or worrying about fitting into a gym suit are often painful memories for people. If a family member teased you about your weight, that will add to your pain and self-consciousness.

"Does your occupation require a certain weight?"

Patients who are athletes, dancers, actresses, models, television personalities, flight attendants, or fitness instructors often come to therapy because their jobs expect a certain level of fitness, size, and appearance. Patients in the public eye often feel constant pressure to lose weight, and this causes an unnatural anxiety and obsession with food and eating.

Ballet dancer Dawn Smith-Theodore (2018) describes how her eating disorder and perfectionism hijacked her love of dance. Her experience can apply to all clients involved with athletics:

> I grew up in front of a mirror and as a dancer it was my best friend and my worst enemy. When I began comparing myself to others and listening to the drill sergeant in my head that never stopped proclaiming that I needed to lose weight, then the mirror became my enemy. The less I ate, the louder my inner drill sergeant barked negative criticism. Soon, the drive to be perfect took over my thoughts. I spent hours planning my caloric intake. Eventually developed

anorexia nervosa where I did not see myself as thin no matter how much weight I lost. I was chasing the rainbow of perfection, an illusion. While perfectionism is part of the temperament of some people, dance further cultivates it. There is a dangerous line where perfectionism becomes problematic, and the dancer begins to lose perspective. The love they had for dance eventually starts to fade away. Thoughts become very black-and-white: If you aren't perfect, you're a failure. Do not let the allure of being perfect steal your love of dance. (Smith-Theodore, 2018, paras. 2–13)

3. Diet History

"Have you ever been on a diet?"

Monica: "What a funny question. I don't know any woman who hasn't been on a million diets. I've tried them all—grapefruit, pills, intermittent fasting. I lost weight and then gained it all back and then some."

Dieting is the norm in our society, especially for women. In my life, I have only met *four* women who never dieted.

"How did your dieting begin? What role did your parents play in your dieting?"

Cindy: "My mother forced me to diet when I was 10 and made me have these awful weekly weigh-ins. My thinner sister, Candy, was given free reign of the kitchen. I felt constantly enraged and started sneaking food."

Cindy's ongoing binge eating served, in part, as a silent opposition and rebellion to her mother's intrusiveness and control. When parents try to manipulate a child's eating, as in Cindy's case, the child loses the inner instinct of hunger and fullness.

"Do you have a way you prefer to diet? Do you fast, skip meals, take diet pills, laxatives, or avoid certain foods?"

The more restrictive a dieting method, the harder it will be to make peace with emotional eating; the more moderate the method, the easier it will be to restore natural eating.

4. Binge History

> **"Have you ever binged? When did it start?"**
>
> Danny: "When I went to an out-of-town college, I really missed my family. All the guys were into sports, and I put myself on a diet to slim down so I could join a team. I cut out bagels and bread. But, then, I started bingeing on them nonstop."

Bingeing often occurs when two factors are present at the same time: A person has suffered an emotional loss in their life and, simultaneously, he or she begins a weight loss diet. Clinicians will need to be on the lookout for that particular pattern.

> **"When are you most likely to binge?"**

We need to explore the emotional states most likely to trigger each client: loneliness, boredom, anger, depression, and sexual tension. Awareness becomes the first step in creating a treatment plan.

> **"On what foods are you most likely to binge?"**

Are there certain foods that provoke a binge, such as cake, ice cream, chips, bread? Is the client restricting those foods, which then leads to a backlash binge? How can we help her make peace with those "forbidden" foods, which will then remove their allure?

> **"Where are you most likely to binge—at home, work, school, in your car?"**
>
> Paige: "At home, after my husband goes to sleep. I'm very controlled during the day, but then I feel a certain freedom to give in to myself."

Very often, the location or timing of the binge has a specific meaning for the person. One woman I worked with binged only at her mother's house even though she was married with a family of her own. Another only threw up before going out on a date. Investigating the meaning of these triggering events can help break the cycle.

> **"What is the longest you have gone without a binge? What helped?"**

I want to know what support systems made it easier for the person not to overeat or starve or purge. What circumstances seemed to help allay the eating problem: when they were away from home or at home? Involved with friends and being sociable? Or following a less restrictive eating pattern?

"Do you binge around your menstrual period?"

If this is the case, I suggest that women increase their intake of complex carbohydrates and reduce protein at the evening meal. This raises the body's endorphin level and lessens cravings. There are also medications that help with premenstrual dysphoria that can reduce cravings.

5. Purge History

"Do you make yourself vomit? Since when? How often?"

Frequent vomiting can cause rupture of the esophagus, electrolyte imbalance, and heart failure. Medical consultation is needed for all bulimic patients.

"Do you take laxatives or diuretics? Since when? How often?"

> Scott: "When I'm being 'good,' I completely give up carbs and take muscle-building supplements. Then I get carried away and start doing laxatives to make weight loss go faster. Then I get into a bad place and start bingeing."

Laxative and diuretic misuse can cause dehydration, leading to malfunction of the nerves and muscles as well as kidney damage and, in extreme cases, death. Medical consultation is needed for all laxative- and diuretic-abusing patients.

"How often can you eat normally without purging?"

I want to understand whether the client considers all foods dangerous or only certain foods that then must be purged. The wider the range of foods that are forbidden, the more severe the eating problem will be.

"How often do you exercise? How compelled do you feel to exercise? Do you use it as a way of undoing a binge?"

Many people are involved in exercise bulimia where their anxiety about calories and weight leads to an addictive relationship with exercise.

> **"How often do you drink? Do you use drugs? Do you feel you ever had an alcohol or drug problem? What about spending too much? Shoplifting?"**
>
> Pamela: "I was a heroin user and an alcoholic. When I got those under control, I realized that my eating addiction has always been my first and foremost problem!"

Since many eating disordered people also have co-occurring disorders, my question delves into a history of substance abuse or other addictive behavior. Many of my patients are cross-addicted with a history of alcoholism and drug abuse. With some newfound clarity, they often come for help when they recognize how fraught their relationship with food has been.

6. Family History

> **"Does anyone in your family suffer from alcoholism, drug abuse, eating problems, anxiety, or depression?"**
>
> Yolanda: "All during my growing up years, Dad was drinking out of control, Mom would get depressed and crawl into her bed, and I would gorge on chips and muffins. There was never enough food that could quell my fears about my parents' problems or my loneliness. Only when I got into therapy did I realize I was using food to try to medicate my own anxiety."

There are strong genetic tendencies among addicted families, one of which is depression. Eating disorders can be a symptom of depression and as such can be successfully helped through psychotherapy and possibly antidepressant medication.

> **"Have you ever been physically abused? Sexually molested?"**
>
> Carlos: "After my grandfather abused me sexually when I was eight, I began eating nonstop. I didn't know what else to do. I gained a lot of weight, and my mother wanted to know if I was eating too many French fries at school. But I couldn't tell her the truth that I was devastated and felt so lonely."

An alarming number of people with eating disorders have been abused as children. Food is the safest, most available drug for numbing painful feelings. If our client has been abused, we need to address this gently but fully to help heal the eating problem.

7. Rounding out the Picture

> **"Have you ever been in therapy for an eating problem before? What was it like?"**

If my client was in therapy before, I want to learn what went right, what went wrong, and why they left. The two most common complaints I hear are "My therapist didn't talk to me enough. I didn't get enough feedback." Or "I learned a lot about myself, but it didn't help my eating problem." My belief is that patients do not resolve their eating problems through insight alone. A therapist needs to be an active participant to help merge working on the emotional issues with concrete strategies for behavioral change.

> **"Is there anything which would be helpful for me to know that we have not discussed yet?"**

I never fail to ask this question because some of the responses can be amazingly revealing. One patient "forgot" to mention that her son had died two years ago, and her husband was hitting her. Another patient "forgot" to mention that although she did not vomit outright, she would bring her food up and swallow it repeatedly. Another client told me her husband was in jail for embezzlement. And still another had just discovered she was adopted.

8. Concluding the First Interview

From the first meeting I have with a new client, I share my initial impressions. "You have an emotional eating disorder," and I name which one. Some people are happy to hear this because they thought their behavior with food is crazy. Now they can put a name to it and have a real diagnosis.

Then I add, "Many people have this eating disorder, and they do get better. If you would like to work with me, we need to focus on two things: First, we will discuss the nitty gritty of what you eat. Second, we need to understand the emotions that are fueling your turning to (or away) from food. I think I can help you." (I only say that if, in fact, I feel that way. If a person's health is compromised, I will insist they get clearance from their medical doctor before we begin working together.)

Then I wait and listen to what the client says. Most often I hear, "OK, that sounds like a plan. What do we do now?"

I respond, "How would you feel about keeping an eating and food journal this week? Just write down what you eat and how you feel. You don't have to do anything different with your food but just observe and share it with me. We'll be like two detectives and figure out what works for you and what doesn't."

Occasionally I hear, "Well, let me think about it and get back to you." And I respond, "Was something missing in today's meeting that makes you unsure whether you want to continue?"

The more we can help our patients verbalize their questions, concerns, and doubts, the more a beginning partnership can develop. We show that putting thoughts and feelings—including negative and doubting ones—out on the table in the clear light of day is a great opportunity to deepen discussion.

9. Special Treatment Issues

Some patients need clearance from their medical doctor first. With others, it is clear that they suffer from major depression, bipolar disorder, or OCD and will be very much helped by medication. I refer them to the psychiatrist I work with for a psychopharmacological evaluation. And sometimes it is not so clear-cut, and the therapist's experience and intuition rule the day.

People who present with severe eating disorders and whose health is unstable may first need to be hospitalized before outpatient treatment begins. If they are emaciated, purging numerous times a day, taking drugs, or drinking alcoholically, therapists may decide not to work with them before they are stabilized. Patients often protest the extreme measure of inpatient treatment; others are relieved they can let go of the exhaustion that comes from being so tightly in control and can finally let themselves be taken care of in a more protected setting.

Melanie, a 26-year-old bulimic young woman, came for a consultation. I was alarmed at how much she was throwing up and told her she needed inpatient treatment. Eating disorders have the highest mortality rate of any mental illness, so we need to protect our patients and also ourselves by not embarking on therapy if a patient's functioning or health is impaired or if they are suffering from malnutrition. We need to make a risk assessment in our first interview.

Melanie asked if I would give her a chance to pull herself together before we considered inpatient. She asked for two weeks of twice-a-week therapy to see if she could reverse the damage she was doing before we considered an inpatient program. I was skeptical because "white-knuckling" and willpower over two weeks does not cure anything in the long haul. But I was impressed with Melanie's prescribing her own treatment and decided to give it a try.

During those two weeks, Melanie stopped vomiting and became interested in working on her relationship issues both with her parents who chronically demeaned her and with the men she chose to date who also demeaned her. Over the years we worked together, Melanie resorted to bulimia from time to time, but she was able to pull herself out by relying on her newfound self-soothing techniques of practicing yoga and her increasing ability to verbalize her conflicted feelings rather than purge them.

Melanie was the girl who prescribed her own treatment, and I'm glad I trusted her and my own instincts. Melanie said it was a turning point that I was willing to listen to her opinion and give her a chance, something she felt her parents would never do. This stimulated her own confidence to listen to her own inner wisdom.

A difficult situation arises for therapists when a patient comes to their initial session with a significantly distorted view of themselves, such as the case of Allison. "Look how fat I am!" she shrieks as she plunks herself down. Allison is skinny and maybe anorexic. What does the therapist do?

I hope that a therapist will not do what I did the first time I was in a similar situation with my first anorexic, Cathy. At that time, I said, "Tell me about your feeling fat." Cathy barked at me, "It's not a feeling. It's the truth." I realized everyone in Cathy's life dismissed her and that she would not feel understood by me if I jumped on the bandwagon like her family and contradicted her reality. Cathy had a psychological need to feel fat, and I realized I would have to join with her perception to cultivate an alliance.

Better prepared now, I ask Allison, "How fat are you?" Allison relaxes slightly and begins a litany of self-hatred about her weight and body.

"That's a terrible way to live," I respond. Allison smiles. We have begun. Unless her health is in danger, I do not want to take away Allison's distortion. I want to understand its meaning and function in her life and help her get curious about what makes her tick.

Conclusion

The questions in this assessment set the stage for the kind of connection we will create with our clients. How we ask, how we listen, and how we respond in this early encounter will communicate volumes about whether we can be trusted and whether we have the capacity to deeply understand the person before us. We want to inspire in our clients curiosity and the hope that healing change is possible.

Therapy is an art. Therapy is a science. And when science and art mesh in a warm, related relationship with our patients in which we bring to bear our training and experience together with our humanity, the healing unfolds in a deep and meaningful way.

3

Treatment Part 1: Awareness Is the First Step

Eating disorders *are* about food: binge eating, purging, starving, and chronic dieting. Yet eating disorders are also *not* about food: they are a creative solution for managing inner turmoil. Although people abuse food in many different ways—gorging, throwing up, or self-starvation—all emotional eaters use food as a drug that can soothe, comfort, and keep them company or even as a weapon to sabotage and hurt themselves because of unresolved guilt and self-destructive needs.

It is because of this complex intersection in which eating disorders are both about food and not about food that makes them so complex and difficult to treat.

The Benefit of an Eating Disorder

All eating disorders have psychological meaning. As social work clinicians, our goal is not to take away the eating disorder from someone who has come to rely on it as a coping mechanism but rather to understand its function, decode its meaning, and help our clients find other self-soothing and self-regulating mechanisms.

Some people even function better with their eating disorder. Although a faulty adaptation, it may serve as protection against more severe illness. Eating disorders can be the glue that holds someone together.* A social

*Dr. Hilde Bruch, the pioneer in exploring emotional issues and eating disorders, addressed how an eating disorder may represent the patient's attempt to stay well or be less sick. She described eating disorders as an "illness of inner self awareness, of inner emptiness, inner loneliness, inner unworthiness" (Bruch, 1973, p. 88).

work colleague who worked in an eating disorder inpatient facility discussed a 600-pound man in rehab who had lost 30 pounds. He then began having terrifying nightmares of repeated sexual assaults as a child that he had not previously remembered. His gorging and obesity had become a shield against these intrusive memories, which now threatened to overwhelm him; compulsive overeating provided a tool to help him dissociate and numb his intolerable memories and created an armor of fat. Clearly, his treatment team could not move forward with their goal of normalizing his eating and weight until his underlying trauma was processed.

In my own practice, I have repeatedly seen the benefit and value of an eating disorder as protection and safeguard from underlying trauma. In the case of David, a bulimic young man I worked with, I came to understand his bulimia was a protection from suicide and therefore needed to be understood and managed rather than resolved before he was psychologically capable of letting it go.

Racing his car down a busy city street, David swerved to avoid another car and accidentally ran over a child who was crossing the street. She died instantly. David was arrested and sent to prison, where he began to binge and purge. When he was released on probation, he began therapy with me. David repeated endlessly in the sessions that he could never forgive himself, that he was a selfish and reckless person who did not deserve to live. My first priority was to monitor David continuously to make sure he was not planning to hurt himself, and he was able to make that commitment to me. Unable to digest the enormity of the tragedy, David "recruited" his bulimia. The violence of bingeing and purging provided release, relief, punishment, and dissociation from the trauma.

With long-term therapy, David became able to internalize my empathy, my caring for him, and my wish to understand his experiences. He began to mourn that he had taken the life of a little child, and he began to cry. Only when he was able to cry did he begin to relinquish his bulimia. Throwing up had been a substitute for tears. I learned from David how an eating disorder can be both perverse and beautiful—beautiful because it helped keep him alive as he struggled to redeem himself. I also learned from him how an eating disorder can be a way of "self-destructive survival" (Gentile, 2007).

An Integrated Approach

Clinicians need to blend and integrate treatments to address both the problematic behaviors around eating as well as the emotions that fuel them. Cocreating a treatment plan with our clients requires a flexible and fluid strategy that will change as the client grows, develops, and evolves.

Many eating disorder patients come to me for a second opinion and express dismay that their previous treatment did not help. Their dismay illuminates how clinicians need to be adept at individualizing a comprehensive treatment plan for each client.

Ellie, a 30-year-old bulimic, expressed her disappointment: "My previous therapist told me if I worked out my emotional issues, my eating problem would get better. But it never did. I now know a lot more about myself and what makes me tick, but I'm still bingeing and throwing up."

Ellie's story demonstrates that if we clinicians solely focus on the patient's inner emotional life to help them resolve their eating disorders, this may not ultimately heal their struggle. In *Help Me! A Psychotherapist's Tried-and-True Techniques for a Happier Relationship with Yourself and the People You Love*, Dr. Richard Joelson (2016), a clinical social work psychotherapist, points out how patients often become "insight rich and change poor." In other words, they can gain great insight and understanding into what makes them tick, but they do not know how to apply these insights to improving their eating behavior.

It has also been said, "A goal without a plan is just a wish." Ellie wanted to figure out how to end her bulimia but was not given concrete, behavioral, and cognitive strategies and techniques in her therapy as to how to accomplish that.

Jessica, a 27-year-old binge eater, had a different therapy experience than Ellie that also left her disappointed:

> My previous therapist helped me with behavioral and cognitive techniques to stop bingeing and lose weight, and it worked for a while. I was happy to lose some weight. But I started bingeing again because the truth was, I was still depressed after my divorce. I realize now I needed to express my tremendous sadness and guilt about the breakup of my marriage and not just work exclusively on my eating issues.

Jessica's story shows that if we solely focus on helping clients regulate their eating behaviors or negative thinking, this will not ultimately heal an emotional eating problem either.

The comprehensive approach for healing an eating disorder is

awareness of emotional triggers and roots	+	action of cognitive–behavioral strategies	=	results

Social work clinicians also need to keep in mind that all eating disorder patients believe weight loss is medicine that will cure all their life's problems. However, weight loss in and of itself is not a cure for binge-eating disorder or obesity. And weight gain in and of itself is not a cure for anorexia nervosa. If the inner emotional issues and the harmful behaviors are not decoded and worked through in treatment, clients will relapse and return to their eating struggles.

Triggers of Emotional Eating: Present Triggers

Clients need to identify what triggers their eating disorder behavior. This includes examining both present and psychological triggers. Present triggers are the current people, places, and situations that promote disordered eating.

Depression: seeking comfort, companionship, or a heightened mood through eating behaviors. Following the death of his wife, Doug turned to binge eating to quell his pain. He was depressed both at the loss of his wife and the conviction that his life was over now that she was dead.

Anxiety: trying to regulate feelings of anxiety through bingeing, purging, or starving. Chloe wanted to "come out" to her parents that she was in a relationship with a woman. Unable to "stomach" the anticipation of her family being shocked and appalled, she stopped eating and began to compulsively count calories.

Anger: biting or stuffing oneself with food to discharge angry feelings. Josh was passed over for a promotion at his office. He discharged his anger at his boss through nighttime overeating with much hostile biting and chewing and then would make himself throw up.

Loneliness: using food to keep oneself company. Intense emptiness and isolation from others make loneliness one of the most painful feelings for emotional eaters who can, at times, even feel lonely among other people. Becca, a high school student, felt lonely every afternoon when she came home from school. Her mother worked late hours, and Becca sought "mothering" in the refrigerator.

Boredom: filling up empty time by bingeing. Boredom is a type of tension, not an absence of tension. Raymond compulsively arranged activities and social engagements for himself but, whenever he had time alone, he felt bored, tense, and uncomfortable. "I have no idea what I'm supposed to do with myself," he complained and resorted to bingeing and compulsive exercise to fill up the empty, boring time until his next scheduled activity.

Entitlement and reward: using food as a reward to compensate for the burdens of life. Molly, an enraged teenager, had to take care of her younger siblings until her parents got home from work. She would binge nonstop and felt entitled to make up to herself for the burdens she felt they inflicted on her. "I deserve all the cookies I want to reward myself for not being able to go out with my friends. Those cookies sweeten the deal," she added poignantly.

Preventive bingeing: overeating to prevent yourself from being hungry at some future time. Yvonne was a saleswoman who drove to meetings throughout the city. Unsure how long each meeting would last and whether she might get hungry and not have a chance to eat, Yvonne compulsively overate in her car to prevent possible future hunger.

Anesthesia: Using food to put yourself to sleep or to numb yourself. Allen was the victim of a violent mugging and suffered flashbacks and insomnia. Gorging on food helped make him sleepy and sedated.

Transitions: bingeing between activities to help you switch gears. Millie, a single mother, arrived home from work, and then her children came home from school. Her evenings involved helping with homework, making dinner, bathing, and putting the kids to sleep. She ate throughout the afternoon, trying to fortify herself for the long exhausting night ahead of chores and child care and responsibilities.

Fatigue: overeating to refuel yourself rather than resting, napping, or sleeping when tired. Victor would pump himself up between his day job and his night job through compulsive eating. Not able to respond to his body's need for rest, he attempted to use bingeing to boost his energy.

Lack of structure: using emotional eating to replace the missing structure of the workweek at night, on weekends, or on vacation. Nancy thrived on her hurried, demanding schedule as an emergency room nurse. When she had days off from the hospital, she felt at a loss without the hectic schedule and manically ate large portions of food to fill in the blanks of free, unstructured time.

Separation or abandonment: using a connection with food to avoid feeling the pain of rejection or the loss of a loved one. Carole struggled with leaving home to attend an out-of-town college and deeply missed her friends and family back home. She began to diet and count calories and became hooked on self-starvation to quell the pain of being homesick.

Procrastination: using emotional eating to avoid or postpone the anxiety of some dreaded task. Earl was a freshman in college but often felt inadequate to the tasks at hand. His evenings were spent bingeing and purging to avoid the anxiety of getting down to his homework and confronting his uncertainty over whether he was truly "college material."

Fear of crying: overeating to avoid crying because it feels too painful or too indulgent or because clients worry that once they start, they'll never stop. Kellie had been blindsided by her husband asking for a divorce at the same time her mother was undergoing treatment for breast cancer. Needing to "stay strong," Kellie buried her sorrow and tears through her eating binges.

Avoidance of sexual intimacy: overeating as a substitute for sex or a way to avoid sex. Brooke was uneasy with sex. She avoided her husband by stalling her bedtime and would stuff herself with cookies in the kitchen pantry instead.

Resentment: "swallowing" resentments and detouring them through emotional eating rather than confronting them directly. Wendy felt strong resentment that her boyfriend of three years was not broaching the subject of marriage. Wanting to avoid conflict and fearful of alienating him, she buried her resentment in compulsive eating and laxative abuse.

Guilt or shame: attempting to alleviate and punish oneself for guilty feelings through overeating. After his father died, Eric grew remorseful and guilty for not having visited him more frequently in the nursing home. He turned to food, his "substance of choice," to distract himself from this gnawing self-blame.

Disappointment or rejection: using food to "make it up to yourself" for feeling deprived. Inez was rejected from the business administration program she hoped to attend and tried to lessen the pain of disappointment with compulsive exercise and calorie restriction.

Chronic physical pain: overeating as an attempt to soothe yourself to feel better. Leah suffered from arthritis of the back, and when the pain flared up, her eating disorder also flared as she attempted to "medicate" her physical pain with food.

Memories of hunger: overeating in response to food deprivation of the past. Vincent was chronically afraid of not having enough food. He grew up with parents who were drug addicts and often did not provide consistent food for his sister and him. He compensated now with overeating in an attempt to make up for the scarcity of the past and reassure himself he would never go without food again.

Overwhelmed: having too much responsibility on your "plate" and seeking an oasis in food. Phyllis worked full-time, had two children at home, was caring for an aging father, and also was involved in a master's program. Food became her oasis in the midst of feeling overwhelmed.

Envy: feelings of greed, jealousy, competition, and envy can be so painful that people turn to food to compensate for their feelings of deprivation. When Annette discovered her best friend was pregnant, she was filled with envy as well as shame. She had been struggling with infertility and could not bear to face her friend's pregnancy. A steady regime of bingeing "helped" her swallow these unacceptable feelings as well as making her belly feel big and full.

Anticipatory grief: preparing for the death of a loved one, a dreaded move, or a medical procedure by padding yourself with excess food to "dial down" the fear. Bonnie's sister was declining from Alzheimer's disease, and to cushion herself against her sister's loss, Bonnie found herself bingeing incessantly.

"Hangry": this is a double whammy trigger combining hunger and anger. Marsha coined this term to describe the two ingredients that consistently led her to overeat.

Dieting: the most common trigger for binge eating when the deprivation caused by the diet invariably becomes unbearable. Samantha found herself on an ongoing diet-and-binge cycle every time she tried to follow a rigid food plan. Breakthrough bingeing would assert itself as her unsatisfied body rebelled.

Triggers of Emotional Eating: Psychological Triggers

Psychological triggers are the emotional roots of the past that have made the client vulnerable to the development of an eating disorder. The psychological roots of eating disorders can be well hidden and can often be traced back to the client's early years and attachment experiences. Treatment helps foster awareness of the events and experiences that have led our clients to conclude that "trusting food is safer than trusting people." This awareness will deepen the treatment and the client's healing.

Three special areas of exploration will help illuminate the roots of eating disorders and restore the client to trust and rely on their own personal emotional global positioning system: (1) frozen grief: unresolved losses and the inability to mourn can keep clients stuck in the numbing behaviors of bingeing, purging, and starving; (2) trauma and sexual abuse: prevalent in the eating disorder population, trauma and sexual abuse need to be worked through to free clients from the need for the anesthesia and punishment of emotional eating; and (3) fear of success: an underexplored dynamic in which clients are unconsciously afraid to give up their eating disorders. People may become stuck in their therapy and recovery because there are "benefits" to not overcoming their emotional eating. Self-sabotage has provided them with secondary gains.

Frozen Grief and Emotional Eating

Emily was a binge eater who came to therapy to get her overeating under control. When we began to discuss her history of overeating and her life experiences, she casually mentioned the early death of her father.

Emily was four years old when her father died. He had been sick for several years, and when he died, her family told her, "Daddy went to Heaven. He is in a better place." Daddy was never spoken about again.

"Tell me about him," I asked. "There's nothing to tell," Emily replied. And with that, she began to cry as the accumulation of 32 years of stifled tears came surging up in a tidal wave of pain.

"Oh my God. I have never shed tears for my father before," Emily sobbed.

With each following session, Emily cried deeply about the death of her father. Then one day she exclaimed, "I wonder if after so many years my fat has been like frozen grief. I think with all these tears, my grief is becoming liquid!"

Grief—frozen by fat, frozen by the numbing of overeating, starving, or purging—can be held in the body for years and even decades. Emily's description of "frozen grief" reminded me of a special moment I spent with my grandmother many years ago. Grandma was 86 at the time and was telling me about her father who had died when she was only five years old. To my astonishment, Grandma began to cry about her father's death—a memory from 81 years before. In that moment, I learned that grief has no timetable. Time does not necessarily heal all wounds. Unspoken loss continues to exert its power. There is no expiration date to memories or pain. I came to see how much loss and grief can play a significant part in the emotional eating of my patients. I thought about how chronic eating disorders can be related to unresolved frozen grief. And I came to see how therapy for emotional eating needs to help people mourn the sorrows that have kept them stuck in bingeing, purging, or starving.

I began asking my patients to construct a list of losses they had suffered in their lives. I discovered that these losses did not always have to do with death but with a myriad of ways that hurt can lodge inside us without resolution. Unable to dislodge the "knot" in their throat by crying and grieving, many eating disorder patients turn to the pain-relieving medication of bingeing, purging, starving, laxatives, or excess exercising.

Andrew came from a wealthy family with houses, a boat, maids, and nannies. He was bulimic since his early teens and, in spite of the family's wealth, had suffered a list of hardships that he had never discussed or sorted through. He revealed,

> I knew early on that my mother was cheating on my father—she had a woman lover. My mother ferried me around to our various homes, and she had a parade of different nannies taking care of me and my brother. Both my parents were heavy drinkers and completely self-involved. My father died of alcoholism when I was 20.

Andrew had suffered ongoing neglect from both parents, ruptures with homes and revolving-door nannies, and the traumatic early death of his father. "Bulimia is an all-consuming compulsion which has helped me ignore my hurt," he explained. "When I'm not eating and purging, I'm very depressed. Frankly, I'd rather be eating and purging."

Mourning for what he did not have, for what he wished he had, and for what he never would have was bitterly painful for Andrew. His bulimia provided a cocoon of deadness. With time, and with therapy plus a support group, he became less detached from his feelings and was filled with great anger and sadness.

Feeling bad was actually progress for Andrew. He was finally feeling rather than numbing. As he absorbed the ongoing companionship and compassion from his therapist and support group, the warmth of these connections helped him speak about his painful experiences and thaw his grief. The comfort and consolation from other people enabled him to relinquish the protection of bulimia and embrace new possibilities of trusting and supportive relationships.

Mourning is the process of sorting out the emotions that follow a significant loss: anger, guilt, crying, loneliness, emptiness, depression, and anxiety. Death is not the only grief that wounds our heart and soul. Any loss or change or trauma or transition in our lives can feel like a threat to our sense of stability and self.

For emotional eaters, bingeing, purging, starving, and rigid dieting are coping tools for despair and powerlessness.

Nicole learned that her father was diagnosed with terminal cancer, and she immediately joined a gym to begin training for a body-building competition. She had a strict eating schedule, replete with color-coded plastic containers for her food and supplements, and a rigid workout schedule. After the competition ended and her father had died, Nicole came to therapy for binge eating. She described how training for this event had completely absorbed and camouflaged her fears and worries about her father's illness. "I didn't feel anything at all!" she said, "and I was grateful for that." But once he was gone and her contest was over, her grief and bingeing broke through. Her pain asserted itself and insisted on being acknowledged; she could no longer hide behind her grueling weight-lifting regime.

Mourning is not a linear progression of moving from point A to point Z and then we are done. Mourning does not have a distinct beginning, middle, and end. Rather, it is like being lost at sea. Some memories and emotions, like strong ocean waves, knock you down by their sheer force. Other waves are gentle, lapping at your feet, making you smile with a soft sadness. Mourning has its ebbs and flows—a high tide with upsurges and hidden riptides that can ambush you and flood you with heartache. And mourning has a low and placid tide.

Why Do Emotional Eaters Freeze Grief?

Our culture, deeply uncomfortable with death, dying, and grieving, encourages us to stifle our feelings. Mourners are advised, *God never gives you more than you can handle. Keep busy! Be strong! Just give it time. Time heals all wounds. He's in a better place. You need to get out more. Keep a stiff upper lip!* (I've always imagined that "keeping a stiff upper lip" is a person's attempt to quiet the "trembling lower lip.")

Emotional eaters, obviously, are not the only people to freeze grief. But emotional eaters are prone to derail, detour, and divert difficult feelings through food. And grief is the most difficult of feelings.

Emotional eaters believe if they open their hearts to feel their pain, it will never end. "If I ever started to cry, I would never be able to stop," Yvette, an anorexic woman, declared. Simon, a bulimic man, stated, "My Dad has been dead two months already. I feel I should be over it already and not feel sad anymore. It's time to move on."

Yvette's and Simon's beliefs about grief reveal common features of people with eating disorders: impatience with themselves, the conviction that strong feelings are scary and should be avoided, black-or-white thinking, and critical and perfectionist commandments to one's self. Emotional eaters prefer a "quick fix" rather than tolerating the process of digesting either food or feelings. No wonder they turn to the numbing and anesthetizing benefits of eating in an attempt to cover up their sorrow and anger and "just get over it."

Unfreezing Grief: Restarting the Process of Mourning

When we are in pain, we naturally seek to protect ourselves from the hurt. And so, after a deep loss, people often sleep, drink, eat, shop, seek compulsive sex, lose themselves on the computer, or engage in any number of activities to dull the ache and fill up the empty space within. But when eating disorders or other addictions become an ongoing pattern and a way to chronically avoid pain, then grief becomes frozen. The substances quell the pain from the outside in. Real and lasting relief comes from unraveling one's emotions from the inside out.

Clients often feel guilty as if healing grief means they have forgotten the person they have lost. We tell them mourning really means that grief finds a place to live in their heart where they are enriched by loving memories and not tormented by anguished ones.

Sometimes grief never gets resolved. Hope Edelman speaks of the "Resolution Hoax":

> I wish I believed that mourning ends one day or that grief disappears for good. The word "resolution" dangles before us like a piñata filled with promise, telling us we only need to approach it from the right angle to obtain its prize. Some losses you truly don't get over. Grief is something that continues to get reworked. (Edelman, 2006, p. 19)

Grieving is ambiguous. It concludes, it continues, it intrudes, it retreats, it pounces, it ebbs, it flares up, it settles down. Perhaps we all need to learn to contain within us the contradiction that life does go on, there are still pleasures to be enjoyed, and yet we are forever altered by having lost and suffered.

The Process of Thawing Grief

Thawing grief includes helping our clients with eight tasks:

1. Recount the story of what happened in detail because their sorrow needs to speak. Abby: "I was raped on my college campus." Robin: "My grandmother died of cancer in our house when I was 12."
2. Describe the impact it had on them when it occurred. Abby: "The rape devastated me because I had never been with a man before. I feel ruined." Robin: "Watching my grandmother grow increasingly sick frightened me beyond what I could bear. She was ugly, and I didn't know her anymore."
3. Express the feelings of anger, guilt, self-blame, or regrets they may have. Abby: "I never should have been walking alone at night on campus. The rape was my fault. But, on the other hand, shouldn't I have the freedom to walk by myself without having to worry I'd get assaulted? I am furious with God for letting this happen

to me." Robin: "I feel like a bad person because I wanted my grandmother to die. It was too much for me to handle anymore."

4. Imagine the effect this loss will have on their life as they move forward. Abby: "I have no idea how I will ever have sex, even if I can find someone to trust. Sex equals trauma in my mind. How will I ever get over this?" Robin: "If anyone knew the real me—that I wanted Grandma to finally die—they would never look at me the same way again."
5. Consider the connection between their loss and their history of bingeing, purging, starving, drinking, taking drugs, or any other addictions. Do they want to eat, drink, run away, or cry? We teach clients that crying is our natural healing process of releasing emotions that well up. Tears are a gift from deep inside. "There is a sacredness in tears. They are not the mark of weakness, but of power. They speak more eloquently than ten thousand tongues. They are the messengers of overwhelming grief, of deep contrition, and of unspeakable love," wrote Washington Irving (1899, para. 9).
6. Remember and reexperience the good memories, if any, connected to this loss. Clients find many poignant ways to keep the memories of their loved ones close to their heart. One woman took bushes from her parents' garden to plant in her yard while another donated a bench in her mother's honor at a nearby nature conservancy.
7. Acknowledge the pain and hurt of the bad memories. Recognize whatever unfinished business is connected to this loss. Accept the fact that one's life does go on despite loss and grief. Create a ritual or a memorial to honor the loss.
8. Cultivate other secure relationships, such as a group or therapy, which will be an outlet of support without the crutch of emotional eating.

Grieving the Loss of an Eating Disorder

As emotional eaters begin to recover, they need to grieve the loss of their best friend and enemy (their "frenemy") of bingeing, purging, starving, and chronic dieting. People often experience grief when they recover from their eating problems because they lose a tried-and-true way of soothing themselves, a way of giving meaning and focus to their life, a well-worn way of coping with stress, and the magical belief that weight loss will solve all their problems, repair their self-esteem, and make them feel happier. Grief also includes the realization of how much wasted time, energy, money, and obsessing the eating disorder has consumed.

Eventually, through the process of healing, clients need to part from their eating problems, honor the help these disorders have provided, say good-bye, and go their separate ways. This farewell does engender grief as the question remains: "Who am I without my eating disorder?"

Rose Ann has struggled with binge-eating disorder, anorexia, and laxative abuse. In her poem, written as she emerges from the bondage of her eating disorders, she portrays the transition from an eating disordered identity to recovering the vitality of her life. She captures the confusion, the hope, the vision of how life could be, as well as an acknowledgment of what it has been like surviving under the tyranny of an eating disorder.

Who Am I without My Eating Disorder?

Rose Ann F.

Who am I without my eating disorder? I am the dirt on which you walk, Or am I the ground for which things grow?

Who am I without my eating disorder? I am the rose about to wilt, Or am I the bud who needs to bloom?

Who am I without my eating disorder? I am the tears that carry sorrow, Or am I the tears that set you free?

Who am I without my eating disorder? I am the eyes that refuse to see, Or am I searching just for me?

Who am I without my eating disorder? I am the heart that anxiously skips a beat, Or am I the pulsing rhythm in my feet?

Who am I without my eating disorder? I am the life that waits for death, Or am I the child still unborn Who waits first breath to greet new dawn?

The more people run away from intense emotions, the more their eating problems run after them. Grief must be witnessed to be healed. Therapy can help to unfreeze grief. Clients learn that pain is not the whole of who they are. Tears thaw grief. Shared pain is soothed pain.

A Grief and Food Timeline

I help clients chronicle their history of loss and grief by creating a timeline from childhood to the present, including any rupture, disruption, change, loss, family death or turmoil, significant illness, accident, or violence.

Then we chronicle a timeline with weight and eating disorder history. Are there any parallels between these two timelines? Can clients relate an upsurge of eating problems to times of loss, transition, or grief?

Doreen made her timeline and described it to me:

> I made a graph of all the losses and changes in my life, and then I superimposed my eating disorder history on top of it. Here is what I learned:
>
> - When I was five years old, I was a normal weight kid. Then my parents moved into a house of our own in the suburbs. The photos after that show me getting heavier and heavier. I imagine I felt bereft to leave my little friends behind in the old neighborhood; they were the very first friends I ever had. My mother was more socially isolated in the new house because she didn't drive, and my father had more financial responsibilities with the mortgage. I think the heightened anxiety level in my house began fueling my compulsive overeating.
> - I had an abortion when I was 24. My guilt, confusion, and shame led to another upsurge of compulsive bingeing in which I gained 30 pounds.
> - When I was 40, my older brother was diagnosed with leukemia. As he became more emaciated, I went through a period of anorexia. Part of me really enjoyed the self-control of starvation. Brad died two years later, and my anorexia continued until I went into treatment. Treatment helped me to eventually start eating again, even though a part of me really prefers being anorexic to being normal. Just a part of me, though.

Doreen felt gratified to lay out her time frame of loss and change and see the connections with her eating struggles. Her self-compassion was fortified when she understood there were significant and major reasons that led her to turn to food for comfort, companionship, and consolation. It also heightened her understanding of the triggers and events that might contribute to her vulnerability in turning to emotional eating in the future. "Forewarned is forearmed. I now know when a stressful experience related to loss comes up, that's when I need to make an extra conscious commitment to my eating," Doreen added.

Sexual Abuse, Trauma, and Eating Disorders

Sexual abuse and trauma shatter the sacred innocence of a child and can become a primary trigger for an eating disorder. In my practice, many of the women and men who come to therapy for emotional eating have been molested as children.

"It was my father's best friend." "It was my father." "It was my brother." "It was my mother's boyfriend." "It was my mother."

"And so I starved myself." "And so I binged." "And so I got fat." "And so I started using laxatives."

The abuser has seized ownership of the child's body for his own use and hijacked the child's sense of self. Abuse shocks and violates the boundaries of the self so dramatically that inner sensations of hunger, fatigue, or sexuality often become difficult for the victim to identify. The person who has been sexually abused becomes plagued with confusion, guilt, shame, fear, anxiety, self-punishment, and stifled rage. She (or he) seeks the soothing comfort, protection, and anesthesia of food as well as the violent relief and release from vomiting and laxative abuse. Bingeing, purging, starving, and chronic dieting are mood-altering behaviors that help detour, divert, and distract a person from inner pain. For many survivors, trusting food feels safer than trusting people.

Carla describes the history of her disordered eating: "My father's best friend molested me in our garage starting when I was seven. I was filled with such anxiety that I began gorging on everything that wasn't tied down. I gained 30 pounds by the time I was eleven, which my mother attributed to my eating too much pizza at the school cafeteria."

Erica was abused by an older cousin who said it was just a game of doctor. "Overeating and laxatives became my way to rid myself of the pain and confusion. I realized I was trying to evacuate my cousin out of my body through those laxatives."

Gary described his shameful memories:

> After my parents divorced, my mother would get drunk and dance around the house in her nightgown. She scared me, but the worst part was I got turned on. To try and get control I began starving myself and developed anorexia. Through therapy, I now understand how I was trying to starve out my horrible feelings about myself. My shame made me feel I didn't even deserve to eat.

As they reach their teen or adult years, survivors often try to de-sexualize themselves. They may work to make themselves very fat or very thin in an attempt to render themselves unattractive. They hope their armor of fat or skinniness will protect them from sexual advances or even wipe out their own inner sexual feelings, which may be too threatening to deal with. Survivors may not be fully aware of how they manipulate food or their bodies to make themselves feel safer. Much of this behavior occurs unconsciously, behind the scenes, until therapy or a self-help program increases the person's awareness. But manipulating one's outer body shape is an unsuccessful attempt to resolve the inner problems of betrayal and guilt.

Some larger-size survivors actually fear losing weight because it will make them feel smaller and childlike, ushering in earlier memories of feeling defenseless that are difficult to cope with from when they were a child. Raquel became anxious as she started to resolve her binge-eating disorder in therapy.

> Even though I've only lost 15 pounds, it's triggering flashbacks of abuse with my grandfather because I feel smaller, like the little girl I was, when he molested me. Although I do realize this is a distortion on my part, it helps me understand why I packed on the pounds to make myself feel bigger and more protected.

Other survivors obsessively diet, starve, or purge, striving to make their bodies "perfect." Striving for a perfect body is their attempt to feel more powerful, invulnerable, and in control so as not to reexperience the powerlessness they felt as children. Of course, no amount of weight loss will ever make an abuse victim feel perfect enough.

In addition to falling prey to eating disorders, victims of trauma may also be vulnerable to depression, anxiety, alcohol and substance abuse, posttraumatic stress disorder (PTSD), pornography addiction, prostitution, and a profound mistrust of intimacy.

The ongoing impact of abuse cannot be minimized. Children do not tell about their abuse for many reasons: They may not have fully realized anything wrong was happening, they were gaslighted into thinking the abuser's behavior was acceptable, they think they are to blame for provoking the abuse, they are dependent on the abuser and cannot risk upsetting the status quo, they fear they will not be believed, they were abused by a religious leader whom the family respects, or they were threatened or bribed to keep silent. A number of women clients have discussed sexual abuse that occurred with their brothers, and the siblings all participated in a family conspiracy of silence.

Physical abuse coupled with a parent's demand for respect can also damage a child's self-esteem and open the door to seeking relief in an eating disorder.

Martina, a bulimic woman in her 20s, recounted the story of her grandmother beating her. Grandmother, confined to a wheelchair, summoned Martina to come across the room so she could beat her for some unknown infraction. Martina dutifully approached her grandmother's wheelchair as the woman raised her cane and hit Martina across her back and shoulders. The idea that she could protest or resist did not occur to Martina as she complied with her grandmother's request. "Did it occur to you to not go to her?" I asked. "No," Martina responded with surprise, "she's my grandmother. I have to respect her."

Simone, a binge eater, was also beaten by her father for some unknown infraction. After he hit her naked backside, her father would demand that Simone kiss his hand. He wanted her to express her gratitude that she had the kind of father who hit her to make her a better person and instill good values. Simone cried as she told this story, "Having to kiss his hand was an additional humiliation after he hit me. But he was my father, and I knew I had to respect him."

The documentary film *Leaving Neverland* (aired on HBO in 2019) relates the history of the two men who accused Michael Jackson of abusing them throughout their childhoods. Both men spoke of their deep love for Michael, the sense of specialness he imbued within them, and how they were "groomed" and seduced by him over a period of time. Their stories poignantly demonstrate how they were willing to go along with the abuse because the connection with Michael felt like love and caring. This is true for many children who have been molested. Not many abusers have the star power of Michael Jackson, but for children, adults, by virtue of their authority, control, size, and power, do wield enormous power.

There are many harmful forms of abuse and betrayal beyond overt touching. Covert abuse—a seductive, stimulating attitude by an adult—also wreaks emotional havoc. Many eating disordered girls I have worked with speak with dismay of their father's scrutiny of one particular part of their body: her hair, her belly, her backside, her breasts. This intrusiveness, even when no touching is involved, leaves the girl feeling encroached upon and self-conscious. Several women with eating disorders reveal how their fathers called them tramps when they began dating. Margo recalled that beginning at the age of 14, her father constantly hounded her as to whether she was still a virgin. And Erin, a bulimic girl, said, "My father never actually touched me, except with his eyes."

Whether the abuse is overt or covert, it damages a child's security and trust in the family and other relationships.

Secrecy, Shame, and Surrender

Sexual abuse and emotional eating share two central elements: secrecy and shame. Many eating disorder patients feel guilty about the sexual abuse in their childhoods, believing they could have prevented it but chose not to because of some defect in themselves. They repress their secret and push it underground and then distract and anesthetize themselves by furtive emotional eating. For some eating disorder sufferers, memories of the abuse remain repressed, and for others, the eating disorder consumes such an enormous amount of time and psychological energy that there is no time to think about any trauma from the past.

Secrecy is intertwined with shame. People who are emotional eaters as well as survivors of sexual abuse are no strangers to shame—shame about how insatiable they can feel at their core for craving food and love, shame about what lengths they have gone to, to sneak food, and shame for the secret gorging rampages, forceful purges, or self-destructive starvation that can override reason. Woven into this self-image is their sense of being damaged, which was injected by the abuse.

PTSD

Many people with eating problems suffer from symptoms of PTSD. Trauma can be caused by other events besides abuse: early extended separation from a parent, experiencing or witnessing violence, emotional or physical abuse or neglect, bullying or teasing, medical trauma, accidents, mental illness or substance abuse in the home, parental divorce, death of a loved one, military combat, a natural disaster.

Posttraumatic stress is an emotional and physiological disorder resulting in recurrent anxiety, depression, feeling chronically "dead" inside, insomnia or nightmares, intrusive memories, experiencing heightened vigilance about one's surroundings, as well as flashbacks. Some victims of posttraumatic stress also become involved in self-destructive behavior by forming repetitive abusive relationships or losing themselves to drugs, alcohol, promiscuity, or self-mutilation. And some victims become so fragmented as to develop dissociative identity disorder, an involuntary escape from reality characterized by a disconnection between thoughts, identity, consciousness, and memory.

Eating disorders mimic the repetitive nature of abuser and victim. Clinical social worker Dr. Judith Scheel (n.d.) posited that

> from an abuse perspective . . . the individual with the eating disorder assumes roles of both the victim and abuser. They are typically at the mercy of the eating disorder symptomatology which can be quite sadistic (e.g., laxative abuse, starvation, binge eating until exhausted and physically in pain) as well as simultaneously assuming the role of the abuser who is in effect doing the harm, perpetrating the assault to her own body. This paradigm fits with the relationship between the individual who is physically and/or sexually abused and the abuser, only this time, the sufferer is able to

> assume "control" by taking on both roles. The individual therefore is able to maintain recurrent and intrusive abusive events through the use of the eating disorder while simultaneously enabling herself to dissociate, distract and sooth the pain through the obsession with food. (para. 12)

Healing from the Trauma of Sexual Abuse

Empowered by the #MeToo movement, many women (and men) are coming forward for the first time to declare the abuse they suffered as children and the sexual violence and exploitation they have experienced as adults. I do not believe there can ever be accurate statistics about the crime of sexual abuse given that children don't tell and, for adults, shame and self-blame runs deep about revealing these experiences. The RAINN (Rape, Abuse & Incest National Network) organization is the nation's largest anti–sexual violence organization, which operates the National Sexual Assault Hotline. They refer to statistics from the U.S. Department of Justice indicating that "Every 92 seconds, an American is sexually assaulted. And every 9 minutes, that victim is a child. Each year, 60,000 children were victims of sexual abuse" (RAINN Organization, n.d., para. 1).

Although there is more media coverage than ever about the prevalence of sexual abuse, this does not relieve the shame that many people feel about their experiences. If they have been a victim of incest, confronting the abuse means facing the agony not only that they come from the kind of family where abuse was perpetrated but also that no one in the family protected them.

Often eating disorder patients feel enormous guilt for having gone along with and even enjoyed the sexual contact with their abuser. Binge eating, purging, or starving then becomes their ongoing self-induced punishment or attempt to dissociate from their feelings. When we scratch the surface of the lives of these children, though, we discover that sexual abuse may have been the only real affection or caring they received. A child who is lonely or starved for affection may revel in the attention, even if it is abuse. But the truth is that children are never the seducers—they are always the victims. The only thing a child is guilty of is the innocent wish to be loved.

Clinical social worker Babette Rothschild (2000) explains in her book, *The Body Remembers*, that the nervous system responds to trauma by fight, flight, or freeze reactions, which are automatic survival reactions. It is important to understand that these responses are instinctive and not chosen after thoughtful consideration. "Many who have suffered trauma feel much guilt and shame for freezing and not doing more to protect themselves. Understanding that freezing is automatic often facilitates the difficult process of self-forgiveness" (Rothschild, 2000, p. 11).

How can we help our clients heal from sexual abuse? Because the experience of sexual abuse is about being out of control, we need to help clients feel they are in a protected setting where their feelings can reemerge and let loose. Releasing pain and guilt is not an intellectual experience, but something that comes from deep within. This can be a wrenching step because exposing one's emotions can feel raw, like a reenactment of the original trauma. The capacity to trust a therapist will take time, because abuse and trauma are about the experience of interpersonal betrayal.

PTSD is a complex psychobiological condition, and therefore it is crucial to give attention to both body and mind in treatment. Somatic interventions such as helping a client become aware of their breathing, temperature, or scanning the body for muscle tension helps anchor the person in the present and helps separate the past. Rothschild (2000) explained, "One of the goals of trauma therapy is to help people understand their bodily sensations. They must first feel and identify them on the body level, then they must then use language to name and describe them" (p. 44).

Confronting shame, releasing pain, and experiencing rage and guilt are part of the process of reclaiming one's inner self as well as one's sexual self. The need to detour feelings through destructive eating will subside when our clients are able to grieve for the little child who was betrayed.

Everyone's healing journey is unique, and everyone's healing time frame is different. Finding a compassionate therapist or a survivor's group can support this process. The healing process emerges slowly over time. It cannot be forced. As Philip Bromberg (1998) has written,

> We do not treat patients to cure them of something that was done to them in the past; rather, we are trying to cure them of what they still do to themselves and to others in order to cope with what was done to them in the past. (p. 237)

The deepest part of recovery is being able to feel sorrow for oneself, to cry, to view oneself with compassion, to acknowledge the loss of innocence, to recognize the impact the abuse has caused. These are all milestones on the journey. Reliving the experiences of pain can set the stage for moving forward, gradually shedding the past, and reclaiming the wholeness that is inherently the person's right. Grieving is a sign that a traumatic experience is being relegated to the past (Rothschild,

2000). The need for emotional eating will ebb with the working through of grief and sadness.

Ilene had worked deeply and wholeheartedly on finding ways to make peace with her incest traumas. The complication for her was that her abusive father was also her more loving parent. Ilene's mother was cruel and unloving, whereas her father could often be appropriately affectionate and supportive. Ilene had to contain and "digest" the contradiction that her father was both an abuser and, at times, a loving parent. It is so much easier when experiences are black and white but, like life itself, they often are not.

Painful residue remains for Ilene, at times threatening to cloud her well-being. However, she created a tiny ritual to bring herself back into loving alignment whenever memories, anger, or bitterness threaten to surge up. "This is very powerful for me," she explained. "I take my own hand and lift it up to my lips. I kiss my hand with great love and tenderness and softness. Through this small gesture, I then feel restored by my own self-love!" Ilene also practiced a series of affirmations such as these (adapted from Fradkin, 2012):

- Recovery is absolutely possible and achievable for me.
- I release and forgive myself for any responsibility I have accepted in the past for my abuse.
- My abuser(s) from the past chose to hurt me. I will not continue that legacy by hurting my own self in any way (food, relationships, drinking) but instead will practice self-care.
- Offering myself daily compassion is necessary for my healing and growth.
- I commit to connecting to the child inside me today so we can play, laugh, and experience joy together.
- Feeling is healing. As I heal, I develop the ability to experience a wider range of emotions to enhance my health and connections to others.

Group Therapy

Group treatment for women with abuse histories and eating disorders can be a powerful tool of recovery. Social work psychoanalyst Gwenn Nusbaum (2006) describes how in the context of an empathic therapy group, women help each other learn to negotiate the intense feelings of shame, guilt, desire, and hunger. In group, members learn to deal with "the delicate balance between too much and too little" as well as "not too hot, not too cold, not too distant, not too far" as they learn to respond to their own needs and to establish boundaries with others.

A Controversy in the Field: Is Forgiveness of Abusers Necessary to Heal?

Many abuse victims, as well as mental health clinicians, believe that the ultimate goal of recovery is to be able to forgive your abuser. Without achieving forgiveness, they claim, you are neither healthy nor healed.

Books on forgiveness exhort us to *Forgive and Forget*; *Unconditional Forgiveness: A Simple and Proven Method to Forgive Everyone*; *Let It Go: Forgive so You Can Be Forgiven*; *I Forgive You: Why You Should Always Forgive*; *Do Yourself a Favor . . . Forgive*; *The Power of Forgiveness: How to Quickly Get over the Past.*

Many counselors recommend a forgiveness formula and instruct us that "forgiveness is a choice, forgiveness is a gift, and you should strive for total forgiveness." The most damaging message of all is that "Unforgiveness is a learned behavior that can become a cancer of the soul that metastasizes if gone unchecked."

I refute and argue against this authoritarian one-size-fits-all notion of forgiveness. Forgiveness may indeed be part of recovery, but *not* forgiving can also be a valid position. No one can tell a person there is one right way to handle an abuse experience. Everyone needs to create a personal road map of recovery.

The outright assertion that "You are not recovered unless you forgive your abuser" can actually be viewed as another form of abuse—psychological bullying and coercion, pressuring someone as to how she should think or feel, just as the abuser pressured and forced that person to do his bidding.

Forgiveness is defined as a change of heart toward someone who has wronged you, in which you overcome feelings of resentment and anger. But, in truth, forgiveness is not such a black-or-white concept. It may include a range of alternatives—from a genuine feeling of pardon to the victimizer on one hand to absolutely never forgiving on the other, with a continuum in between. And it may change over time.

In *The Courage to Heal*, the authors state,

> Developing forgiveness for your abuser, or for the members of your family who did not protect you, is not a required part of the healing process. It is insulting to suggest to any survivor that she should forgive the person who abused her. This advice minimizes and denies the validity of her feelings. Yet the issue of forgiveness is one that will be pressed on you again and again by people who are uncomfortable with your rage. . . . You should never let anyone talk you into trading in your anger for the "higher good" of forgiveness. (Bass & Davis, 1994, pp. 160–162)

There is also an important distinction between understanding and forgiving. You may understand the dynamics of the abuser and why he or she resorted to violence or abuse. You may learn that the abuser also was a childhood victim. This is not the same as forgiveness, because understanding someone's behavior does not exonerate them. I think a more accurate slogan rather than "To understand all is to forgive all" would be "To understand all is merely to understand all."

Chris Anderson, a former executive director of MaleSurvivor.org, states,

> I believe it is absolutely possible to be on the healing path without addressing whether or not we forgive those who have hurt us. If there is anyone that survivors need to be able to forgive it is ourselves. Many of us attack and blame ourselves for the dysfunction and destruction others brought into our lives. If we can let go of that pain, we are better able to live better and more satisfying lives. For those burdened by the pain of the past, it is a great challenge to live in the present. But it is by living in the present that we increase our chances of recovering. By living in the present we can better connect to people who give us more of what we need—hope and support—so that we can heal. (Chris Anderson, personal correspondence, September 20, 2019)

If survivors on their own, without outside pressure, can organically arrive at a place in their hearts of being able to say, "I forgive you," it may well serve as a step toward healing. But forgiveness should not be demanded as a component of recovery.

The Importance of Self-Forgiveness

Self-forgiveness, however, is a crucial component of recovery. Victims often worry they were complicit in allowing themselves to be abused; they do not fully appreciate their vulnerability and helplessness. After all, it is psychologically more protective to believe "I am a bad child" than to believe, for example, "my father is a bad father." Children need that father to protect them and cannot run the risk of losing him. They turn the "badness" on themselves. Therapy can help generate self-compassion for the untenable situation the victim found him- or herself in.

Recovering from abuse includes any path that will lead you to feel whole and healthy, with compassion for yourself and the ability to be genuinely intimate with the people you love. In her book *Apology*, Eve Ensler (2019) finds her own unique way of making peace with the horrific sexual and physical abuse perpetrated by her father. She writes a letter to herself in her father's voice in which he apologizes; it is the letter she wished for but can never receive from the man who has been dead for decades.

Through the healing power of therapy, people can often rework their pain and emerge with *posttraumatic growth*, an enhanced resilience toward coping with emotional struggles.

Cornerstones of Recovery

No one can heal their shame, secrecy, abuse, or eating disorders alone. Just as hurtful relationships were the cause of isolating with food in the first place, so supportive and loving relationships will be the medium of healing. Connecting with other people who can validate clients' pain and accept them for who they are is key. Through a support group or therapy, they can create a second-chance family.

Another cornerstone of recovery is the ability to achieve sexual intimacy with a partner. Sexual intimacy is the opposite of emotional eating. Whereas emotional eating is about controlling, rigidity, fear, and isolation, intimacy is about surrendering, enjoying, sharing, and letting go.

Our goal as therapists with eating disordered and sexually abused clients is to help them recontact their inner vigor and vitality and sink their teeth into life, not into their relationship with food.

Overcoming the Fear of Success in Resolving an Eating Disorder

Michelle, a clinical social worker, came for a consultation to discuss a case she was working on:

> Hannah is an obese 24-year-old binge eater who began with me six months ago. We developed a good connection; she worked hard to use the behavioral techniques I suggested to reduce her binge eating, and she was quite open about her struggles and frustrations with dating. She also went to a commercial weight loss group and was losing some weight, which made her endlessly pleased. But then she abruptly stopped coming to sessions. I have no idea why. She hasn't answered any of my messages. What went wrong?

I responded, "The problem is that everything went right!"

Michelle, like many other clinicians whose clients terminate their therapeutic relationships prematurely, are intrigued to learn how pervasive is the dynamic of self-sabotage and the fear of success with eating disorder clients. This is an underreported yet key dynamic in the field.

Why would someone sabotage their success and turn their back on the gains they have made? Why would someone drop out of treatment when they were making traction on resolving their problems?

As Michelle described Hannah's history, we began to get some clues about why she terminated therapy prematurely. Hannah came from a very religious family. When she broke away from their strict teachings, her wish to lose weight became her new "religion," a central organizing focus that gave structure to her new life. In one recent session, Hannah had briefly mentioned, "As I'm getting a little thinner, I think I'm also getting a little depressed." Michelle now realized this was a signal that her client was communicating some struggles with her newfound success.

Hannah's story reminded me of others I have heard over the years. For emotional eaters, so much of their lives center around worries and preoccupation with calories, weight, and body image; the eating disorder has consolidated a shaky and vulnerable identity. One client realized, "If I get better and don't have to spend my time worrying about losing, gaining, dieting, and calories, what will give my life meaning? Telling myself I am fat and ugly has been like a daily mantra for me! What am I going to replace that with? If I give up my obsession with food and weight, I worry about feeling empty inside and without purpose."

As clinicians, we know that the road to resolving an eating problem is filled with fits and starts, obstacles and overcoming. But for certain clients, even the beginning stages of letting go of their eating disorder usher in feelings of disorientation, confusion, and fear.

As a client begins to feel better and more in control of her eating, we need to be alert to clues that she may become uncomfortable and therefore want to undermine her progress. Hannah's brief mention of an increase in depression was a clue. As therapists, we should be aware that giving up emotional eating can create its own stress that can be addressed with the therapist. And although all emotional eaters will fervently claim the wish to lose weight, many clients unconsciously fear being thin, which holds multiple and unique meanings for them.

I often say to clients, "If we could cure your eating disorder by the end of today's session, what would your life be like?" They often look at me blankly and answer, "I have no idea!" I then add, "What would be the worst thing about getting better?" Although most people say,

"Nothing. It would all be great," this question injects a note of curiosity and inquiry into the sessions that we can call upon in the future.

Some people become thoughtful and do have an answer to the worst thing about recovery, which helps them understand why they may sabotage their success:

> **Leslie:** When it came to light that my brother had been abusing me, my family went into therapy to understand what had gone wrong. They now realize I gained a lot of weight when I was 12 as a frightened reaction to his abuse. I'm afraid if I stop bingeing and lose some weight, everyone will think I'm now okay, and it will let them off the hook for what happened. I'm not ready to let them off the hook and have them believe I'm all better. I'm afraid they would not feel guilty anymore for what happened to me.

> **Mindy:** My father was fat all his life, and in the last two years the doctors convinced him to lose weight because his health was in jeopardy. He finally did lose 40 pounds but died six months later from a stroke. I always felt that if he hadn't lost so much weight, he never would have died. It made me scared that could happen to me if I ever stopped compulsively eating and got to lose some weight.

> **Elizabeth:** I think I'm having an identity crisis now that I lost 65 pounds after lap-band surgery. My distress is making me start to binge again. At my new thin weight, I now have to learn how to navigate my body at this new size—how to walk down the street, even how much space I need to sit on a bus. It scares me. All of this is so new. I don't even know what style clothes I like or what size I should wear. Even my face doesn't look familiar!

Elizabeth no longer had her cocoon of fat to hide behind. In reaction, she started to undo her progress by bingeing again. Her therapy helped her realize there is a transition in adjusting to a thinner body that needs to be taken one step at a time. We delved into a detailed inquiry about the feelings and body sensations of all these changes so she could "digest" them slowly.

> **Lourdes:** That's an easy question! If I weren't bulimic anymore and stopped throwing up, I'd have to seriously think about divorcing my husband! And I don't want to think about that.

> **Colleen:** This might sound selfish, but giving up my anorexia makes me afraid to lose the special treatment my parents have been giving

> me. I am an identical twin, and since I became anorexic, no one mistakes me for Tara anymore. My anorexia made my family more worried about me than her and that gave me a feeling of secret power. Now I realize that getting attention by staying so skinny is a hollow victory—getting special attention for being thin is not the same as being special for being me! But, I have to be honest that I will miss my parents' extra attentiveness and worry.

Colleen was afraid to lose the special treatment her parents had given her when she was in the throes of her anorexia. Colleen needed to work on her lifelong competition with Tara in treatment rather than recruit her anorexia to be the more important twin.

Fears of Change and Loss: Issues behind the Fear of Success

Human beings often experience any change—even change for the better—as a loss. Additional examples of fears of loss that might derail a client's progress are included here.

Losing the Status Quo in Relationships. Sometimes, weight conflicts are an integral factor in the balance of power, trust, and dependency in relationships. Eliminating that dynamic means having to find new ways of relating.

Craig's wife and daughter badgered him constantly about losing weight. In despair, they finally joined a family support group that helped them realize the futility of trying to control Craig's behavior. As they backed off from criticizing him, Craig discovered how much he missed their complaining about his weight. Their attention had made him feel cared for and special.

Craig explained, "It was similar to my family of origin where my mother repeatedly berated my father to stop drinking. I never realized how I interpreted her reprimands as a way of showing my father love and attention. I'm beginning to see that my need to be scolded by my wife and daughter is some kind of misguided attempt to get their affection. Unfortunately, it is really eroding their respect for me."

Losing Family Loyalty. Sometimes being successful feels like being disloyal to one's family, and so clients sacrifice themselves to continue to belong. Gayle came from a family of obese parents and two obese brothers who shared an ongoing camaraderie about their weight. When Gayle went away to college, she joined a women's overeating group and became more in touch with her own rhythm of eating and lost 20 pounds. But when she came home for Christmas, her family treated her as if she had deserted them. "Boy, look at you," they mocked. "College makes you think you're too good for us. We have two weeks to fatten you up again!"

Gayle was devastated by her family's ridicule and began to feel guilty about her weight loss, as if she had done something wrong. She began overeating to undo her achievement and "return to the fold." In therapy, she realized that regaining the weight was her way of trying to keep the bond with her family intact. She also came to understand that her success—whether it was enjoying her body more or achieving a college education—would entail some degree of growing beyond and apart from her family. As she slowly resolved this anxiety and guilt about separating from her family, she got back on track with her newfound patterns of healthy eating and receiving support from her women's group.

Losing the Power to Spite Someone. Patricia experienced her mother as constantly pressuring her to be slim and to marry a rich husband. But try as she might, Patricia could not stop bingeing or lose the extra 50 pounds her mother wanted her to lose, and she only seemed to manage to meet unavailable guys. "Since I was a little girl, my mother measured out my food and weighed me weekly. I hated scales. I hated measuring cups. I hated her! Whenever her back was turned, I would sneak candy and cookies. Keeping myself fat was perfect revenge. Even though I'm now 25, my mother is still trying to control my weight and marital status—and I'm still rebelling!"

"What's pathetic about my story," Patricia continued, "is that I'd really like to have normal eating habits and get married someday. But another part of me enjoys spiting her more than getting my life together. I'm in such a bind!" The battle between Patricia and her mother now continued within Patricia herself—a civil war. She knew if she did lose weight, she would also lose a powerful weapon against her mother. Bingeing and staying larger is her way of communicating, "I'm going to be my own person, and there's nothing you can do about it!"

Only when Patricia learns to separate her wishes and hopes for herself from the coercion and pressure she experiences from her mother will she be able to permit herself to attain her natural weight. This means using her mouth for speaking and not for overeating and asserting herself directly with her mother rather than letting her body do the talking for her. Then her decisions will come from within her and not from her mother. As a social work colleague of mine once said, "Maturity is doing something even though your mother wants it!"*

---

*Thanks to Carole Gladstone, ACSW, for this turn of phrase.

In *Self-Realization and Self-Defeat*, Samuel Warner (1966) explains that self-defeat is a technique to achieve power over others and get indirect revenge.

> All of us learn in childhood that we can "get back" at others by defeating ourselves. It is an element of childhood's repertoire mechanisms for dealing with life. And thus the stage is set for the utilization of self-defeat as a way of venting unconscious resentment in life. Self-defeat is always self-and-other defeat. (p. 218).

Families Can Be Affected When Their Loved One Gets Better. Diane was an obese, married 42-year-old woman who had made good strides in curtailing her binge eating but decided to have bariatric surgery to help reduce her weight of 330 pounds. Following the surgery, she was thrilled to watch her weight come off. But when Diane proudly lost 50 pounds and began dressing more stylishly, her husband Ethan became paranoid and convinced she was cheating on him with various men. He peppered her constantly with accusatory questions, even waking her from sleep to torment her with his angry onslaught. Diane was horrified that her marriage was falling apart; she blamed herself for causing the rupture by dramatically losing weight and began to anxiously binge once again.

In her therapy, we realized Diane was unwittingly backsliding in an unconscious effort to undo her weight loss accomplishment, as though this would save her marriage. She realized she harbored the fantasy that gaining weight and returning to her original size would restore Ethan to his previous, more stable level of functioning.

Although the outcome of this couple remains to be seen, it illustrates how nobody resolves an eating disorder in a vacuum. Family and friends may have strong reactions to their loved one's success, ranging from happy to jealous to fearful and, in the case of Ethan, paranoid.

Clinicians need to be aware that as our clients get better, there may be family reverberations that we need to look out for. This is reminiscent of the case of Caroline whose husband badgered her to lose weight. When Caroline did, indeed, resolve many of her binge triggers and lost weight, her husband brought her a present to celebrate—a large gift box of Godiva chocolates. Caroline read between the lines that Neil was subtly instructing her, "Change back to the way you were. I was more comfortable that way."

When a client discusses concerns about family members sabotaging them, we need to look at how this client's getting better has destabilized something in the family dynamic. That destabilization must be addressed, or relapse will occur. Couples or family sessions can be key in addressing the anxiety around these shifts of balance, power, and control.

The Negative Therapeutic Reaction: The Wish to Thwart the Therapist. Certain clients do not want to succeed in resolving their eating problems because they have an investment in trying to spite the therapist. Their interest in robbing the therapist of the pleasure of helping them and being important to them is based on early issues of envy and competition with a parent. The wish to get even with controlling and authoritative parents leads these clients, often unconsciously, to undermine their own progress in therapy. They try to defeat the therapist but wind up defeating themselves as well.

Geneen announces that she will stop being bulimic during my summer vacation, which is seven months away. She has decided not to improve until then. "Why wait so long?" I ask. Geneen replies, "Because if I work on not throwing up now, you will take the credit for my success. You will think it has to do with your help, and I don't want to give you the satisfaction."

Geneen's hostility to me and her wish to thwart me is a direct translation of her rage at her mother's lifelong intrusiveness and attempts to control her daughter's eating. I suggest to her that she secretly get better behind my back and not tell me. Geneen is pleased and intrigued by this "solution." Of course, her interest in spiting me will still be up for discussion as we move forward.

Guilt and Self-Sabotage. People often do not feel entitled to success in resolving their eating disorders because of guilt. In his book *Why People Fail*, social worker Dr. Herb Strean (1992) describes the psychological meaning of failure and how if we believe our success will make others suffer, or if we feel that in becoming successful we have stolen happiness away from someone else, we will arrange to defeat ourselves not to feel guilty. If we surpass our rivals, we may view our accomplishments as provocative acts that hurt others, which then makes us then feel obliged to undo our success.

People do not feel entitled to resolve their eating disorder for many reasons related to guilt and their distorted conclusion:

- "I don't deserve to be happy."
- "If it weren't for me, my parents wouldn't have gotten drunk [divorced, sick, fought so much, died, and so on]."
- "My mother was never able to lose weight, and I don't want to make her feel bad. We always shared weight loss schemes, and I

don't want to rub salt into her wounds by getting healthier and maybe losing some weight."
- "I was sexually molested as a child, and part of me enjoyed that attention. Why do I deserve to be happy?"

Many patients who come to see me for therapy make great strides in improving their relationships and professional lives. When they can also declare peace with their eating problems, they often worry they will now "have it all." Amy cried, "My sister has cerebral palsy. How can I let myself feel good about still another accomplishment when she's never had anything?"

Unless this guilt is recognized and worked through, clients will weaken their own progress as penance for the idea that they are hurting other people who are not as lucky as they are.

Social work psychoanalyst Jane Hall (2004) describes these "inner roadblocks":

> Once a journey toward self-understanding has begun, impulses to turn back may threaten the process. When the road becomes dangerous or disappears, it is the therapist who must build bridges, ford rivers, cross deserts, and brave storms, all the while keeping her fearful patient/companion from abandoning the journey. (p. 1)

These images evoke the idea of psychotherapy being akin to a safari as the therapist guide leaves no stone unturned to clear the path of health and healing.

Overcoming the Fears of Change, Loss, and Success

Most people believe that successfully resolving an eating problem means losing weight. I never met a person—even the thinnest anorexic—who did not want to lose weight. But true success means eliminating behaviors of binge eating, compulsive overeating, bulimia, anorexia, chronic dieting, and mentally obsessing about size and the number on the scale. Success also means making peace with one's body, finding other nourishing ways other than food that will help regulate difficult emotions beyond the Band-Aid and temporary relief of emotional eating.

Clinicians need to teach clients that resolving an eating problem can arouse strong feelings of anxiety, especially when success involves so many intense changes. Consider the following questions to engage clients in becoming thoughtful. If you were living in harmony with your body and expressing your feelings without detouring them through dieting, bingeing, purging, or starving,

- How would your family life change? Your work life? Your friendships?
- In what ways would these changes be negative or frightening?
- In what ways would these changes be positive or exhilarating?
- Are there any other "dangers" about declaring peace with your food and eating that could get in your way?

Each of the fears of change you discover needs to be tackled with a three-pronged approach:

1. Identify and confront the feelings of loss that emerge as you begin to succeed.
2. Find an outlet of self-expression that can give meaning to your life outside of the consuming passion with weight and food.
3. Move beyond the loss to new ways of empowering yourself by joining a support group, entering therapy, or developing an inner spiritual life.

Compassion for one's self is the antidote to self-punishment and self-hate. Compassion is a state of forgiveness, of benevolence, of declaring peace with ourselves. We can help clients generate self-compassion

- by accepting the fact that achieving success in our lives means, to some degree, abandoning the cocoon of our families.
- by accepting that we can love and hate someone all at the same time, and these feelings, although conflicting, are fully human and not worthy of self-punishment.
- by accepting that we can entertain all kinds of thoughts in the privacy of our heads from murder to adultery, but thinking these thoughts is not the same as acting on them and therefore not worthy of self-punishment.
- by accepting that putting our own needs first is not selfish but based on self-love and self-preservation. To be "people pleasers," on the other hand, is to ignore our own healthy self-interest.
- by accepting that the daily living of life is not a dress rehearsal for some future performance. The present moment is all we have, and we have a responsibility to make it the fullest and richest life we can. "Growing pains" got this name because sometimes growing hurts.

We help clients work out their fear of success by encouraging them to "feel the fear and do it anyway!"

4

Treatment Part 2: Action Strategies

The first action an eating disordered person usually takes when they decide to get their weight, food, and eating under control is to go on a diet. And they can choose a diet from every letter of the alphabet: Atkins, blood type, carbs (low), DASH, Dukan, elimination, F-factor, gluten-free, high-protein, intermittent fasting, Jenny Craig, juice fasting, ketogenic, locavore, macrobiotic, Mediterranean, Nutrisystem, organic, Paleo, raw foods, South Beach, TLC, vegan, Weight Watchers, Zone.

The beauty of these diets? They all work! Diets help clients

- feel virtuous and confident they are regulating their eating.
- feel in control by structuring their food.
- feel motivated by focusing on counting calories or points.
- distract, detour, or divert themselves from examining emotional issues that have fueled their disordered eating.
- lose weight. This inspires a person to reduce their food even more to achieve even faster weight loss results.

Diets are seductive because they promise all these benefits and extend the hope that the person will once and for all resolve their eating and weight problems. This current diet will be the one—they hope—that will finally work.

But embedded in these diets are the seeds of their own destruction. Most often, the hopeful client eventually becomes disillusioned and returns to bingeing, purging, or starving. Ultimately, diets don't work because

- the body perceives dieting as the equivalent to a famine and therefore slows down metabolism to conserve energy.

- their restrictive nature stimulates hunger for forbidden foods and for bigger quantities than permitted on the diet.
- diets require compliance to an external authority rather than determining what one's body and appetite are truly hungry for.
- diets provoke rebellion because nobody wants to be told what to do and how to eat. It is too reminiscent of a scolding parent telling you to finish your lima beans.
- the emotional issues that have stimulated eating disorders in the first place are not addressed. Then the need for the "medication" of emotional issues once again resurfaces.
- with time, following a diet gets boring.
- the diet increasingly demands obedience and strictness. When people cannot perfectly meet these rigid standards and begin to "cheat," they feel they have failed and are ashamed.
- the diet turns into a dictator rather than a guiding companion.
- diets are the gateway to eating disorders by promoting this vicious cycle: dieting → weight loss → deprivation → breakthrough bingeing → guilt → increased restriction. The cycle repeats with yo-yo dieting.

But restrictive diet plans are not the only thing that sets an emotional eater up for failure. When people place their own arbitrary restrictions on what they can and cannot eat, this also boomerangs and can lead to out-of-control eating.

Jean goes out to lunch with her girlfriend. Lucy orders dessert, and Jean looks longingly at the chocolate mousse but reminds herself she is on a diet and not allowed to eat sweets during the week; she silently criticizes her cravings to have some dessert. Jean then goes home and binges on cookies for the rest of the afternoon.

I ask her, "What if you had joined your girlfriend in having dessert?"

Jean responds, "Who eats dessert on Tuesday afternoons?"

"Your girlfriend Lucy does and so do a lot of other people!"

"I can't eat dessert during the week. I save it up for the weekends," Jean says.

"Do you think you would have binged when you got home if you had satisfied your dessert craving at lunch?"

Jean pauses. "I never thought of it that way."

Jean does not allow herself to be attuned and respond to her inner promptings because of her ingrained belief, "Who eats dessert on Tuesday afternoons?"

It is sad and a bit funny that Tuesday afternoon in Jean's mind is a day when dessert should be forbidden. Jean carries around these rigid, arbitrary, and unnecessary rules of what is permitted and what is not, but the trouble is this doesn't work for her. External rules and regulations do not promote her self-knowledge about what ultimately serves her best.

Questions for Jean include: Why has she given up her internal voice with its helpful promptings and instead become obedient to an external capricious voice? And whose voice is that external capricious voice, anyway?

I share with Jean my favorite mantra, "Eating to satisfaction is the single most important ingredient in preventing a binge." I am trying to restore Jean's connection with her inner voice, her inner hunger, and her inner decision making rather than relying on the outer dictator of her eating disorder. Our work deepens as Jean realizes she never knew she had an inner voice and thought she would always need to be told what to eat. With a nod to the book *Tuesdays with Morrie*, I laughingly suggest we should write a book together called *Tuesdays with Mousse (Chocolate)*.

In her exposé against the diet industry, Jessica Knoll (2019) writes in the *New York Times* article "Smash the Wellness Industry":

> I called this poisonous relationship between a body I was indoctrinated to hate and food I had been taught to fear "wellness." This was before I could recognize wellness culture for what it was—a dangerous con that seduces smart women with pseudoscientific claims of increasing energy, reducing inflammation. . . . But at its core, "wellness" is about weight loss. It demonizes calorically dense and delicious foods, preserving a vicious fallacy: Thin is healthy and healthy is thin.
>
> The diet industry is a virus, and . . . when you have to deprive, punish and isolate yourself to look "good," it is impossible to *feel* good.
>
> Wellness also contributes to the insulting cultural subtext that women cannot be trusted to make decisions when it comes to our own bodies. . . . We must adhere to some sort of "program" or we will go off the rails. (paras. 5, 16, 19)*

We might reconsider all eating disorders as actually stemming from "dieting disorders."

Action Strategies That Do Work

Action strategies that do work are based on the empathic connection between therapist and client. A relationship of trust and connection

*For articles on dieting, wellness, and body positivity, see Brodesser-Akner (2017), Knoll (2019), and Markowicz (2018).

imbues the client with hope that these recommendations will work; the best strategies in the world will not reach or touch the client without the nutrient-rich broth of the therapeutic relationship.

In *The Body Remembers*, Rothschild (2000) discusses the primal importance of working to help a client feel secure in the therapeutic relationship. She states, "The therapeutic relationship may be the whole of the therapy, building resources and resilience that were never developed" (p. 81).

Cognitive Strategies

Albert Einstein is said to have declared, "We can't solve our problems with the same thinking we used when we created them." Eating disorder clients are often immersed in hurtful and destructive thought patterns that keep them stuck in distorted inner dialogues. "I am fat and ugly" is the refrain most proclaimed by emotional eaters.

Negative thought patterns are learned through internalizing our culture's critical messages about appearance or through family or peer messages. And therefore, they can also be unlearned by challenging their distortions. By bringing dysfunctional thoughts out to the light of day, we help our clients examine, understand, and modify their self-criticism. These hurtful thoughts can then be replaced by helpful self-talk—a wonderful companion as a person struggles to free themselves from the snare of an eating disorder.

These six styles of thinking trap emotional eaters into self-destructive conclusions and hopelessness. We help them intervene with alternative and supportive messages.

1. **Imperative thinking** refers to the perfectionist expectations clients place on themselves that dictate what they are allowed or not allowed to do. They must not deviate from a certain path. Their thoughts are peppered with "I should" or "I'll always" or "I'll never." Instead of "I must exercise every day. If I don't work out today, I'll get off track and never do it again," substitute *"Skipping a day or so of exercise never hurt anybody. I need to respect my fatigue and only work out when I'm feeling more rested. I have to trust that my wish to exercise won't abandon me if I take time off."*
2. **Magnification** occurs when clients blow out of proportion the significance of a negative event in their lives and, at the same time, minimize their success. Rather than "I weigh more this summer than last. I will not go to the beach until I lose at least

30 pounds," consider "*I'm sorry I've had problems with my food this year, and I need to look at why. But I won't let that get in the way of enjoying my summer to the fullest. I deserve to have fun regardless of my size.*"

3. **Dichotomous thinking** refers to the "all or nothing" mind-set with which emotional eaters often struggle. Either "I'm good on my diet or I'm bad." Either "I'm fat" or "I'm thin." Dichotomous thinking is called black-or-white thinking because it leaves no room for shades of gray or nuance. Instead of "If I have ice cream, I will never be able to stop myself from bingeing on it. I'll wind up totally out of control," tell yourself, "*I can have ice cream and enjoy it. Only if I deprive myself will I start bingeing to make it up to myself and then spin out of control. I have to trust that if I make ice cream a part of my life, it will lose its stronghold on me.*"
4. **Superstitious thinking** involves linking together two ideas that are not related. Replace "If I eat this one cookie, I know it will make me fat" with "*A cookie never made anybody fat. That's just my anxiety talking.*"
5. **Selective abstraction** means focusing on and drawing conclusions from an isolated detail of a situation even though there may be evidence to the contrary. "My stomach got so bloated after lunch that I'm sure I've gained weight. How am I ever going to lose that fat?" can be reframed as "*Everyone's stomach gets bigger after eating. The anorexic in me is so critical and demanding. I know when I'm finished digesting my food, my stomach will go back to the way it was before I ate.*"
6. **Personalization** is thinking that all situations revolve around one's self. People with eating problems in particular tend to overestimate the importance of their appearance to others. Instead of assuming "Those guys were laughing when I walked by. They must think I'm fat and ugly," remind yourself, "*Who knows why those guys were laughing? My tendency to be mean and pick on myself makes me feel the whole world revolves around criticizing me. I have to trust that not everyone sees me through the same judgmental lens that I do.*"

Cognitive strategies, including 12-step programs, can often include teaching clients some wonderful mantras: *Easy does it. Keep it simple. Strive for progress, not perfection. One day at a time.*

Then there was my pithy cognitive strategy that almost backfired. Vanessa was obsessing for the millionth time about how her jeans did not fit perfectly. She had been in treatment with me for two years, we liked each other, we understood the roots of her body obsession, and she had learned to treat herself with much more loving kindness.

At her current upsurge of obsessive thinking, my annoyance rose to the surface and I yelled, "Would you shut up already!" (And I might have used an expletive). The room grew quiet. Vanessa stared at me and, in that moment, the end of my career flashed in front of my eyes as I imagined her suing me for abuse and malpractice. She then burst out laughing and through her loud guffaws exclaimed, "That is just what I needed to hear!"

In her following session, Vanessa announced she had repeated my phrase several times during the week to bring herself back from obsessing, and it worked very well. "I told myself to shut the f*** up, pictured your face, and wound up laughing instead of obsessing. Thank you!"

Of course, I knew from our previous work that Vanessa was open to a bolder engagement, and I certainly wouldn't use this technique with just anyone.

I filed this intervention under "Therapist's Creative Use of Self," and I reminded myself that a good enough therapist is not perfect but simply dedicated to ongoing self-discovery and lifelong learning (Cozolino, 2004).

Behavioral Strategies

Helping clients focus on their behaviors around food and eating starts with suggesting that they keep a "food and mood" journal. Patterns emerge that help us intervene with supportive recommendations. Most clients' diaries reveal these deficits in feeding themselves:

- Clients undereat and restrict during the day and overcompensate at night. We help them modify their food intake and spread it more evenly throughout the day.
- Clients do not eat sufficient carbs throughout the day (bread, rice, potatoes) and then binge on carb-heavy food.
- Clients do not eat sufficient protein and then do not feel satiated. Or clients avoid foods with fat, thinking that dietary fat will make them fat rather than helping with satiation. These nutritional distortions need to be addressed.
- Rather than clients getting fuel from food, they use caffeine beverages to rev up energy.
- Nighttime bingeing and purging is common, and individualized behavioral strategies can be created for self-care and calming oneself at night.

- Eating disorder clients often go to bed quite late, depriving themselves of restorative sleep, which leads to more snacking. Sleep patterns need to be addressed.
- Habitual automatic eating generally begins after work, after children are asleep, or while watching television. Clients need to focus on whether they are really hungry at these times or responding just out of habit and routine.
- Journals will reveal the moods and time of day that may be most stressful for the client, and self-soothing techniques can be created.

As part of helping clients make behavioral changes, I have created a daily self-monitoring diary to enhance awareness of eating behaviors and to also serve as a tool for relapse prevention (see Figure 4.1).

Figure 4.1 The Daily Eating Diary

1. Did I encourage myself to eat from physical hunger?
2. Did I eat at the *first* signal of hunger rather than letting myself get overly hungry?
3. Did I overeat, purge, or undereat for emotional reasons today?

   Boredom ______ Anger ______ Depression ______
   Anxiety ______ Fatigue ______ Frustration ______
   Sexual feelings ______ Transition between activities ______
   Other ____________

4. How could I have handled those emotional triggers without food?
5. Which times of the day and evening were the most troublesome for me with food?
6. What alternatives did I take during those times?
7. What alternatives could I have taken?
8. What are the ways I took good care of myself today?
9. What are the ways I needed to give to myself today?
10. What emotional needs do I anticipate for tomorrow and how can I plan to take care of them?
11. Did I practice HALT (not letting myself get too Hungry, too Angry, too Lonely, or too Tired)?
12. Did I forgive myself for any eating difficulties today, knowing I did the best I could, and tomorrow is a new day?

Dialectical Behavioral Therapy

Dialectical behavioral therapy (DBT) emphasizes that difficult feelings are a normal part of life and need to be accepted and even honored. The problem, as DBT founder Marsha Linehan (2014) explains, is not so much the difficult emotions that all we humans experience but our lack of coping methods to deal with them. Emotional eaters, for example, would rather detour, divert, and distract themselves from pain and find relief in bingeing, purging, or starving as an escape. DBT recommends four coping methods and mindfulness skills to help clients cope with pain:

1. **Emotional regulation techniques:** The first step is for clients to fully observe, accept, and describe their emotions in detail without fear or judgment. The next step is for the therapist to help clients understand that all feelings have a beginning, middle, and end *whether or not you eat over them.** The discomfort will not last forever, the distress will pass, and resorting to eating behaviors only leads to more pain.
2. **Distress tolerance:** Sometimes nothing can be done to immediately change a painful situation. Breathing through the pain, learning to accept a certain degree of powerlessness, developing patience, and tolerating a difficult reality puts one in a stronger position to cope with stress without resorting to emotional eating.
3. **Dialectical thinking:** Clients are encouraged to accept themselves just as they are. Emotional eaters are inclined to be self-disparaging and judgmental. Self-compassion coupled with commitment to change is a growth-promoting position for clients that helps eliminate their need to beat themselves up when they have a hard time with food.
4. **Chain analysis monitoring:** Emotional eating is made up of links on a chain, beginning with a "prompting event" that then leads to eating behaviors. Chain analysis helps clients "to slow down the process, to 'freeze frame' each link one after the other, so that eventually they can break the chain by substituting more adaptive links than the behaviors they have used in the past" (Safer, Telch, & Chen, 2009, p. 62). With chain analysis, clients realize that bingeing or purging does not appear unexpectedly out of the clear blue but involves a series of steps that build momentum, leading to a binge. Clients can learn to intervene and find alternatives earlier in the chain before hurtful eating becomes the only "solution."

*Thank you to Aaron Cohen, MSW, for this phrase.

Intuitive Eating

Once upon a time, we were born with the innate wisdom to know when we were hungry and when we were full. Intuitive eating is a philosophy that encourages and teaches people to return to eating based on that innate wisdom. In "ditching the diet," clients are taught to break their allegiance to the external authority and rules of a weight loss plan. This may be a particularly difficult step because most clients do not trust themselves to make healthy decisions about food and eating. And because their sole focus has been to lose weight, clients may be reluctant to focus inward to reconnect with hunger and fullness. Nevertheless, we need to foster their curiosity about their inner signals—about what hunger feels like, how to recognize fullness, how to find the willingness to stop eating when satisfied, learning what tastes good and how different foods make one's body feel. Intuitive eating is a skill that can be taught.

Intuitive eating is the opposite of mindless eating, which is fueled by anxiety and leaves people exiled from their inner signals of hunger and fullness. With mindless eating we are on autopilot; with mindful eating we are present and attuned to our bodies in the current moment. Mindless eating is reactive to external cues; mindful eating is responsive to internal cues. Mindless eating is about emotional hungers and cravings and fearful attempts to control and manipulate one's food and weight; mindful eating is about pleasure, enjoyment, and savoring tastes, textures, and flavors. Reclaiming one's pleasure in food is a key benefit of mindful eating.

The express track to intuitive eating is twofold: to breathe and to chew. So many people hurriedly grab, gulp, and swallow that they don't allow themselves the time to chew, breathe, and relish their food. Other keys to intuitive eating involve teaching clients to slow down while eating, pay attention, observe without negative judgment, focus their awareness on the present moment, honor their inner messages, not restrict food for weight loss reasons, and practice self-compassion. With mindful eating, we help clients make peace with all foods; there are no good or bad foods. We are like matchmakers working to help clients match their desire to which foods and how much will satisfy them at any moment when they are hungry. A social work colleague, Aaron, created a prayer he would recite before each meal, "Thank you for this food I am about to eat and for the willingness to be mindful," and he would then take three slow breaths before eating.

Clients need to learn that making a commitment to this way of eating requires a transition—at times a lengthy one—of exploring and questioning so their bodies can relearn their hunger cues. We also teach that we never get this perfect because every day and every meal is unique, so we are constantly "trying on for size" whether we are hungry, what we are hungry for, and when we are full.

Tamara, who dubbed herself a "full-time mindful eating student," arrived at her session quite delighted about how her eating on Saturday night turned out:

> When I asked myself what I was hungry for, my inner voice piped up, "Pizza with mushrooms and spinach and a beer with lime." I immediately knew that was exactly the right answer! And I proceeded to order just that. In the past, even if I had known what I wanted, I would have doubted myself or argued that it was too caloric and not dietetic. But then I would have felt cheated and wind up bingeing later that night. This worked out so well for me!

Others are not so delighted to learn intuitive eating: To her regret, the compulsive overeater learns how much less food she actually needs to satisfy her hunger than she had been relying on. And the anorexic is horrified to realize how much more food she needs to satisfy her hunger than she had been allowing herself.

In her blog post "Disordered Eating to Intuitive Eating," registered dietitian Alex Raymond (2019) discusses the four phases to help clients move forward with intuitive eating:

1. **Nutritional healing:** Clients begin with a flexible meal plan to use as "training wheels." Raymond emphasizes how important it is in the early stages to eat enough—every two to four hours. "It's very likely the body's hunger/fullness cues are suppressed. The body has to get used to getting fed every few hours in order for the body to start producing those cues."
2. **Embodiment:** Helping clients understand that declaring peace with emotional eating involves letting go of controlling one's body shape and size. All the body manipulation in the world, with food restrictions and excess exercise, will not help us learn to live in the body we have right now.
3. **Transition:** Clients work on accepting the body they have. This doesn't mean they always love the way their bodies look, but they are working to respect and deepen the ability to listen to their hunger and fullness cues.
4. **Intuitive eating:** Clients become attuned to their body signals of hunger and fullness and eat accordingly.

Hunger

Hunger is a complicated emotional, chemical, and physiological reaction that people experience in a variety of ways: rumblings in the stomach, feelings of light-headedness, fatigue, headaches, or food cravings.

Hunger comes in varying intensities. Many people go to extremes—either eating before they are actually hungry or letting themselves get overly hungry. Helping clients pay attention to the nuances of hunger by rating it can reacquaint them with their body's signals. The key is for people to feed themselves on demand at their body's initial signal of hunger:

0. **Empty:** Feeling empty, famished, starving, dizzy, faint.
1. **Inner nudge:** Beginning to feel an inner nudge of hunger and the physical sensation of wanting to eat.
2. **Comfortable:** Feeling comfortable, neither overly hungry nor overly full.
3. **Emotional:** Feeling emotionally "antsy," anxious, in a tense state of wanting to eat.
4. **Out of control:** Bingeing, eating compulsively or purging, out of control, in the throes of addictive behavior.

Fullness

Just as there are stages of hunger, there are also stages of fullness of which clients need to become aware:

0. **Empty.**
1. **Full enough:** Just full enough that the edge is off your hunger, but you still want more to eat.
2. **Satisfied:** Feeling comfortable and satisfied both physically and emotionally with what you have eaten.
3. **Too full:** You have eaten too much and are overly full.
4. **Stuffed:** You are decidedly uncomfortable and bloated, and you vow you will never eat again.

Learning to stop eating when you are satiated takes a lot of fine-tuning. Permitting emotional and physical satisfaction with every meal helps to avoid compulsive eating.

Many people know when they are full but find it difficult to stop if there is still food on their plate. I call this "separation anxiety," and I encourage patients to develop strategies to help them "wave good-bye" to the food until the next time they are hungry:

- Taking three more forkfuls "for the road" and really savor them. Then stop eating.
- Planning an after-meal activity that is a comforting transition away from eating—something to look forward to rather than a distasteful chore like cleaning up. Overeating is a great way to

avoid the chores at hand. Leaving the table and reading a newspaper with your feet up on the couch is a perfect alternative.
- Creating an after-the-meal ritual like brushing your teeth or saying a little thanksgiving prayer asking for the willingness to stop eating.

Learning to eat mindfully is an act of self-love and self-care. Reclaiming one's pleasure and satisfaction with food and honoring one's hunger is a healing process for emotional eaters that empowers them to trust themselves. The joy of mindful eating is that clients' eating is not directed by rules, regulations, scales, or diets. It is directed by their own unique inner experiences. Therefore, they become their own expert on their food and eating. And that is very empowering.

When clients are on the road to intuitive eating, they will still need to work on strategies to cope with anxiety, boredom, and the host of emotions that originally sent them to binge, purge, or restrict. Coping with feelings without turning to food is the work of psychotherapy, but the growing ability to savor one's food, eat to satisfaction, and honor one's hunger and body will pave the way along this journey.*

Health at Every Size

The diet industry promotes losing weight and being thin as the sole measure of happiness, health, and success. Yet for most people, this focus on weight loss invariably creates guilt, shame, body insecurity, yo-yo dieting, and a persistent sense of failure as they either cannot lose the "required" amount or repeatedly fail to keep it off. The Health at Every Size (HAES) movement flies in the face of the dieting "authorities" and instead encourages people to adopt a healthy lifestyle for the purpose of well-being rather than weight loss.

HAES is a nondiet, weight-neutral approach developed by a group of health professionals in the 1990s that has recently caught fire as a therapeutic antidote to the rigid, diet-driven culture we live in. HAES celebrates and respects natural body diversity where people of all body shapes and sizes can be motivated to embrace their bodies, eat with pleasure, and exercise in an enjoyable way that will lead to health but without the stress or negative judgment associated with weight stigma and dieting. This is a corrective remedy for clients with emotional eating

*Additional resources on intuitive eating include Intuitive Eating Pros (see a list of articles at https://www.intuitiveeating.org/resources/articles/), Chosen Bays (2017), Thich and Cheung (2010), and Tribole and Resch (2012).

problems who have chronically felt despair and discouragement that their body size makes them feel like a failure.

Dr. Linda Bacon, author of *Health at Every Size* and *Body Respect*, researcher, social justice advocate, and nutrition and health professor, states that lifestyle factors such as exercise, sleep, stress levels, and eating a balanced, nourishing diet are much better predictors of internal health than weight alone. Because people of any size—big or small—can be sedentary or eat unhealthy diets, studies increasingly show that we should focus on physical activity and fitness-based interventions rather than weight loss–driven approaches for clients' health and well-being.*

HAES seeks to help people treat themselves well by caring for the body they have right now, rather than waiting until some future time when they hope to lose weight and their life begins. Indeed, life is not a dress rehearsal for some future ideal time. Teaching our clients the principles of HAES will support them in making peace with their body size and eating behaviors and get off the weight cycling merry-go-round. The four principles are as follows:

1. **Weight inclusivity:** This helps our clients accept and respect the inherent diversity of body shapes and sizes and reject the tendency to idealize thin bodies. Just as a woman with a size 8 shoe cannot squeeze comfortably into a size 6, it can be difficult for people to reshape their bodies because heredity and genetic makeup are mainly responsible for our shape and size. We have very limited control in manipulating body shape and sustaining weight loss.
2. **Eating for well-being:** This helps our clients learn flexible, individualized eating based on hunger, satiety, nutritional needs, and pleasure, rather than following an externally regulated eating plan focused on weight control.
3. **Life-enhancing movement:** This helps our clients discover physical activities that are enjoyable and inspires people of all sizes and abilities to participate in enjoyable movement.
4. **Respectful care:** This encourages our clients to trust they are entitled to medical care that does not shame them because of size. And, as clinicians, we must also acknowledge our own weight biases.†

*Health at Every Size resources include Bacon (n.d.), Bacon and Aphramor (2011), and Redefining Wellness (2019).

†See Association for Size Diversity and Health (n.d.-a, n.d.-b). Health at Every Size and HAES are registered trademarks of the Association for Size Diversity and Health.

The National Association for the Advancement of Fat Acceptance argues that fatness is a form of body diversity that should be respected, much like diversity based on skin color or sexual preference.

I had to confront my own unwitting weight bias as I greeted my client after an extended summer vacation. Ginny said, "You look like you lost weight." And I responded, "Thank you." I was embarrassed at my response as if weight loss were a compliment that automatically merited an appreciative thank you. I wish I had thought of a more neutral response such as "Yes, I did. Your reaction?"

Because HAES supports clients in accepting their bodies regardless of size, some clinicians worry that this approach may normalize obesity or even send the message to ignore the health consequences of obesity. Rather, this philosophy helps people build a more trusting relationship with their bodies, which, up to now, they may have ignored or abused due to shame. If we can help clients achieve a less critical, more peaceful relationship with themselves, they will improve their health, their habits, and their self-esteem. Their relationship with food and body will then be based on self-care, not self-control.

Nutritionist Christy Harrison (2018), who has dubbed dieting "the life thief," compares conventional weight management tactics with the HAES philosophy. Weight management approaches are based on the belief that peoples' food and activity choices always determine their size and that, with enough effort, people can lose weight and keep it off permanently. HAES, in comparison, has demonstrated that, in truth, people have very little long-term control over their body size, and diets only lead to weight gain rebound and chronic dieting dissatisfaction.

The HAES philosophy gives eating disordered clients hope by dismantling the conviction that only thin bodies deserve exercise, good nutrition, and self-love. If our clients (and ourselves) believe that all bodies deserve care and attention, then we provide them with loving kindness and self-compassion—wonderful ingredients for living in and respecting one's body. HAES heals.

EMDR

Eye movement desensitization and reprocessing (EMDR) therapy was developed by Dr. Francine Shapiro, PhD, to help process and resolve traumatic memories. A strong connection exists between trauma and the development of eating disorders, and EMDR can help the client "metabolize" and "digest" traumatic memories so emotional eating will not be needed as a coping strategy.

Experiencing a traumatic event causes unprocessed information to be dysfunctionally held in memory networks in the brain and can lead to symptoms of PTSD. Those with eating disorders attempt to numb and self-medicate trauma through their eating behaviors. But our brains do have a natural way to recover from these traumatic memories and events, and EMDR therapy seems to have a direct effect on healing the way the brain processes information.

During the therapy, the client reflects on the traumatic event while focusing on the side-to-side movement of the therapist's fingers. These bilateral (side-to-side) eye movements or binaural (left and right sounds on a headphone) are believed to help process and desensitize the trauma and the eating disorder.*

With a successful EMDR course of treatment, the client no longer relives the images or emotions when the traumatic event comes to mind. EMDR appears to be similar to what occurs naturally during dreaming or REM (rapid eye movement) sleep. The bilateral movements or sounds keep the client focused in the present, so they are not retraumatized while processing the disturbing event. The goal is to reprocess these memories in an adaptive way—eliminating emotional distress and reducing physiological arousal. The experience is still remembered, but the fight, flight, or freeze response from the original event is resolved.

EMDR therapy helps the brain metabolize these memories and allows normal healing to resume. When no longer triggered by traumatic memories, emotional eaters will no longer need the anesthesia of their bingeing, purging, or starving.

Food Addiction

The word "addiction" comes from the Latin *addictus*, referring to a transaction in which an individual is given into slavery. Our contemporary understanding of addiction is that an afflicted person is enslaved to a harmful solution for dealing with emotional pain. The following client behaviors indicate addiction:

- Clients describe that their need for the gratification of the moment becomes more urgent than their rational self.
- They lie to others about what they are eating and secretly sneak food.
- They avoid socializing or going to work to binge, purge, or starve.
- They cannot stop eating compulsively, vomiting, starving, or abusing laxatives despite their best efforts.
- They are ashamed and humiliated by their behavior but feel powerless to change.

---

*EMDR resources include Forester (2019), Seubert (2018), and Shapiro and Forrest (2004). See also https://www.emdria.org/ and http://www.emdr.com/.

Physiological Illness and Psychological Obsession

Addiction is a complex physiological illness coupled with a psychological obsession that progresses over time. Physiologically, food addicts need to consume increasingly large amounts of food to feel good. Usually the addict is drawn to foods high in sugar, fat, salt, or wheat products. Unlike normal eaters, food addicts have a very high tolerance for consuming large amounts of these foods and will experience withdrawal when they cannot get their food. Symptoms of withdrawal may include crying spells, insomnia, irritability, difficulty concentrating, anger, depression, fatigue, and headaches. The withdrawal symptoms then set up further cravings for consuming even more food.

Increasing evidence suggests food addicts may have a metabolic abnormality of their body chemistry that causes them to crave refined carbohydrates, such as sugar, in the same way that alcoholics crave liquor. Carbohydrates cause the body to release the chemical serotonin, which is a natural calming agent that eases feelings of stress and tension. Bingeing becomes an attempt at self-medication—a way of raising the body's serotonin level (Addiction Hope, n.d.; Ross, 2012).

Starvation also produces a "kick" for people with anorexia because endorphins are released by the lack of food. Compulsive exercise provides a similar "high" as well. People may become "committed" to their addiction not because they lack willpower but because of strong biochemical forces.

A food addict also develops an intense mental obsession with food, and this "consuming" preoccupation can interfere dramatically with day-to-day living, as well as drain one's energy from the pursuit of more enriching life goals.

Overeaters Anonymous and Eating Disorders Anonymous

"I admitted I was powerless over my eating, and it has made my life unmanageable." So begins the first step of Overeaters Anonymous (OA). OA states that eating disorders are an addiction that cannot be cured but only arrested one day at a time. The first OA meeting was held in 1960, and since that time it has grown to about 7,000 meetings in more than 80 countries—about 54,000 members.

Recovery from Addiction—The OA Approach

Recovery for addicted eaters begins when they recognize that their lives have become unmanageable and they are powerless over food. For the food addict, relief may come with a program such as OA (Bill B., 1981; Wilson, 2015).

OA is a self-help group of men and women, which offers a resource of structure, support, and compassion for breaking free of the bondage of eating problems. In the meetings, people share their experience, strength, and hope with other members. The 12 steps become a road map of surrender, self-exploration, and trust in a higher power. It is one of the many ways to heal from struggles with food and eating.

OA believes that eating problems are a threefold disease: physical, emotional, and spiritual. The problem is emotional, the symptom is physical, the solution is spiritual.

The program is composed of three ingredients:

1. **The steps:** Only one of the 12 steps deals directly with food; the others address a person's relationship to oneself, to others, and to a higher power. Because the steps talk about God, many people believe that OA is a religious program. However, the program emphasizes that each individual should choose a concept of a higher power that fits their belief system. This personal higher power then becomes a strength they can turn to for guidance that is greater than their momentary desires and compulsions for food. Some believe that God refers to Good Orderly Direction. Others define the concept of God as their own true, inner voice—the part of themselves where their most honest and caring self resides. When we think about how clients have made food—or the craving for thinness or the number on the scale—their God, the idea of choosing a healthier concept to rely on for help and guidance becomes easier to appreciate.
2. **The meetings:** OA meetings can help break through the isolation that is so typical of eating disorder sufferers. The group becomes a second-chance family where clients can share their innermost selves and feel understood. Clients need to learn to relate to one another to recover, replacing their self-contained world of food for the richness of human relationships. In *Fat Is a Family Affair*, Judi Hollis (2003) discusses how "we have tried to get nurturance without being vulnerable. The only way to do that is with food" (p. xvii). The group teaches how to be vulnerable without food.
3. **The tools:** According to Alcoholics Anonymous, "The alcoholic is absolutely unable to stop drinking on the basis of self-knowledge." Similarly for the food addict, self-knowledge brings a

person just so far, and then it must be coupled with action: preplanning your food each day rather than relying on the whim of the moment to dictate what to eat, working with a sponsor who becomes a personal guide, and using slogans such as the Serenity Prayer ("God grant me the serenity to accept the things I cannot change, the courage to change the things I can, and the wisdom to know the difference").

Controversy

Many clinicians as well as clients bristle and object to the idea that people can be considered powerless over their food and therefore take issue with the OA model. Critics of the addiction model believe that diagnosing people with a lifetime food addiction disempowers them and destines them to despair that they can never be healed.

Strong controversy exists between clinicians who adhere to the addiction model and those therapists who believe in the no-diet approach of learning to eat when you are hungry and stop when you are full.

Food addiction is a chronic, progressive, and potentially fatal disease; addicts are powerless over certain foods. This is a concept subscribed to by many eating disorder and addiction therapists (Ross, 2017; Sheppard, 1993; Tarman, 2019).

The no-diet approach says we do have power over food: "The first step in breaking free is to attune one's eating with hunger and fullness. No food is forbidden if the person remains conscious" (Roth, 1993, p. 6). Addiction experts say, "Food is a drug. Every addict has to learn that the relationship is harmful" (Hollis, 2003, p. 33).

No-diet experts say, "Each time you feed yourself when your stomach is hungry, you are nourishing yourself"; the cure is "to feed yourself on demand" (Hirschmann & Munter, 2008, p. 140).

Therapists who work with the addiction model believe that for some people, eating certain foods is a form of substance abuse, like drinking is to an alcoholic. They believe that eating disorders are a physical, emotional, and spiritual disease. An OA-type program would encourage a client to choose a sponsor to help design a daily eating plan to eliminate personal binge foods.

Therapists of the no-diet/no-deprivation approach explain that structured food plans do not work because they deprive us of the foods we love and set us up for an inevitable cycle of bingeing on those very foods. People can learn to eat normally by paying careful attention to their own inner cues of hunger and fullness.

Resolving Controversy

How do we clinicians know whom to believe? Whose advice shall we follow? How do we figure out what is best for our clients? Experts from each side believe they are right. So, what is the truth?

The truth is, I believe, they both are right, but they both have left out the key variable in this controversy: the individual client, with his or her unique mosaic of strengths and vulnerabilities, needs and desires, heredity and beliefs (Jasper, 1989).

Each person's eating struggle is as unique as a fingerprint. Every emotional eater is not created the same. What works for one may not work for another.

The ultimate goal of either approach is to help our clients move increasingly from reactive eating, which is vulnerable to external stress, toward responsive eating, which is attuned to either one's own personal food plan or to one's inner physical hunger. Emotional eating is reactive eating. Responsive eating would be one of the following:

1. Preplanning your meals with a structured food plan.
2. Preplanning your meals with a structured food plan and then learning, in time, to eat when hungry and to stop when full.
3. Learning to eat when you are hungry and to stop when full.

Eating Disorders Anonymous

Eating Disorders Anonymous (EDA) is a variation of OA, which, arguably, could be considered a more contemporary approach to 12-step programs. Whereas OA focuses on abstinence and talks about food as if it were addictive, EDA does not. In EDA, the focus is on balance—not abstinence from anything. EDA encourages sound nutrition and discourages any rigidity concerning food, weight, and body image. EDA members don't count anything—no weighing and measuring, no calorie counting, no scales, no numbers at all. Rather, EDA appreciates "milestones of recovery"—a self-defined marker on a person's journey in recovery. Members underscore that even on their worst days, people need to also acknowledge the things they are doing right to support their recovery. EDA believes people can fully recover, and the program's motto is HEALTH: honesty, equality, accountability, love, trust and humility.*

*For more on Eating Disorders Anonymous, see http://eatingdisordersanonymous.org/. Another OA-type organization is Food Addicts Anonymous (http://www.foodaddictsanonymous.org/).

Conclusion

There are many paths to declaring peace with emotional eating. In my first book, *French Toast for Breakfast: Declaring Peace with Emotional Eating* (Cohen, 2016), I discuss the misguided approach of one of my colleagues, a psychologist, who hypnotizes clients for weight control and intones, "If you ever put a piece of chocolate in your mouth again, little eggs in that chocolate will crack open, and tiny worms will come out. . . . You will never be interested in eating chocolate again." Resolving eating problems can never be about cultivating within the client fear or disgust about eating or food.

Everyone's eating problem is as unique as a fingerprint and, in this chapter, we have explored the variety of action approaches to help our clients make peace with their emotional eating. Knowledge, flexibility, and empathic attunement about who will benefit from which approach will help clinicians blend together the science and the magic of psychotherapy.

As Zen Buddhist master Thich Nhat Hanh reminds us,

> We spend hours worrying about our future, blaming ourselves for what we've eaten or how inactive we've been, and completely missing the present moment—the moment in which we actually have the power to make real change in our lives. (Thich & Cheung, 2010, p. 2)

5

Medications and the Eating Disorder Client

"Are you one of those shrinks who believes just take some pills for all your ills?" Ellyn challenges me. "You know, better living through chemistry?" she provokes.

I have just suggested to Ellyn that her depression and bulimia could be helped by medication. I respond, "So your daily vomiting, how's that working out for you?"

Ellyn laughs at my tough-love challenge because she is learning that the aggression she vomits out can now be vented in spirited conversation and confrontation between us. But I also think to alleviate her depression, we need to consider medication.

"But, in truth," Ellyn asks, "If I take medication, aren't I just turning to a pill as a crutch the way I've always turned to food? Aren't I just substituting one dependency for another?"

I answer, "In the time we've been together, you've been working on getting to the bottom of your depressed feelings and also improving your bingeing and purging. And you have definitely made some progress. But I think there is also something biological going on here as well, and medication can help restore whatever chemical balance is out of alignment."

"And what's making you come to this conclusion?" Ellyn wonders.

"I think you have had a low-grade depression for many years, but it got worse when your father died, and your bulimia got worse at that time, too. Sometimes when we go through a trauma or loss, it can wear us down. The chemicals in our body, endorphins, are responsible for our feelings of well-being, and they can get depleted.

"Also, your father and grandfather suffered from depression and alcoholism, so there may be a genetic component to what you're going through as well.

"I recommend that you have a consultation with the psychopharmacologist I work with. Let's just hear what he has to say. And, if he recommends antidepressants, which I think he will, I believe you will feel much better. And you deserve to feel better!"

Ellyn agrees she will go for the consultation, and we will take it from there.

When I suggest medication, clients often challenge me warily like Ellyn. Fear is often prompting that reaction. Fear and apprehension are frequent reactions when clients are told medication can be helpful. They worry that taking medication means that

- they must be really crazy.
- they will get addicted and need increasing amounts.
- they will gain weight.
- they will never be able to get off the medicine.
- they will have to keep this a secret.
- family and friends will make them feel ashamed.
- they will turn into zombies.
- no one will ever want to marry them if they are on psychiatric medication.
- the medication will not work, so why even try? They are too far gone.
- they are a failure for not resolving their emotional and eating problems on their own.

Not all eating disorders stem exclusively from emotional issues. Our complex internal biochemistry also controls our eating patterns and our perceptions of hunger. Over the past 40 years, scientists have made great strides in understanding how our brains work. Their research points to the enormous role that hormones, neurotransmitters, and enzymes play in affecting our behavior. The pathways in the brain that regulate our eating behavior are made up of networks of brain cells. Messages are passed from one cell to another by chemicals called neurotransmitters. If there is a neurological dysfunction in the brain because of an abnormal conduction of neurotransmitters, these pathways can go awry and lead to eating disorders, depression, anxiety, or OCD. Medications such as antidepressants can be used as a way to re-regulate the functioning of the transmitters in these brain pathways. They "remind" the body of the correct route to become balanced again. Rather than a crutch, medications can gently restore one's inner chemistry and improve functioning.

Researchers have also discovered that certain foods influence the chemicals in our brain, which directly affect our mental energy, mood, and behavior. Foods rich in carbohydrates, for example, serve as natural tranquilizers. They can trigger the release of neurotransmitters, which, in turn, elevate our mood and make us feel better. Eating disorders have been called an attempt at self-medication. So, when clients binge on donuts, cookies, or chips, they may actually be trying to alleviate their anxiety or depression. Donuts do lift the spirits—but only temporarily.

If we suspect our eating disorder client can benefit from psychiatric medications, social work clinicians will need to consult with psychopharmacologists. Much has been written on medication for eating disorder patients that is helpful for us to study (H. Davis & Attia, 2017; Eating Disorders, n.d.; EDReferral.com, n.d.; Healthline, n.d., Karges, n.d.; Metro Health, n.d.; Montecatini, n.d.; Muhlheim, 2019).

Psychiatric Diagnoses in Eating Disorder Patients

Eating disorder patients often suffer from depression, panic and anxiety, OCD, bipolar illness, and premenstrual syndrome (PMS). These disorders respond well to psychiatric medications.

Depression

Research currently shows that almost three quarters of all patients with emotional eating problems also suffer from a depressive disorder (WebMD, n.d.).

Biologically based depression, which is related to abnormal neurochemical functioning, is different from the occasional depression or sadness that many people experience from time to time.

There are several types of depression. A partial list follows.

Major Depression. Major depression refers to an acute episode of depression lasting more than two weeks with five of the following symptoms:

- Depressed mood
- Lack of interest or pleasure in life
- Significant weight loss or weight gain not related to dieting or an increase or decrease of appetite every day
- Insomnia or oversleeping every day
- Psychomotor agitation or retardation every day (feeling "hyper" or "dragged out")
- Fatigue or loss of energy every day
- Feelings of worthlessness or excessive or inappropriate guilt
- Diminished ability to concentrate or make decisions

- Recurrent thoughts of death, suicidal thoughts, or suicidal behavior

Persistent Depressive Disorder. A chronic state of depression that has lasted for at least two years. Even the person's achievements and successes do not alleviate the depression, except temporarily.

Bipolar Disorders. Illnesses in which the person's mood swings between lows and highs, ranging from deep depression to inappropriate elation (formerly called manic-depressive illness). Bipolar disorders can range in intensity from mild to severe. People with a diagnosis of bipolar II do not reach the extreme highs of those with bipolar I.

Atypical Depression. Symptoms include increased appetite, weight gain, bingeing, oversleeping, heaviness in the arms or legs, and sensitivity to rejection, particularly romantic rejection. This depression tends to be chronic and more common in bulimics. Atypical depression is the opposite of typical depression, which usually involves loss of appetite, weight loss, and insomnia.

Seasonal Affective Disorder. Another form of biological depression often connected with eating disorders. It occurs during autumn and winter months and abates with the increase of sunlight in spring and summer. Seasonal affective disorder may respond to light box therapy with natural spectrum light of 10,000 LUX and antidepressant medications.

Premenstrual Dysphoric Disorder. Severe and disabling depression occurring five to 11 days prior to a woman's monthly menstruation. It includes a marked depressive mood, irritability, and tension. The symptoms abate with the onset of menses.

Postpartum Depression. Severe depression that women may experience after giving birth. It generally occurs soon after delivery or even up to a year later. This depression can make it difficult for the mother to find the energy to care for herself or her child and can impair her ability to bond with her infant. A doctor or psychiatrist can recommend which antidepressants can be used during breastfeeding with the least side effects for the baby.

Panic and Anxiety

Patients with eating problems often suffer from panic disorder and anxiety. Panic attacks refer to a sudden explosion of symptoms such as heart pounding, shortness of breath, trembling, and a sudden fear of impending death or feeling "crazy." These attacks feel very intense—coming on suddenly, peaking to a crescendo, and then persisting for minutes to hours. They often seem to occur for no obvious reason.

A panic attack occurs sporadically, whereas panic disorder refers to persistent worry or maladaptive behavioral changes related to the attacks.

Phobias

Many eating disorder patients also experience anxieties such as social phobia (fear of being in social situations), simple phobia (fear of a specific object or situation like spiders or closed spaces), or agoraphobia (fear of being in crowds or public places).

The psychodynamic meaning of the specific phobia is worth investigating. This was brought home to me in the case of Carmen, a bulimic patient. Carmen described going out to lunch at an outdoor restaurant with her boyfriend when a winged cockroach landed on the table. Carmen became hysterical, crying, shrieking, and ran to the ladies' room, where she proceeded to make herself throw up. "It was this horrible *cock*roach," she explained in session. She continued to describe the *cock*roach with a heavy accent on the first syllable. At first, I attributed this to her being a Spanish speaker with a thick Spanish accent who maybe did not know how we pronounce the word in English. But then I remembered one of the words for insect in Spanish is *bicho*, which is also a slang word for penis.

"Why do you keep saying *cock*roach, and why were you so afraid of it?" I asked and exaggerated the pronunciation even more.

"Because my uncle put his cock in my mouth when I was seven," Carmen blurted out, and she sat there stunned and in shock because she was not aware she even had that memory.

Needless to say, this unexpected and disturbing recovered memory opened the door for a deeper understanding of Carmen, her bulimia, her phobia, and the trauma she had endured.

OCD

Eating disorder clients often suffer from OCD. Obsessive preoccupation about weight gain and calories as well as compulsive behaviors such as frequently weighing and checking oneself in the mirror are common. Obsessive rumination often presents itself around nonfood issues as well, such as worries about germs or having done something bad. Compulsive actions include repeatedly washing one's hands or checking that the door is locked and the stove is turned off.

PMS

PMS refers to a wide range of symptoms that women suffer during the week prior to their monthly period, including irritability, tearfulness, fatigue, anxiety, depression, bloating, and increased food cravings. The emotional and physical symptoms of premenstrual dysphoric disorder are more severe than PMS and can affect daily functioning. The symptoms usually stop when the woman gets her period.

Nutritionists recommend increasing the amount of complex carbohydrates in one's diet such as oatmeal, brown rice, beans, flax seeds, and quinoa. Complex carbohydrates increase the level of serotonin, one of the endorphins in the brain that contributes to feeling calm; PMS has been associated with lowered levels of this chemical.

Women on low-carbohydrate diets often suffer more PMS symptoms. This is important to share with our clients so that women know there is actually something they can do to improve their mood. Fruits, vegetables, and dairy have high fiber, protein, and other nutrients and can balance blood sugar, which will help control mood swings and fatigue. Healthy fats such as avocado, salmon, tuna, nuts, and canola oil can also improve one's mood. Iron-rich foods such as red meat, poultry, and eggs can help with fatigue. PMS-related bloating is actually caused by dehydration, so drinking water will increase urination and relieve some of the water retention.

If these changes in diet and exercise do not sufficiently alleviate the PMS symptoms, a woman should then rule out underlying medical, gynecological, and psychological conditions with a physician. At that point, medication should be considered.

Medications for Eating Disorder Behavior and Related Symptoms

Medication can be beneficial for eating disorder patients in three different ways:

1. Medication can target and alleviate eating disorder behavior directly.
2. Medication can help relieve the symptoms of depression, anxiety, OCD, or premenstrual syndrome that often accompany and give rise to eating disorder behavior.
3. Medication can provide a combination of effects by relieving some of the eating disorder behavior as well as the underlying symptoms of depression, anxiety, or OCD.

When people feel better, they then have more inner resources to face the underlying emotional issues that fuel their eating problems.

Types of Medications for Eating Disorders and Related Symptoms

Many different kinds of chemical abnormalities underlie the various depression and anxiety disorders, and many types of medications are available to treat them. Sometimes a trial period is needed until the most effective medication is found for each person.

This is a partial list of some of the most effective medications currently used for depression, anxiety, and premenstrual dysphoric disorder in the eating disorder population. With an improvement in mood, many patients are better equipped to resolve their bulimia and binge-eating disorders. A psychiatrist with experience in eating disorders will choose from a wide range of options for each client's individual needs:

Selective Serotonin Reuptake Inhibitors and Serotonin and Norepinephrine Reuptake Inhibitors. Selective serotonin reuptake inhibitors (SSRIs) include Prozac, Lexapro, Zoloft, and Celexa. These antidepressant medications can help people increase their control over their eating and lessen the urge to binge and purge. Norepinephrine reuptake inhibitors (SNRIs) have a dual effect on two neurotransmitters and include Effexor and Cymbalta. When the patient is ready to come off them, both SSRIs and SNRIs need to be tapered gradually. New research has demonstrated that withdrawal from antidepressants can at times be protracted and difficult (Carey, 2019b).

Wellbutrin. This antidepressant medicine is also helpful for seasonal affective disorder. Unlike other antidepressants, which may cause weight gain, Wellbutrin can cause weight loss. It also has a low risk for sexual side effects. However, it should be avoided by individuals who have had anorexia or bulimia because of an increased risk of seizures.

Topamax. This medication can result in weight loss and has proven helpful in the treatment of bulimia and migraines and can reduce binge-eating episodes. Side effects can include serious kidney problems, kidney stones, fatigue, and forgetfulness.

Vyvanse. Vyvanse became the first medication approved by the Federal Drug Administration for the treatment of moderate to severe binge-eating disorder in 2015; the drug has been proven to reduce binge-eating episodes. However, Vyvanse is an amphetamine and is highly addictive. Side effects include insomnia, agitation, and mania, and it has been associated with elevated blood pressure and a higher risk of heart attack and stroke. This medication and its side effects should give patients pause before taking it, and it should be carefully monitored by a doctor.

Monoamine oxidase inhibitors. Monoamine oxidase inhibitors (MOAIs) such as Nardil or Parnate appear to be particularly effective in the treatment of atypical depression. These medications require that a patient comply with special dietary restrictions, such as avoiding red wine and aged cheese, which can cause dangerously high blood pressure. Doctors may not want to use these medications with those binge eaters who have trouble following dietary instructions.

Lithium. Lithium is used to treat bipolar illness and to enhance the effect of other antidepressants used for depression. Blood levels of this drug need to be carefully monitored to achieve the correct therapeutic effectiveness and to avoid toxic levels, kidney failure, and low thyroid function. Seventy to 80 percent of bipolar patients respond favorably to lithium.

Abilify and Seroquel. These anti-anxiety and antidepressant medications can also help treat the severe agitation that some eating disorder patients experience. These medications also alleviate symptoms of bipolar disorders. The side effects may include weight gain, metabolic syndrome (prediabetes), and neurological side effects.

Buspar. Buspar can be helpful for anxiety for people who have addictive potential.

Klonopin, Xanax, and Ativan. These benzodiazepines can be helpful for anxiety and panic disorders. Users develop a tolerance and physiological dependence, which means that these medications need to be tapered off slowly. For people with a substance abuse drug history, these medications can be addictive.

Ambien or Lunesta. These sleep medications can be helpful for insomnia for short-term usage. Side effects may include sleepwalking and eating at night in a forgetful state.

Ketamine. Ketamine was approved in 2019 by the FDA for the treatment of severe depression. It is administered as a nasal spray or intravenous infusions. Ketamine works within minutes and is mainly prescribed for people with treatment-resistant depression who have not had improvement on more traditional antidepressants. This drug is also a recreational club drug referred to as Special K (Carey, 2019a).

Zulresso. Approved by the FDA in 2019 as the first drug for women suffering from postpartum depression, the medication works within 48 hours, but it is an expensive infusion and requires a stay in a medical center (Albert & Block, 2019).

Naltrexone. An opioid-like medication used to treat alcoholism, Naltrexone can help decrease the amount and frequency of drinking. This medication may also help decrease cravings in binge-eating disorders and is a new option to consider if other medications have not been fully effective.

Considering Medication for Our Clients

First of all, it is important to realize that for everybody, good nutrition is good medicine. Anorexics often suffer from malnutrition and, to a lesser degree, so may bulimics and binge eaters. Symptoms of a malnourished person include depression and moodiness, so ensuring that our clients are eating all food categories including protein, carbohydrates, and healthy fats can be an important goal. Collaborating with a nutritionist who has experience with eating disorder patients is a cornerstone of good psychotherapy practice.

An astonishing—almost magical—example of the benefit of collaborating with a nutritionist occurred in my treatment of Maria, a woman who had not menstruated in 30 years despite being of childbearing age. The registered dietitian with whom I consulted, Laura Shammah, recommended that I advise Maria to eat half an avocado every day. Within several weeks, Maria's period returned and has continued ever since. The dietitian explained that avocados are rich in the healthy fats that help regulate hormones, which in turn help ovulation and the menstrual cycle. My graduate training in psychotherapy for eating disorders never taught me about the beneficial role of avocados in treatment.

As social work clinicians, how do we decide if a client can be helped by medication? In my practice, I always try to determine the severity of a patient's state of mind and mood to see whether we should first give psychotherapy a chance or proceed with a medication evaluation from the beginning.

If the situation is not urgent, I recommend a trial run of therapy with a two-pronged approach. I would blend behavioral work, which focuses on improving the client's eating patterns, together with psychotherapy to address the emotional issues underlying their eating problems. If there is no change in their eating behaviors after this initial therapy (about three months), then I suggest a consultation for medication.

However, if the situation is urgent at the outset—if a client's depression, anxiety, or panic are out of control or if the person is struggling with suicidal impulses, alcoholism, or drug abuse—then a medication evaluation is definitely required. This type of evaluation would also be required if an anorexic has life-threatening weight loss or medical complications due to bulimia. Sometimes hospitalization is necessary to help someone stabilize this type of crisis.

Before the medication evaluation, we should alert our clients about what to expect: the psychiatrist will review the background of the client's eating problems as well as other emotional, physical, and behavioral symptoms they may be experiencing. The doctor will also review past psychiatric, medical, and family history because addictions, mood disorders, and anxiety disorders are often hereditary.

It is especially helpful for social work clinicians to work with a psychiatrist who has expertise in the treatment of eating disorders. For instance, the commonly prescribed dosage of Prozac for depression is 20 milligrams a day. However, it is now known that many patients with bulimia do not respond to this dose but may respond to a higher one of 60 milligrams. A doctor with expertise in eating disorders will know that antidepressants will not be as effective for patients with a sluggish thyroid. Thyroid medication may sometimes be prescribed for those patients who have normal thyroid function to boost the effect of the antidepressant medication.

Just as with psychotherapy, medication requires a certain length of treatment; the usual course for relief of depression is about nine months. After six to nine months, when the patient's eating disorder and mood swings are stabilized, medications can be tapered off.

Many patients are able to sustain the benefits of improved mood and improved eating behaviors after they complete their first trial of antidepressants. Some, however, may occasionally relapse because they experience a resurgence of symptoms; medication then needs to be continued for another course of treatment. If this happens, some patients worry that they have to continue on medication because they have become dependent or addicted. This is not true. If a depressed patient continues to need medication, he is dependent on it only in the same way that a person with high blood pressure is "dependent" on medication: he must control the symptoms of a continuing underlying illness.

With all my eating disorder patients, I recommend a current medical evaluation by an internist or family physician with routine lab tests.

The physical examination will look for medical conditions, such as thyroid or endocrine problems, anemia, hepatitis, mononucleosis, ulcers, tumors, or other health concerns that could be affecting mood or eating behavior. A medical condition, such as described above, does not necessarily preclude taking psychiatric medications.

When Our Clients Take Medications

Medications can be extremely helpful in treating eating disorders, depression, and anxiety. They also have side effects that make it important to be regularly monitored by a psychiatrist or another medical doctor.

To get the best result from medication, clinicians need to instruct clients, as follows:

- Have patience as it can take several weeks for the medication to become effective.
- If you have side effects, discuss them with your doctor. Sometimes they will resolve with time, or you may require a change in dosage or prescription.
- Make the commitment to be consistent in the time and dosage of your medicine.
- Before stopping medications, speak with your doctor about how to taper off to avoid possible withdrawal symptoms.
- Avoid alcohol and recreational drugs, which can worsen depression or heighten the effect of the prescribed medication.
- Discuss with your doctor any herbs, supplements, vitamins, birth control pills, or over-the-counter medications you are taking as these may interfere with the psychiatric medication.

When Medications Are Not Indicated

No specific medication is recommended by the Food and Drug Administration for the treatment of anorexia, although trials show that Zyprexa used off-label can help to restore normal weight in anorexia patients.

It has been said that the best medicine for anorexia nervosa is food. Dr. Timothy Walsh (2013), one of the world's leading authorities on eating disorders, believes there is far more evidence supporting nutritional rehabilitation and psychotherapy for treating anorexia nervosa than supporting treatment with medication.

Medication is not the answer for clients if they are hoping for a diet aid for quick weight loss. Nor is it the answer if they have poor eating habits, have a medical condition that resembles a weight problem, such as hypothyroidism, or are actively involved with drugs or alcohol.

Although active involvement with drugs usually requires treatment in a detoxification or rehabilitation facility first, most of the medications I have discussed are not habit forming or addictive, with the exception of certain anti-anxiety medications. If patients are in recovery from alcohol or drug abuse, medications may be taken safely under medical supervision.

Other clients who may not benefit as much from medication are those for whom the eating disorder has provided a "glue" for a shaky sense of self. Hilde Bruch (1973), the pioneer of eating disorder treatment, argues, "There are people who function better with the extra weight. Obesity, although a faulty adaptation, may serve as a protection against more severe illness: it represents an effort to stay well or to be less sick" (p. 4).

I would add that this may be true of the other eating disorders as well. Because eating disorders are creative solutions for inner turmoil, they serve a protective function against that turmoil overwhelming the person. Therefore, healing an eating disorder must proceed at a pace that the person can "digest."

When Medication Is Worth a Try

Patients sometimes worry that their true feelings will be covered up by medications or that they will feel like "zombies" while taking medications. This is not the case. Unlike street drugs, which create an artificial high or a lulling sedation, the medications discussed here can help clients restore their natural mood and balance.

Depression usually gets worse over the long-term if left untreated. Not only does it cause significant misery for the depressed person and their family, but chronic depression causes a breakdown in the immune system that can lead to other illnesses. I explain to clients that trying to "tough it out" without medication may sound admirable, but in many cases this will not provide relief. A biological illness does not improve through willpower.

We now know that medication alone is not as effective as medication coupled with psychotherapy, where people can tackle both the emotional and the biological components of their eating problems (Muhlheim, 2019).

Ongoing research in the field of eating disorders continues to shed light on the complexity of eating disorder syndromes and their biological underpinnings. Leaving no stone unturned to help our clients with their eating problems, such as a trial run of medication, can be a truly compassionate act that clients can choose on their own behalf.

Hospitalization and Other Treatment Options

Determining when a higher level of care is needed should become part of a clinician's ongoing assessment of their patient. Sometimes a higher level may be needed at the outset of treatment, and sometimes a client may decline during the course of the treatment if they are faced with a physical or emotional crisis that they cannot manage in their outpatient therapy.

Hospitalization Guidelines

Medical complications can compromise the health of eating disorder patients, and therefore nonmedical clinicians will need the ongoing support of physicians to monitor these possible crises, which will require hospitalization:

- Severe malnutrition (weight is less than 75 percent of average body weight for age, sex, and height)
- Dehydration
- Electrolyte disturbances
- Cardiac dysrhythmia
- Physiologic instability (severe bradycardia, hypotension, hypothermia, orthostatic changes in pulse or blood pressure)
- Arrested growth and development
- Failure of outpatient treatment
- Acute food refusal
- Uncontrollable bingeing and purging
- Acute medical complication of malnutrition (syncope, seizures, cardiac failure, pancreatitis)
- Acute psychiatric emergencies (suicidal ideation, acute psychosis)
- Comorbid diagnosis that interferes with the treatment of eating disorders (severe depression, OCD, severe family dysfunction).

Hospital Day Treatment Programs

Day treatment programs are structured and generally require attendance of a half day or more, several days a week. Day treatment can include medical care; group, individual, and family therapy; structured eating sessions; and nutrition education.

Residential Treatment for Eating Disorders

With residential treatment, clients temporarily live at an eating disorder treatment facility. A residential treatment program may be necessary if the person needs long-term care and rehabilitation for the eating disorder or if they have been in the hospital a number of times and now need a structured aftercare plan.

Conclusion

The complexity of eating disorders as both biological and psychological illnesses requires us to weave together an individualized treatment plan for each client. One size certainly does not fit all. Collaborating with a psychiatrist with expertise in eating disorders will help us with the possible medication treatment of our clients.

6

The Therapeutic Relationship: Cultivating Hope and Connection

Psychotherapy is a "healing conversation" that provides an opportunity for our clients to repair the inner emotional wounds that have led them to conclude that *trusting food is safer than trusting people.** The nurturing and collaborative relationship with the therapist "sets the table" for clients to understand their early history and how that history relates to their present eating difficulties. By integrating both the past and the present, emotional eaters improve their capacity to regulate their emotions, learn to tolerate discomfort, trust in others for security and support, and learn to love.

These six vital ingredients help deepen the therapy relationship and encourage an intimacy to bloom between therapist and client:

1. The power of hope
2. Explaining what to expect
3. Curiosity
4. Shame, secrets, and self-esteem
5. Healing power of tears and laughter
6. Eating disorders mirror our relationships

1. The Power of Hope

H.O.P.E. = Hold On, Pain Ends

The most important ingredient we can offer our clients is hope—hope that their eating disorder can get better, that they can live more at home

*Thanks to Andrea Levin, LCSW, for this turn of phrase.

in their bodies, and that their relationship with food can become easier and less fraught with struggle. Hope is the opposite of despair. Hope kindles clients' interest in beginning therapy, and it sustains the bumps along the way.

Hope is looking forward to something you want with some glimmer of confidence that you can achieve it. This is different than optimism, where people strive for a positive outlook and "whistle a happy tune whenever they feel afraid." Whereas optimism is about a positive attitude, hope has a goal and a specific plan of action to achieve that goal. It is not just a wish but a building of practical strategies for improving one's future. Hope sustains personal motivation.

Therapists inspire hope by teaching our clients that the goal of therapy is "progress, not perfection." Rare is the person who achieves perfect eating because there is no such thing, so we help clients become more flexible, more realistic, and less judgmental. We teach them "anything worth doing is worth doing imperfectly."

Clients come to us hungry for hope. If they have battled weight for a very long time or cannot stop overeating or throwing up after they binge, they may despair at ever making positive changes. They believe they will never get better.

When clients feel hopeless about making progress with their eating or weight issues, they generally do one of two things:

1. They become paralyzed and stuck in their misery and do nothing. Because nothing changes, their despair deepens. Eating and weight issues become a chronic way of life with an increase in emotional and physical limitations. A lack of hope engenders passivity, becomes a self-fulfilling prophecy, and then resignation sets in.
2. They make a sweeping overhaul to change themselves quickly and dramatically. They begin following restrictive or fad diets and punishing exercise regimes. They fall prey to quick-fix schemes like "lose 10 pounds in 10 days." But a quick fix is rarely sustainable because it takes so much energy and deprivation. Then people wind up eventually reverting back to their old patterns.

Neither choice provides much hope or traction for long-lasting change. How do we help clients move from hopeless to hopeful to healing to wholeness?

Jackie, age 24, taught me an unusual lesson about hope and how it can be found anywhere. In our first consultation appointment, after listening to Jackie's story, I told her she had a diagnosis of binge-eating disorder. A slow, bright smile lit up her face. She seemed thrilled.

I was so surprised at her happy reaction that I asked why she was grinning. "Because up until now, I just thought I was crazy!" Jackie explained. "I have been so ashamed and guilty and felt so alone with my chaotic and sneaky eating. I've spent a ton of money on food and even hide food from my family. Now that I know I have an official diagnosis, I'm relieved that my eating problem is not my fault, and hopefully there is something I can do about it. I never even heard the term 'binge-eating disorder,' so I guess I'm not the only one who has it. I like that I'm not alone."

Nadine, a new patient, also taught me something original about hope. A bulimic married woman, Nadine was struggling to go even one day without bingeing and purging. We had been working on alternatives to her bulimia, and in her next session she declared, "I did it! I didn't binge at all last week!"

"That's great!" I responded enthusiastically. "What helped?"

"Every time I wanted to binge, I took a shower instead. I wound up taking seven showers every day!"

I was surprised at Nadine's "solution" and worried that she was becoming obsessive–compulsive about a brand-new behavior. But she explained, "I know that sounds crazy, but it gave me hope that if I can find alternatives to detour my cravings, then maybe I have a chance to get better."

Debora also discovered a unique solution to improve her binge eating that gave her hope she could get better despite spending many evenings after work gorging on cake and cookies. As we strategized alternatives, Debora came to her next session and announced, "I found a new plan that seems to be working. Rather than bingeing on chocolate chip cookies this week, I started eating four heads of iceberg lettuce with mustard every night." I was also startled at Debora's "solution" and hoped she wasn't developing a brand-new compulsion around food. But she then explained, "I realize I can't spend the rest of my life devouring lettuce, but if I can at least break the cookie habit, I feel more hopeful that I can keep doing better."

Jackie, Nadine, and Debora recognize that creating hope means taking any step away from one's entrenched destructive habits. Even a small change in behavior can engender the belief "I can do better." Taking showers and bingeing on lettuce provides a better alternative than hurting oneself with food and teaches clients that there are alternatives to make their goals more of a reality.

These emotional eaters realize that just wishing for a different outcome with their eating struggles does not change anything. Instead, taking action—any forward action—is the key ingredient to growth, change, and creating hope.

In the field of addiction, the concept of "harm reduction" theorizes that people may not be able to refrain from alcohol, drugs, gambling, cigarettes, or hurtful food behaviors so quickly. But there is value in just reducing one's negative behavior and committing to doing better even though the problem is not yet fully resolved. The fundamental strategy is to set an intention that is doable. Pablo pledged to throw up only once a day as opposed to multiple times and to distract himself whenever he felt the urge to purge. He gave himself permission to indulge his bulimia until he was ready to do better, but he committed to placing some boundaries and limits on what he allowed himself to do.

To help our clients generate hope with their eating struggles, we encourage them to do just one thing differently. Because change is composed of a series of progressive steps, taking even one step forward can provide a glimmer of hope. No step is too small to acknowledge. Hope begets hope, and we continue to build strategies with our clients to create small victories (adapted from Richardson, 2012). The following sections include other strategies to cultivate hope.

Lessening Our Clients' Perfectionism

The identity of many emotional eaters is based on performance, pleasing, and striving to be perfect; they are convinced this is what makes them lovable. However, evaluating their life and eating behavior through the lens of "I must be perfect" will sign them up for a lifetime of frustration and self-doubt. The antidote to perfectionism is believing that "good enough is good enough."

Chelsea lamented she was no longer a size zero, "my ideal size." I had known Chelsea at size zero as a gaunt young woman with angular collarbones that jutted out alarmingly. Fortunately, Chelsea caught her self-criticism in midstream and backed off even before I shared my perspective with her. She added, "OK, I know that after three children, I have to learn to be more realistic. I'm allowed to be a larger size with a tummy to show for all my hard work of carrying three kids. My perfectionism could lead me straight back to anorexia. I need to remember it was my learning healthy eating that allowed me to get pregnant in the first place."

Trust

Clients need to find people they trust and to whom they can speak from their heart. Helping clients vent their stress in words rather than acting out with food lightens their burden.

"I love coming to therapy," laughs Maddie. "Because you're my shrink, you have to listen to me, but I don't have to reciprocate by being polite and asking how you're doing! Frankly, I don't care how you are. I just want to talk about myself!"

Maddie's candor and sense of humor inspires hope in me—that this is a girl who can learn to take care of herself and speak her mind rather than stuffing down her thoughts and feelings with potato chips and brownies.

Changing What They Can, Accepting What They Can't

The Serenity Prayer from the 12-step program of Alcoholics Anonymous provides a tool of hope for our clients:

> *Grant me the serenity to accept the things I cannot change*
> *The courage to change the things I can*
> *And the wisdom to know the difference*

Accepting a certain amount of powerlessness is often a tough lesson for emotional eaters who need to be in control of everything. We teach them to take all necessary steps to fix a problem, then let go of the results.

In the midst of a grueling divorce, Ruth recognized that all the chocolate layer cake in the world was not going to relieve her hurt and anger. She continued her plan of action to solve her legal dilemma while working valiantly not to compound her own pain by overeating.

Encouraging Clients to Talk to Themselves and Become Their Own Guidance Counselor

The ability to have a private, encouraging conversation with oneself is a key component to hope and healing.

Antonio groans,

> Today was a horrible day with my boss. I really wanted to binge and throw up to make myself feel better. But I've learned to just keep distracting myself until that mood passes and have a healthy carrot juice instead. I'll feel a heck of a lot better tomorrow for not giving in to stress eating. The biggest realization in my recovery is that my agitation will pass whether or not I binge and purge.

It is key for people to realize, as Antonio says, that "my food cravings will pass whether or not I give in to them."

Practicing Self-Care and Creating Rituals

Self-care rituals provide balance and inner harmony for our clients: enjoyable exercise, meditating on one's breathing, nutritious abundant food, deep sleep, relaxation, and times of peace and quiet to recharge one's batteries.

This can be difficult for emotional eaters who have not been taught early in life how to soothe themselves and that it is a positive thing to pay attention and care for one's needs.

Tova comes from a family who survived the Holocaust, and self-sacrifice is considered a virtue in this family. Tova finds it hard to feed herself meals. We've been working on the goal of eating breakfast, something that sounds so simple, but for her it's not. She has a lot of inner resistance, as if breakfast were too self-indulgent.

"Well, I did better this week," she announces. "When I woke up, I got the box of cereal out of the closet."

"And did you eat it?" I ask.

"No, I'm not there yet. But I carried it around my apartment before I left for work, and I thought of you," she replies.

I find Tova's answer sad and funny and also a drop hopeful. Nobody has ever carried around a box of Corn Flakes and thought about me before (as far as I know). Maybe I can also get her to hear my voice gently urging, "Sit down. Eat some Corn Flakes. They taste good and they're good for you."

The Value of Self-Expression

Complaining, crying, even howling, and not bottling up hurtful feelings can be a satisfying way of expressing oneself that does not involve detouring emotions through eating behaviors. By developing a variety of techniques of self-expression, emotional eating does not have to be the only game in town. The comedian Lily Tomlin once declared, "God gave humans the gift of language, so we could complain!" And sometimes using your mouth for "purging" frustration in words and not using it for overeating brings satisfaction from tension and relief.

Channa, an anorexic patient who was taught all her life to "suck it up," enjoyed my giving her permission to complain loudly and often. She enjoyed this newfound freedom so much that she gave me a coffee mug with this scene painted on it: A customer goes to the Complaint Department of a store, and the clerk asks what his grievance is. The customer replies, "Pretty much everything!"

Tolerating Feelings

Although they can be very intense, feelings are not facts and thoughts are not facts. Sometimes, in the heat of the moment, we distort how bad things really are. Bad feelings will pass whether or not we binge, starve, or throw up. Tolerating, expressing, and digesting challenging feelings, rather than acting destructively, builds "resilience muscles" for the next time a wave of strong emotions threatens to overtake our clients and lead them down the path of emotional eating.

Finding Perspective

Dr. Tian Dayton (2008) writes, "Resilient people tend not to let adversity define them. They see their problems as temporary rather than a permanent state of affairs and tend not to globalize. They find reasons and ways—whether religious, creative, or good common sense—to place a temporary framework and perspective around the problems in their lives" (p. 103).

The Therapist Needs Hope, Too

I hope all my clients will get better and learn to sink their teeth into the vibrancy of life and not into their obsession with food. I have tremendous hope and belief in the healing power of psychotherapy as, over the years and decades, I have seen countless clients grow and develop and become happier with themselves and their bodies as well as enhance their capacity for love.

Occasionally, my hope for a client is tentative and sometimes it even dries up.

I was not very hopeful when I received a new referral of a 22-year-old anorexic and bulimic girl who had six hospitalizations by the time she was 20; she basically spent her teenage years in hospitals with little sustained improvement. What could I bring to her treatment that would make a difference when numerous other professionals had tried and did not really help?

Working with Christina was a bumpy ride filled with silences, her hostile sullenness, door slamming when she left her sessions each week, and very little traction moving forward with her anorexia and bulimia. Not only does the anorexic not want to take in food, she does not want to take in nourishment from the therapist either. I felt like I was riding a bucking bronco and trying to hold on for dear life. In true eating disorder fashion, I wondered if in agreeing to work with her, I had "bitten off more than I could chew." Sometimes I wished she would just leave treatment and go away. I studied my own "bulimic" response of when I wanted to throw her up and get rid of her.

Christina brought in the following dream: "I am vomiting into the toilet, and I see my mother's head in the bowl. I don't know whether to scoop her out or flush her down."

Christina's dream uncannily mirrored my own ambivalence to her: Should I scoop her up or get rid of her? It also mirrored Christina's ambivalence to her mother, to food, and to treatment: Should I fish myself out of the toilet or flush myself away? Should I even try to get better or just throw it all out?

Slowly, Christina began sharing stories about her early life that evoked sadness and compassion within me. She never had a doll. Her mother was chronically ill. She began to "flesh out" what her life was like as opposed to just the "bare bones" version—a really important step for an anorexic. Her story began to "take shape." Slowly, Christina had periods of eating like a semi-normal person.

Christina and I have worked together for years; our relationship has deepened and become more "full bodied." In one session she asks, "I know I was really impossible to you for a long time. Why didn't you get rid of me?"

I answered, "Because you kept coming regularly to your sessions and that made me feel at least a part of you wanted to be here and that made me want to continue to work with you. But I always wondered since you were so miserable here, why didn't you get rid of me?"

She answered, "Because you kept letting me come to my sessions and didn't fire me for being mean and impossible. Maybe I thought you believed in me, even when I didn't believe in myself."

I realized that the ingredient in Christina's therapy she never had before was the long-term consistency of our therapy relationship. Rather than repeating the actions of the hospital staff who "ejected" her (threw her up and out) after each discharge—which paralleled her bulimia—I hung on to the bucking bronco; this provided Christina hope that an ongoing healing and empathic relationship could be possible over time. While Christina was getting rid of her food, I was trying hard to contain my wishes to get rid of her. I had to "stomach" her being so difficult in sessions.

But sometimes hope dries up for therapist and client, especially when the client is hell-bent on ruining the relationship. Hope then dies on the vine. Kate had done productive work in her sessions and was no longer bulimic. I enjoyed our work together until I discovered she had forged my signature on her insurance form and added extra sessions on the form to get a larger reimbursement check.

I am angry at Kate and tell her that although I want to understand why she did this and try to work it out, I will consult a lawyer to find out what I need to do to protect myself from fraud. Kate cries and tells me that I am betraying her by speaking with a lawyer. "I'm betraying you?" I asked, surprised. "I do want to continue our work and understand what went wrong here. And I also want to protect myself."

Kate does not come back. She has ruptured my trust, although I'm willing to try to repair the connection. In retrospect, I now realize I had a blind spot in my relationship with her. Kate had revealed to me how she cheated in all her relationships—she cheated on every boyfriend she ever had, she regularly cheated at work on her time sheets, and most of all, she has cheated on Mother Nature. Mother Nature designed the digestive tract to be a one-way street going from north to south. When a bulimic throws up, she breaks the rules and turns her digestive tract into a two-way street—a betrayal of what Mother Nature created.

I understand the significant deprivation in Kate's life and why she has such need for power and control, but I lost hope when she did not come back to figure out what went wrong. I wish her well and hope that in the future, when a client tells me she cheats in every relationship, I am more aware that will include me too.

Clients prove that hope, resilience, and creativity can be found even in the most unconventional ways. Author Anne Lamott writes, "Hope begins in the dark, the stubborn hope that if you just show up and try to do the right thing, the dawn will come. You wait and watch and work: You don't give up."

2. Explaining What to Expect

Clinicians are often so steeped in conducting psychotherapy that we may forget many clients are new to this process and need an introduction about what to expect. Even clients who have been in therapy before may not know what to expect from an eating disorder–informed therapy.

Evelyn called in despair. "I need to lose weight. I'm out of control with my eating. Can I come in to see you?"

Evelyn came for a consultation and described her bingeing problems. She also came prepared with a series of questions to find out how eating disorder therapy works; her questions provide a helpful framework regarding what our clients wonder about and what we need to communicate to them. Providing these answers helps to build the therapeutic alliance.

How Can Psychotherapy Help Me with My Eating Problem?

We want our clients like Evelyn to understand that people binge, purge, or resort to self-starvation as an attempt to "solve" their emotional problems and to provide themselves with a coping strategy for difficult feelings. These problems most often are triggered by anxiety, depression, anger, resentment, sadness, loneliness, boredom, sexual difficulties, rejection, trauma, or the illness or death of a loved one. We explain that psychotherapy for emotional eating can help in two ways:

1. By identifying the trigger points that provoke emotional eating, clients then become more aware and alert to their personal patterns and better equipped to intervene with alternatives.
2. By helping strategize a program of behavioral change and developing supportive habits, we help clients interrupt their automatic reflex of emotional eating.

The short version of what therapy for emotional eating is all about:

Awareness + Action = Results

In the initial stage of therapy, Evelyn and most emotional eaters are often relieved to hear that turning to food (or even away from food) can come from a healthy place. After all, it is a positive intention to try to make oneself feel better. Communicating this to clients helps relieve their shame and guilt about having a problematic relationship with food.

Food is the cheapest, most available, and socially sanctioned mood-altering substance around, but we don't want it be the only "game in town" to help someone feel better; we need to expand clients' ways of soothing themselves. After all, bingeing, purging, or starving does not work in the long run because trying to solve life's problems just with food eventually backfires, and people are left feeling empty, unfulfilled, and unhappy with their bodies.

Another technique we can offer our clients to improve their emotional eating is to develop "non-food nurturing" (NFN) strategies that clients can use to alleviate stress and comfort themselves instead of turning to unwanted eating behavior. We devise alternatives unique to each person, which may mean taking a nap, listening to music, taking a shower, going for a walk, or writing in a diary. The women in my emotional eating recovery group share what they now call their "NFN successes" of the week. One of the benefits of group therapy is that clients now replace "isolation with pastry for intimacy with people"—a chance to get outside oneself and use one's mouth for talking, sharing, confiding, laughing, and not overeating.

Should I Just Go to a Diet Program?

Evelyn asked if going to a diet program would be a good path for her. I believe that some programs may be a helpful resource by providing structure, a way of organizing one's food, and encouraging more conscious eating. The key is to make sure the program is well versed in sound nutrition and healthy behavioral techniques and that no food groups are off limits.

Many programs offer quick fixes that provide a spurt of motivation, but their stringent advice cannot be sustained over the long term and will backfire, derailing and discouraging clients' attempts to get a handle on their eating. Many therapists in the field of eating disorders reject any program that sounds like a diet, believing that the only way to empower people is to help them contact their inner hunger and fullness rather than rely on an external agenda.

In my experience, however, I have found that especially at the beginning of treatment, clients feel supported by the structure and scaffolding of a program. When they become less panicky and more in control of their eating, then we can work on incorporating the principles of inner, intuitive eating—eating what you want, when you're hungry, and stopping when full.

In the book *Putting Together the Puzzle Pieces of Full Eating Disorder Recovery*, Catherine Gillespie (2018) explores how much structure around food and eating is optimal for a person in recovery. Gillespie believes that

> most clinicians would agree that it depends on the person's stage of recovery, usually beginning with more structure (often starting with prescribed meal plans) and then progressing to less and less structure (possibly culminating in intuitive eating). Letting go of rigidity around food is clearly a sign of progress for many in recovery, as rigidity around food is associated with eating disorders. And yet to the person in recovery, lack of structure can feel chaotic and overwhelming. Rigidity is maladaptive and related to anxiety. But structure can be supportive and actually reduce anxiety. Structure around meals and snacks can provide an opportunity to relax around food choices. My personal conclusion was that structure

> around meal and snack times combined with permission to eat what I wanted during those meals and snacks was perfect for me. It allowed me to take the risk of experimenting with different types of foods while at the same time being reassured that I would be eating again in a few hours. . . . Structure is not another form of food restriction. Rather, structure can support continued progress in eating disorder recovery. (Gillespie, 2019, para. 17)

For clients who have struggled with eating problems for many years, like Evelyn, all the structured eating plans or nutritional advice in the world will fall short if they have not resolved the emotional tensions that stimulate bingeing, purging, or starving.

Evelyn believed if only she lost weight, her self-image problems would be solved. We learned that she was depressed in her marriage and often felt belittled by her husband or ignored by his heavy work demands. Left alone with little support, Evelyn suppressed her loneliness and anger and overate at night as a way of compensating for not getting enough affection. Therapy helped Evelyn face her resentment, and she began to see that she squashed this resentment with food. Evelyn realized she needed to speak up more directly to her husband about her unhappiness. She had never previously made the connection between her nighttime binges and her stifled anger. Once she made this link, she was faced with a dilemma—continue eating and stifling her resentment or face her fear of expressing herself out loud; this was not a comfortable choice.

So, did making this connection help her eating? The answer is yes and no. Rather than running mindlessly to the refrigerator, Evelyn began asking herself what she was feeling en route to the kitchen. Sometimes, this gave her a chance to stop in her tracks and think about what was bothering her and how to handle it. Other times, she had no idea what to do and she kept her rendezvous with the ice cream. And then, at other times, instead of using her mouth for eating, she went back to the living room and used her mouth to tell her husband how she was feeling.

The point of Evelyn's story is that change does not happen all at once. Improvements—especially long-lasting ones—take time and patience. But every time she stopped herself from mindlessly bingeing, she strengthened her belief in herself and her resilience to handle the next stressful time. As she developed greater self-awareness and reflected more about the feelings that prompted her binge eating, Evelyn was able, little by little, to put a stop to her mindless visits to the kitchen.

What Actually Goes On in Therapy Sessions for Emotional Eating?

Evelyn wanted to know what an actual therapy session looks like and what she was expected to do. I explained how sometimes we spend the session talking about a person's week with food—what went right, what was not so great. We try to understand the inner emotions and stresses that fueled the eating problems during the week, and then we plot what to do next. Sometimes people keep a "food and mood" journal to describe their week with food, which illuminates the people, places, or things that cause stumbling blocks.

Sometimes during a session, the topic of food never even comes up that week. This does not mean the person is not actively working on their eating problem. It means they are bringing out to the clear light of day other meaningful issues that have provoked emotional eating.

As we saw with Evelyn, an eating disorder is about food and not about food at the same time. In each session, we focus on the unique interplay between food and emotions.

What Should I Eat?

Clients want to be told what to eat and how much. Dieting has become such a normal, everyday way of life that clients want to hear what new diet I have up my sleeve as director of the New York Center for Eating Disorders. A difficult part of the therapy relationship is handling the disappointment clients often feel to learn a new magic bullet of a diet does not exist.

With each client, I evaluate how in touch they are with their body's inner promptings of hunger and fullness. The more someone can access cues from their inner self, the easier it is to give up dieting. Then they can relearn to feed themselves when hungry and stop when full and achieve intuitive eating.

For many people, this is out of reach because they have lost touch as a result of years of dieting and yo-yo bingeing. In this case, we create a scaffolding to support and structure their eating until they can, I hope, take the reins back. Key to this technique is not allowing the scaffolding to become a diet of restriction and punishment. Something flexible works best: having meals and snacks and learning that each encounter with food has a beginning, middle, and end.

I often encourage people to write their own personal roadmap as to what they think will help with their food. This empowers the person to believe they can be the expert of themselves rather than relying on outer "authorities" to pronounce what's best for them. This prompts the person to turn inward and reflect on what they imagine will work for them by combining some intuition and some structure. Evelyn created her own manifesto that included short-term recommendations to herself and long-term ones:

Evelyn's Manifesto

Interim Goals

- Pay attention to my hunger—and if it is physical hunger, eat!
- Pay attention to my satiety and eat to a reasonable level of satiety but not to a state of feeling sluggish after a meal or, worse, uncomfortably full.
- Replace the habit of mindless snacking with healthier habits.
- Become more comfortable with meditation and take a moment to pause in stressful situations in my life.
- When I feel the urge to eat and decide it is emotional hunger, let me take the time to observe it, think about why I might be experiencing it and what action I might take to make myself feel better, more fulfilled, more satisfied, and less anxious.
- Don't be judgmental about choosing to eat when I am experiencing emotional hunger.

Long-Term Goals

- Eventually I don't want to write down what I'm eating or even write down how I feel about what I eat. Just eat according to hunger without a huge amount of mental time and energy going into it.
- Reach a stable weight that isn't constantly fluctuating.
- Sometimes if I eat too much or even too little, I don't want to obsess over it. It is what it is.
- Get to the point of identifying physical hunger and not keep questioning myself 100 times.
- Plan ahead to have food available when I expect to be hungry next.
- Stop eating when I am full.

Will I Definitely Lose Weight in Therapy for Emotional Eating?

Maybe. When you no longer use food as a reaction to inner stress, you will begin to reconnect your eating with physical hunger, not emotional hunger. The key is to eat because of hunger in the stomach and not hunger in the heart.

Eventually you will arrive at your set point, the weight range that your body was naturally meant to be. If you are committed to a size 4 when your natural body type and genetics dictate a size 12, you will be disappointed. You have a choice. You can redouble your exercise and food restrictions (which most times results in a backlash of overeating). Or you can bemoan your fate and hate the way you look for the rest of your life. Or you can try to understand why you are wedded to achieving a weight that is clearly not in harmony with your heredity, genes, and metabolism.

This can be tough, especially because we live in a culture where appearance and image are everything. Many women often flounder at this point in their recovery because of the ingrained notion that the thinner you are, the more beautiful you are. This dooms them to a life of perpetual dissatisfaction and needs to be discussed and understood in their therapy. Self-acceptance takes time to achieve, but it is worth the effort because you are going to have to live with yourself for the rest of your life. Evelyn eventually concluded, "Maybe I'm never going to really learn to fully love my body, but at least I can stop waging war on myself and learn to declare a cease-fire."

Dr. William Davis (2009) adds additional insight:

> Dealing with weight itself is not the point. Instead . . . weight change may be a byproduct of learning to listen to oneself and care for oneself in a new, more accepting and more wholesome way. Healing occurs when someone comes to value knowing, nourishing, respecting and guiding all of herself. In this circumstance, physical health and emotional health are joined in a positive, life-affirming manner. (p. 5)

How Long Will This Therapy Take?

Unless your problem just began yesterday, recovery is a process over time. We saw in Evelyn's case that she experienced many layers of self-realization before healing her eating problem.

After four sessions of psychotherapy, Joyce's husband did not notice any discernible weight loss for Joyce. As a successful businessman who was used to quick, concrete results in his business, he wanted to know why she wasn't cured yet. His pressure made Joyce ashamed that she wasn't working hard enough. Joyce was convinced that her only problem in life was that she was too fat. If she could only lose weight, she thought, she would be fine. Since she wasn't losing weight in therapy fast enough, she was ready to give up on the work.

I pointed out to Joyce that she was in mourning for her mother who had recently died, she was in the process of buying a new house, and she had a long history of binge eating since her teenage years. Joyce underestimated how all these tensions in her life were causing a resurgence of her eating struggle. She needed time to appreciate and "digest" all the losses and changes she was undergoing. Joyce also needed to learn that eating disorders are very often a person's attempt to distract herself from the grieving process. When she became aware of this, she decided to take the time she needed to fully sort through her problems without feeling convinced she was a failure.

The process of therapy is a journey of self-exploration over time. With self-reflection and self-compassion, patience and perseverance, Evelyn, Joyce, and all our clients can discover how to declare peace with emotional eating. They can learn to sink their teeth into life, not into excess food.

Will I Ever Finally Get Cured from My Eating Disorder?

Clients often ask this question, and it's a tricky one. I tell them it depends on what they mean by "cured." If cured means never bingeing or overeating again and reaching their ideal weight for the rest of their lives, then the answer is no. If cured means developing a relationship with food that is basically attuned to hunger and fullness and that bingeing, purging, and self-starvation are basically behaviors in the past, then the answer is yes.

The best definition of recovery is when people learn flexibility with food. They can have dessert without freaking out, feeling guilty, or having to compensate by purging, starving, or overexercising. They can have dessert and enjoy it. Food is meant to be enjoyed rather than producing anxiety, worry, and obsession. Enjoying one's food predicts a very good outcome for the recovery of emotional eating. A successful recovery also includes feeling at home in your body, treating it as a friendly ally rather than an object to be yelled at or criticized. This healing has little to do with thinness or fatness and can be achieved by people of all shapes and sizes. Enjoying your body—whatever its size—and having enjoyable sex and regular exercise, not exercise based on fears of weight gain, is part of healing. And successful recovery also means mostly dealing with one's emotional stress directly rather than detouring through food.

Most of all, recovery means tolerating imperfection. Some days are better than others, some days food is messier than others, some days we may overeat or undereat or not sleep enough or have the occasional binge. Some days our emotions are chaotic and all over the place. But the ability to bounce back and get back on track is key to a successful recovery. Recovery is about big dollops of self-compassion and cultivating humor about the foibles of life. It means learning other nourishing ways of comforting and soothing oneself.

Healing an eating problem is about reclaiming the vitality of your inner self that has been hidden by your consuming relationship with food. Healing is about hope and about cultivating a deeply rich relationship with your inner self, your hunger for food, and your hunger for life. As the saying goes, "Anything worth doing is worth doing imperfectly."

3. Curiosity

> *We keep moving forward, opening new doors, and doing new things, because we're curious and curiosity keeps leading us down new paths.*
>
> Walt Disney

If "curiosity killed the cat," then psychotherapy will be on its way out as well. Sparking curiosity in a client is an essential goal of the therapist. Curiosity ignites a flame that needs to be consistently stoked in therapy. Curiosity fosters self-exploration and self-reflection, kindles new perspectives, and inspires motivation. It is the primary ingredient that leads the client to resolve emotional eating problems and other life issues.

Most clients come to therapy to get "fixed"—just help me lose weight, just make me stop bingeing and purging, just help me stop overeating at night. With behavioral techniques, we may be able to do the job, but, with curiosity, clients will dig deeper and get to the roots of why bingeing, purging, chronic dieting, body image dissatisfaction, and starving have distressed and haunted them. Beyond resolving the present situation, curiosity about discovering personal triggers will also build in protection and prevention for future eating issues as well.

Growing up, many people get the message that curiosity is for "nosy bodies" and something to be ashamed of and avoided. Children are told, "curiosity kills the cat," implying that to be curious is dangerous. Or their curiosity is dismissed with "it is what it is" or "just let it be" or "you're reading too much into everything" or "utilize, don't analyze" or "some things are better left unsaid."

But when a therapist consistently demonstrates nonjudgmental curiosity, one hopes that the client internalizes this approach and joins the therapist in wondering about what motivates the client. The clinician's curiosity affirms that the client's life is valuable and worth paying attention to. Difficult material can be brought out to the clear light of day when therapist and client are open to this spirit of inquiry.

Curiosity is the antidote to the constricted inner world of the emotional eater who has subsumed the meaning of life behind struggles with food and weight and numbers: How can I lose 20 pounds as quickly as possible? How can I fit into a size 8? I'll just have an apple for lunch—it's only 100 calories.

But with this added ingredient of curiosity, clients discover how their eating disorder may have helped as well as hindered their life. This expands their perspective beyond this constricted focus on calories, the number on the scale, and weight.

Suzanne has made great strides in her binge eating but comes to session discouraged by her overeating on Saturday night. "Don and I had great sex Saturday night," she begins shyly. "So why did I get up in the middle of the night to overeat? I hate myself for doing that."

I want to rescue her from her self-hate but, knowing she has cultivated much curiosity about her behavior, I wait in silence. Sometimes it is hard to stay quiet when you don't want to see a client suffer unnecessarily. After a couple of moments, Suzanne says, "I think I know what's bothering me, but I kind of don't want to face it. I think it's time to talk with Don about our looking into fertility treatments. We've been trying for a year and nothing. I'm afraid of his reaction, so I've been keeping it inside. That's what was bothering me." Suzanne is both sad that she is hurting about not getting pregnant but also triumphant that she has figured out the stress behind her midnight binge.

Now we get to talk about her fears of Don's reaction, and her own fears and shame about fertility treatment, and we break into bite-size pieces how she might approach this. She feels relieved to have identified her binge trigger and to have created a plan of action as well.

"And, let's point out," I add, "that the binge did calm you down and put you back to sleep. It worked in that moment to soothe you. And now we can move on to find other ways that support you better."

"Once one becomes curious about one's thoughts and feelings, rather than embattled with them, an emotional distancing occurs, which allows for a shift in the patient's perspective" (Carroll, 2014, para. 11; see also Barre, 2019; Kunst, 2012; Ofer & Durban, 1999).

When patients, like Suzanne, are encouraged to wonder about their feelings, reactions, and behavior, they develop alternative methods instead of overeating, purging, or starving.

Kindling Curiosity in Clients

With many clients, like Suzanne, curiosity leads to an in-depth understanding of why they have turned to the "solution" of eating disorders. Curiosity leads to the truth.

We learn about the life issues that have stimulated clients' beliefs that trusting food is safer than trusting people. This was also the case of Roselle and Marjorie.

Why Did Roselle Accept Her Husband Who Was a Bigamist? Roselle suffered from anorexia and was deeply unhappy in her marriage. She came to therapy after discovering her husband was also married to another woman. He had children with this other woman and an ongoing relationship with his second family.

Roselle had suspected her husband led a secret life for quite some time and began to explore why she denied all the warning signs. Rather than beating herself up about her blindness to the situation, we tried to cultivate her curiosity about why she allowed her "not knowing" to continue for years and how her anorexia served to numb her feelings and awareness.

Roselle revealed her father had sexually abused her when she was young, which instilled guilt in her and made her feel she was to blame for stealing him away from her mother. This guilt from the past left her fearful of having any man exclusively to herself. "Sharing" her husband with his other wife secretly relieved her by limiting the marriage to a part-time relationship. She concluded that having a full-time husband felt too threatening and incestuous. Decoding and appreciating the meaning of her behavior gave Roselle more clarity and freedom to decide what further steps she might want to take regarding her marriage. It also helped her to tackle the necessary self-care to make progress with her anorexia.

Why Did Marjorie Want Me to Be Raped? Marjorie, a binge-eating client, presented a difficult challenge for me. In one of her therapy sessions, Marjorie described a movie she had seen in which a psychotherapist gets brutally raped. Then she announced calmly, "I wish you were that therapist who got raped."

I was startled and recoiled at her cruel fantasy. Rather than retaliate with hostility, I summoned up my curiosity. "What would be so good about my being raped? How would that help?" I asked.

Marjorie then revealed for the first time she had been raped twice as a teenager. Her wish for me to be raped as well was her desperate attempt to compel me to more fully understand her suffering. By injecting into me the traumatic horror she had experienced, Marjorie did succeed in making me viscerally understand how raw and terrified she had felt. In the end, her cruel fantasy deepened our bond and my understanding of her anguish. Connecting more directly with the brunt of her rage and vulnerability helped Marjorie diminish her binge eating over time.

Curiosity Doesn't Always Lead to Conclusive Answers

Encouraging curiosity in our work with clients may not always yield a conclusive answer as to what makes them tick, but the spirit of inquiry does shed light and relief on a person's struggles. This was the case of Pauline and Eleanor.

Why Was Pauline Blind to Her Own Body? Pauline, a woman in her early 30s with a binge-eating disorder, discussed how her social isolation and loneliness often prompted her to overeat. She also admitted that she had never looked at her own naked body. She claimed to have never seen herself without clothes in a full-length mirror, never looked down while showering, and never had a sexual relationship. During her short time in therapy, Pauline, a bright and sensitive woman, could not remember any significant history or experience to explain her dread of looking at her own body.

Although we searched for the meaning of her unusual body phobia, we never discovered it. However, in our discussions about her life and feelings, Pauline felt accepted and understood. She came from a large family that gave her little attention; she felt "unseen" by her parents. Just being listened to and valued was a new experience for her. Shortly into her therapy, Pauline met a man whom she grew to trust and love. She had sex for the first time, they married, and she felt happy and at ease. Although we never unraveled her mystery, Pauline managed to overcome inner barriers that had blocked her from forming an intimate relationship. Years later, Pauline wrote to me expressing enjoyment in her life and her increased freedom from binge eating.

Why Did Eleanor Binge and Purge on Pregnancies? Eleanor, a physician's assistant with an extensive medical background, allowed herself to become pregnant seven times and had seven abortions. She also presented with a significant history of bulimia. Why would an educated woman with medical knowledge and resources allow this to happen repeatedly? How does her bingeing and purging on pregnancies relate to her bulimia?

We need to encourage Eleanor's curiosity so we may uncover the meaning of her compulsive pattern and protect her from further risky behavior.

With Pauline and Eleanor, although curiosity did not offer concrete answers, it did teach them an attitude of self-inquiry and self-reflection that will last a lifetime.

When the Therapist Struggles with Curiosity

Sometimes a therapist can get thrown off kilter and has to struggle to find that nonjudgmental spirit of curiosity. I struggled in my work with Rhonda to keep my balance and not to scream.

Why Did Rhonda Accept Life-Threatening Violence? Rhonda was shot three times by her jealous boyfriend. Albert was arrested and sent to jail. The doctors retrieved only one of the bullets from Rhonda's body because of the dangerous position of the other two. Months after she recovered, Rhonda secretly married Albert in jail and told no one. She came to therapy for anxiety, depression, and bulimia.

When she confided that she had secretly married the man who shot her, my curiosity almost flew out the window and my natural human impulse was to yell, "What the hell is the matter with you? Are you crazy? That man almost killed you!"

Had I responded that way, I would have lost Rhonda and lost the opportunity to help her. It was not easy for me to return to my spirit of inquiry, but I worked to get back my equilibrium despite my agitation. Over time, as Rhonda sensed my genuine wish to understand her, she herself became more curious and self-reflective about why she accepted Albert's behavior. She began to delve deeper, "My father was a womanizer who abandoned our family when I was five. My father's rejection made me yearn for a man who really cared for me. When Albert shot me in a fit of jealous rage, I believed this proved he truly loved me. The strength of Albert's jealousy has always felt like love."

Rhonda then added with a rueful laugh, "I also realize that with Albert in jail, I will always know where he is on Saturday nights, unlike my poor mother who never knew where my Dad was!"

Our relationship, based on trust and curiosity, was new for her. In time, Rhonda grew more reflective and self-protective. She began to wonder about the impact of her father's abandonment on her present life, which helped free her to make more conscious, healthier choices. Her bulimia ebbed as she discovered new self-soothing skills and her self-assurance grew.

Cultivating curiosity with Rhonda helped me in other cases where clients presented with domestic violence. Although I express my fear and shock, I cannot be the only one in the therapy room who is worried. I realized in the case of Connie that whenever her girlfriend beat her up, I became more agitated than Connie was. I realized I was experiencing and expressing the emotions Connie was disassociating from and not letting herself feel—she was volleying them over to me. As I stopped accepting the volley, Connie became more anxious and was forced to figure out what it meant to her to live in a heightened state of violence. Like Rhonda, Connie also claimed that her girlfriend beating her felt like an intense expression of love. Both women had mothers who physically abused them during childhood, and the shadow of this parental expression of love had set the stage for future relationships. The work of therapy involved grieving their past hurts and traumas, and it opened up exploration about deserving and accepting love not tinged with hate.

Client's Questions about the Therapy Relationship

Some clients do not express curiosity about the therapist and dislike the idea of even developing a relationship or becoming dependent on the clinician. So they ignore or avoid discussing feelings about the therapist. They say, "I just want my eating disorder to get fixed," or "I don't want a relationship with you," or "Just let me get on with my life." As long as the treatment is flowing productively, I believe it is not necessary to focus on the therapeutic relationship. Only when there are the eventual and inevitable stalemates, enactments, or resistances do we need to directly ask clients for their impressions about how it is going with us.

Other clients come to session with strong curiosity about the therapist and the therapy relationship. Although these personal questions may make the therapist squirm, they can sometimes deepen the treatment into richer, more alive concerns.

When clients pose pointed questions, they reveal their personal fears about the trustworthiness of the therapist and the integrity of the treatment process. Questions from eating disorder clients about the therapist will invariably reveal something about their hunger for connection or hunger for control. And curious therapists believe every client question has value and meaning that needs to be deciphered.

Therapists need to respect their patients' inquiries, as uncomfortable as they may be. When clients ask difficult and intrusive questions, it is also possible they are turning the tables on the therapist and putting the therapist on the hot seat. Sometimes curiosity can be an expression of a client's hostility to the therapist.

These are some of the questions I have heard over the years from my clients and from social workers I have supervised:

- "What if you become a crutch to me, just like food?"
- "What if I need you more than you need me, which I assume must be the case?
- "How can you really care for me if this is just a business to you and I pay you?"

- "I feel like a fool revealing all my inner insecurities and I know nothing about you. It doesn't feel fair."
- "Did you ever have an eating disorder?"
- "Are you happy with your weight?"
- "You have so many other patients. Do you feel the same way about everyone?"
- "What if I get close to you and never want to leave therapy?"
- "How will I know when I'm ready to leave? Will you let me leave? After all, you'll be losing the money you get from me."
- "My last therapist died during my therapy. How do I know the same thing won't happen here with you?"
- "How do you remember what I say? Do you write down notes about me or secretly tape-record our sessions?"
- "What if I say something that hurts your feelings and you don't like me anymore? Will you pretend to help me but instead lead me on the wrong path out of spite?"
- "What if I have sexual feelings to you?"
- "Do you ever have sexual feelings for your patients?"
- "Do you ever pretend to care when you really don't?"
- "Will you think about me when you're on vacation, or do you forget all about your patients when you're out of the office? Will you miss me?"
- "Did you know that the word 'therapist' is actually 'the-rapist'?"
- "Did you ever lie to a client? Would you ever lie to me?"
- "If I get better, will you take all the credit?"
- "Do you love me?"

Obviously, these questions are laden with meaning that a mere yes or no can't answer. The therapist's stock answer is "What do you mean by that?" or "Tell me more" or "Why are you asking now?" Turning the questions back to the clients often leaves people feeling rebuffed and patronized. However, the therapist's intention in asking these questions is valid—to discover and explore the thoughts and ideas of each person. Formulating how to best answer clients' questions depends on many variables unique to each client and unique to each therapist.

If, for example, a woman asks me, "Do you ever have sexual feelings for your patients?" and she is someone who has been the victim of sexual abuse, then I surmise she is trying to determine if I can be trusted not to act out sexually or impulsively. But the question could mean she is struggling with her own homosexual feelings toward me; or it could mean she wants to be mothered intimately like a little girl. A sensitive therapist will help patients identify their specific concerns.

If a young teenage boy poses the same question, he may wonder what kinds of sexual feelings are acceptable and normal. I may kid him and say, "Is the idea of my having sexual feelings to you something you wish or you fear?" or "What would it feel like if I did?" or "Is there something specific you would like to do with me?"

Of course, every therapist has their own theoretical beliefs and comfort level with self-disclosure. Some self-disclosure enhances the therapeutic alliance, sometimes it is unnecessary, and sometimes it can burden and interfere with the treatment.

Curiosity Leads to Self-Reflection

Curiosity is the key that opens the door to the self and stimulates psychological growth, self-discovery, and creativity.

A transformative psychotherapy is reminiscent of Alice in Wonderland peering through the looking glass as she remarks with amazement, "Curiouser and curiouser!" Venturing through the looking glass is the perfect image for entering therapy—a journey toward self-reflection and self-discovery.

As Lori Gottlieb (2019) reminds us about self-discovery in *Maybe You Should Talk to Someone*, "The story a patient comes into therapy with may not be the story she leaves with. The patient's own role might change—from bit player to protagonist, from victim to hero" (p. 378).

The roots of the word *curious* are closely related to the words *care* and *cure*. As Albert Einstein declared, "The important thing is not to stop questioning. . . . Never lose a holy curiosity!"

4. Shame, Secrets, and Self-Esteem

Emotional eaters are no strangers to shame—shame about how insatiable they can feel at their core, shame about what lengths they have gone to sneak food, and shame for the secret gorging rampages that override reason, the purging that wrenches their guts, the spitting out and hiding of food that the anorexic pretends to have eaten. Emotional eaters are fearful their secret relationship with food will be found out, and they will be exposed to ridicule because then everyone will know how greedy and insatiable they really are.

During his childhood, Charles hid food in the family clothes hamper to gorge on later in secret. One day he forgot to retrieve a hunk of cheese, and it began to smell. His father located the cheddar in the hamper and, realizing it must be Charles' doing, made fun of him forever more. Charles never lived down his new nickname of Chuckie

Cheese, and the shame about being a fat, hungry, sneaky kid followed him for years.

The origins of shame tend to come from a deep-seated conviction within a person that there is something inherently and shamefully wrong with who they are. Inner shame is rooted in experiences from childhood, experiences with friends, or from absorbing toxic cultural messages. Emotional eating begins as a way to cope with these intolerable emotions. But then people feel shame not only about who they are but also what they do with food.

The painful paradox is that overeating, starving, or purging, which they originally turned to for relief of shameful feelings, turns on them in time and becomes a source of shame in its own right. The very method they used to help themselves with pain then begins to generate its own pain and shame.

Barbara's father was alcoholic, and this was well known in the neighborhood, leaving Barbara ashamed that her family didn't measure up. As a teenager, she became a laxative abuser with the hope of becoming thinner and more popular. The laxatives were also her unconscious attempt to evacuate her shitty feelings out of her body. But her original feelings of shame and inferiority lessened only when she began attending meetings for Adult Children of Alcoholics. She discovered she was not the only girl who suffered with an alcoholic father and who believed getting thinner and prettier would "redeem" her family in some way and make them more acceptable.

People often wonder about the difference between guilt and shame. These emotions are similar in that they both make us feel bad about ourselves, but they differ in emphasis. We feel guilty for something we do or for harboring some "bad" thought. A guilty person thinks, 'I shouldn't have done that," or "I shouldn't think that way." Shame, in contrast, is about feeling deficient or defective in the core of one's inner self. The shameful person feels, "I am ashamed of my *self*. I should not be that way."

The saddest case of shame I heard was the story of Sonya. When she began therapy for a binge-eating disorder, she told me her mother had died three years after she was born. Only after she came to know me better and decided she could trust me did she reveal the truth: her mother had died while giving birth to Sonya. I wondered, why did Sonya begin with one story about her mother's death and then change it to the truth? She then said, "By the very act of my being born, I murdered my mother."

Her shame and guilt caused her to push people away so no one would discover her true "badness"—that she had caused her own mother's death. Confessing this secret helped us better understand the connection between this birth trauma, her conviction about being a toxic person, and her need for the comfort of bingeing. In time, we also understood Sonya's fear that she might kill off anyone she loved just as she believed she had done to her mother.

She then told me another confidence. Every time it rained, she would cry for all the broken, discarded, unloved umbrellas that were left by people in garbage cans because they had gotten ruined in the storm. Sonya truly lamented for these umbrellas, and we came to see that she considered them "orphaned umbrellas," much like she herself felt like an orphan in the storm of life.

Sonya died many years ago, but her legacy lives on in me—I can never see an orphaned umbrella on the street without thinking of her and her tragic, magical way of imbuing them with sorrow and abandonment.

When we help our clients express their inner shame, we deepen the therapeutic relationship with us. We help them bring out to the light of day their inner sense of shame about their history and eating behaviors. They feel relieved about sharing their hidden burdens and accepted without judgment by an empathic therapist.

Trisha's biggest shameful secret is that she had worked as a prostitute dominatrix for several years. But the darker, more shameful secret was the incest by her brother and uncle she had endured as a child. Trisha had never previously told anybody about her history or her descent into anorexia. I understood that her becoming a prostitute and dominatrix was an attempt—although destructive in many ways—to take charge of men in the sexual act and reverse the vulnerability and shame of what had been done to her. She was trying to master her trauma by assuming an active and sadistic role with her male clients rather than being a passive, helpless child. Together we uncovered how her choice of work had rhyme and reason based on what she had gone through, and her anorexia also made sense as an attempt to numb and starve out the painful betrayal. Trauma requires grieving and feeling sorrow for the little child that was used as a tool. Her grieving opened her heart to more self-love, and Trisha is now in chiropractic school. "I'll still be in charge of people and get to boss them around," she laughs, "but now I'll be a force for healing. Now I'll get to crack bones, not crack the whip!" Trisha illuminates a beautiful example of moving from PTSD to posttraumatic growth.

The Origins of Shame

How does shame come to live inside us? We all need parents who love us unconditionally. Although they do not have to gratify us all the time, we should feel we can depend on them to respect, acknowledge, and respond to our needs compassionately. But if we grow up in a family where we are made to feel ashamed of our needs and wants, our real self goes into hiding. Shaming responses can set in motion the child's attempt to cover up her real feelings by portraying a make-believe self to the outside world and hiding behind food for comfort.

> When one feels empty inside, hungry to feel a part of someone, desperate to be held close, craving to be wanted and admired, respected, and loved—but these have become taboo through shame—one turns instead to food. But food can never truly satisfy the inner need. Longing turns to shame. And so one eats more to anesthetize the longing. (Kaufman, 1985, p. 121)

Ashamed for Being Needy. Children who are made to feel ashamed of their natural human needs will often try to satisfy these needs through a relationship with food.

> **Amina:** In my family there was always competition for who was the thinnest and who had the strongest personality. Even to rest or relax is considered a weakness in my family. To this day, my mother, who is retired, feels obliged to comment, "I was so busy today that I didn't have time to sit down even once!"
>
> My whole life has felt like a performance—pushing myself to be the best in everything. When I'm into starving myself or using laxatives, I feel triumphant, as if I have no needs and I'm totally in control. But everything fell apart when my husband left me. Even though I was devastated, my parents kept telling me, "You're a Patel. We Patels can make it on our own. We don't need anybody." I was ashamed that for the first time I couldn't get out of bed, I couldn't stop crying, and I couldn't stop eating. It was like a dam had burst, and all my years of pretending to be strong started to crumble. I'm also ashamed that I had to go for therapy. My parents would practically disown me if they knew, but I just don't have the energy left to act as if I don't need anything or anybody.

Ashamed for How One Looks. Children who feel used as an ornament by their parents come to believe their real selves are not good enough to make their parents proud. This can set up a child's need to find comfort through food to quell the shame of feeling inadequate.

> **Liza:** My mother always wanted a curly, blond-haired daughter. One summer, when I was 13, she dyed my hair blond and gave me a permanent. When I went to a new junior high school in the fall,

> she told me not to tell anyone it wasn't my real color or style. I went along with her. I guess I believed that my hair was not that great, but I also remember feeling ashamed that I wasn't pretty enough for her to love me just the way I was. I gained a lot of weight in junior high, which only added to my feelings of never being good enough.

If children are given the message that their looks are disappointing, they can discharge their anger and hurt through bingeing, purging, or starving.

Ashamed for Trying to Comfort Oneself. The eminent British child analyst D. W. Winnicott (1953) discussed how "security blankets" (a doll, a stuffed toy, special pajamas) are objects that help children make the transition between running to their parents for comfort and being able to independently soothe themselves. This capacity for self-comfort in moments of distress or pain that we learn in childhood becomes a rich, inner resource in adult life when we are sad or lonely or hurting.

Where there is a breach in the parents' ability to respond with empathy, there will also be a breach in the child's ability to soothe himself. Rather than appreciating the "security blanket" stage as a healthy part of development, parents may feel annoyed by the "babyishness" of it and discourage or humiliate the child with phrases like "When are you going to grow up?" or "Take your thumb out of your mouth." Parents may simply throw out the blanket or toy, much to the child's grief. The child is then cheated of the pleasure and assurance of knowing how to soothe his own needs, and food becomes his pacifier instead.

> **Kevin:** I had a stuffed dog, Lucky, who I took everywhere with me. Lucky was my friend and I felt he really understood me! I came home from school one day to find Lucky was gone. My parents said, "Big boys don't play with stuffed animals." That was the end of my life with Lucky. I couldn't believe my parents didn't understand how much I loved him. My overeating really spiraled out of control that summer.

Ashamed for Not Being Perfect Enough. For parents who need their children to be perfect, nothing is ever good enough. Many of my patients have described bringing home report cards from school with grades of 90 percent only to be ridiculed, "What happened to the other 10 points?" Emotional eaters use food to assuage their disappointment, fear, and rage at not meeting their parents' standards.

Pilar: My family has strong religious values. I was always being criticized for not having enough humility or for having too much pride. They always reminded me that "pride comes before the fall" whenever I'd express some excitement about being chosen class president or making the school swim team. In my home and in my particular church, we were taught to devote our lives to "J.O.Y."—Jesus first, Others second, and Yourself third. Through my therapy, I came to realize that my anorexia was about trying to disown all my needs—hunger included—to make myself a more perfect little girl in the eyes of my family. Now my goal is "Y.O.J." in which "Yourself" goes first! Unless I put myself first and focus on my own recovery, I won't be any good for Others or for Jesus! I will remain that skinny girl who keeps trying to starve herself to become more and more perfect.

Ashamed for Needing or Wanting Therapy. If a teen or young adult asks their parents for therapy because of weight concerns, an eating disorder, or issues related to anxiety or depression, they are often made to feel ashamed. Because of parental fear or parents' lack of knowledge about what therapy is, children are often made to feel embarrassed for requesting this. Even in this day and age, when the stigma around getting help for emotional problems has definitely improved, clients have told me of the following reactions from parents:

- "If you're so worried about your weight, just go on a diet."
- "We don't have the money to pamper you. We have other kids in this family to take care of also."
- "When I was your age, people had real problems then."
- "Therapy is about blaming your mother for everything."
- "Only crazy people need therapy."
- "You'll outgrow it."
- "Why are you depressed? We give you everything."
- "Why can't you talk to me? I'm your mother who knows you better than anyone."
- "Why do you want to air our family's dirty laundry to a stranger?"

Heidi ruefully came to therapy 20 years after she had originally wanted to seek help as a child, but was scared to ask her parents:

Heidi: I'm here to get therapy for my compulsive overeating, which got worse after my husband died from a drug overdose. I've been thinking about wanting therapy for a really long time. When I was 12, my older brother died of an overdose. My parents were so lost in their grief I didn't want to bother them. They never even believed in getting help for Tony when it was clear he had a drug addiction. I looked up psychotherapy in the yellow pages when I was 12 without telling them. I would study the different centers but didn't feel like I knew what to do. Somehow even knowing those centers were there made me feel better. Now that my husband has died, it feels like I'm back in the same place as with my brother. So here I am.

The Cycle of Shame

As adults, feeling shame can continue to fuel people's emotional eating, and they develop a "shame cycle" that keeps them locked into a fixed pattern.

Frank, who struggled with compulsive eating, described the efforts he made to suppress his anger toward his elderly father. "Dad is always getting on my nerves by directing me and criticizing me about how I should run my business. But he's really such a nice guy. He wouldn't hurt a fly." Often Frank's anger and frustration broke through, and he would start screaming at his father. He would then feel ashamed for having "lost it," eat to try to calm down, and then binge again to help him suppress his anger once more.

Connie had another version of the shame cycle. As the oldest of seven children, she learned to swallow and deny most of her needs because they were too overwhelming for her parents to deal with. Any feeling or need she experienced—longing for attention, anger, jealousy, sexual feelings—led her immediately to feel ashamed, to binge, and to purge.

Unlocking Shame with the Key of Psychotherapy

Just as hurtful relationships were the cause of clients' turning to emotional eating in the first place, the empathic relationship with a therapist can be a channel of healing. It is not the shame our clients suffer in childhood that makes them emotional eaters but the inability to tell their hidden stories and express out loud the feelings of shame. People cannot heal their shame alone.

The key of psychotherapy validates clients' pain, rejections, and hurt and accepts them for who they are. Support groups also create a "second chance" family. When clients realize that this new family or therapist accepts the parts of themselves they have "discarded" because of shame, they learn to accept themselves as well.

As Charles Whitfield (1987) so poignantly described in *Healing the Child Within*,

> Recovery is about telling the story of our suffering to safe and supportive others. What we expose and share is our Child Within, our True Self with all its weaknesses and all of its strengths. We need others to help us heal ourselves. They validate our predicaments and our pain and they accept us as we are. And when we hear others tell their stories and share their shame, we help them to heal. (p. 51)

When she was 15, Linda had been deeply shamed by her father for her budding sexual interest in boys. He had caught her kissing a boy on their porch and let her know in no uncertain terms that she was a whore. He repeated this message so unrelentingly that this shame came to live inside Linda. She became fatter and fatter, and the rest of her teenage years were spent in retreat from those early, dangerous sexual feelings.

When Linda began therapy with me and had some success gaining control of her binge eating, she became worried that I was secretly judging and criticizing her. We discovered that when her weight subsided as the issue in her life, feelings of wanting a relationship with a man emerged. She began to feel that if she became sexual, I too would see her as a whore and would roundly disapprove of her interest in the opposite sex.

The shame she had internalized from her father's disapproval was now coming alive again in the relationship with me. This gave Linda an opportunity to relive with me, in the role of her disapproving father, the memories and pain stored within her all these years—the pain that had been hidden by her eating and her weight. The relationship with me, however, did not repeat the pain of her past, because she came to experience me as an accepting person. Through our nonshaming connection, Linda became more accepting of her own self and realized her sexuality could be gratifying and enjoyable, not something to be censored or condemned.

We can only heal what we feel. In Linda's case, she experienced anger, fear, grief, and hurt as she unraveled the shame behind her eating disorder. The pain of recovery is like peeling the layers of an onion—tears and all.

By helping our clients get in touch with their most authentic and genuine selves, we enable them to begin to move away from the despair caused by shame. In the past, they sought relief through food, leaving them defeated and alone. Now they have other choices: connection, communication, and intimacy.

5. Healing Power of Tears and Laughter

Tears

Sharing tears and laughter deepens the therapeutic relationship and the intimate connection between therapist and client. It brings a humanity and vitality to our work and imbues it with a special spark. The comedian Victor Borge once said, "Laughter is the closest distance between two people." One could say that is true of tears as well.

Feeling Sorry for Crying. Magdalena comes for her first consultation about her binge eating and to speak about the recent death of her husband. She begins to cry and says, "I'm sorry."

Isaac comes for his first appointment about his purging and how rejected he feels since telling his parents he is gay. He begins to cry and says, "I'm sorry."

I think that crying can be a wonderful use of therapy, so why the need for an apology? I have asked many clients why they apologize for crying in session. They respond,

- "I don't want to get too emotional." (I answer that therapy is about feeling and expressing emotions. That's why we are here. Better to get emotional than stuff all that down with unwanted eating.)
- "I don't want to bring you down and get you depressed." (You feel like you have to take care of me. Why? This is your session. And if what you say does bring me down, then we'll go through it together.)
- "If I start crying, I'll never stop." (That's because you've been choking down your tears for so long, and now they feel like they are backed up into infinity. Let's give you a chance to let them out and understand what your tears are saying.)
- "I thought I was stronger than giving in to crying." (You speak as if being strong means never being vulnerable nor having upsetting feelings. And why do you feel you have to be so strong anyway?)
- "I'm crying over the death of my dog [cat, parakeet]. It's only an animal, and I'm making such a big deal." (Many people feel that their pet was the closest they've ever had to unconditional love. Why wouldn't you grieve that loss?)

- "My abortion was 20 years ago. Why am I crying about it now?" (An abortion can be a profound loss. Maybe you never fully grieved it, or maybe something in your present life is making this hurt come alive again.)
- "I didn't get the job promotion. But why should I cry? It's not like I got cancer." (You are right. Not getting the promotion is not cancer. But you're hurt and disappointed, which is a good reason to cry. Does it have to be as dramatic as cancer to be worth your crying over?)

One of the more intriguing apologies for crying came from a tearful Julia, who said, "My father died last month. I should be over it by now." Julia is bulimic, and I realize how her need to get over her feelings so quickly is parallel to her need to get rid of her unwanted food so quickly. Unable to "digest" her inner emotions, Julia tries to eject them from her system. Unable to allow her food to "digest," she ejects it from her system as well.

Being Shamed for Crying. In my work with eating disorder patients, I have repeatedly seen how family prohibitions against crying can be very strong and damaging. Parents—hoping to prevent their child from suffering or if they themselves are uncomfortable with crying—will scold or shame a child away from tears.

Parents shame their children by saying,

- "Big girls don't cry."
- "If you don't stop, I'll really give you something to cry about."
- "Stop it! You know how your crying upsets your mother."
- "You're such a crybaby. When are you going to grow up?"
- "You're making a mountain out of a molehill."
- "Don't be a sissy—boys don't cry."
- "When I was your age, I really had something to cry about."
- "You can cry to your heart's content, but it won't get you anywhere."
- "Your crying will be the death of me."

Substituting Vomiting for Crying. I believe that vomiting can be a substitute for crying, as can the use of laxatives, compulsive exercise, and self-harm or cutting. For many bulimics, like Julia, vomiting makes them feel less vulnerable because they can decide when to purge, whereas they do not always have that power over unbidden tears.

I tell my patients that stifling tears leads to emotional eating: furtive bingeing, secret purging, or starving themselves to exile their pain.

I tell my patients that we are the only creatures that Mother Nature granted the ability to cry, that it is a gift. And when people are crying, they are rarely engaging in eating disorder behavior at the same time.

I tell my patients that there is no time frame to get over a loss—death of a loved one, abortion, divorce, the loss of a pet—and it is mostly their judgmental self-criticism that makes everything, including their eating problems, worse. I explain that the root of the word *condolence* means sharing your pain with another and we can be companions in grief.

I add that tears are a language like eating disorders that can speak about matters of the heart. And I will often say, "Tell me what your tears are saying." This invitation often prompts stories to flow.

Crying with Your Client. On certain, exceptional occasions, a patient's tearful story will also make me cry, such as an anguished recounting of childhood sexual abuse or a horrific story of the Holocaust or a client's car crash where he accidentally ran over and killed a child. If my tears come, I do not try to hide them; they are another instance of our shared humanity.

Claudine, a French client of mine, recovered from bulimia and working on her overeating, comes to session with tears rolling down her face. We have just heard that the Cathedral of Notre Dame in Paris is on fire and burning down. "I'm so stupid to be crying about a building," Claudine says. "This is so stupid." By the end of her description, I tell her I have counted eight "stupids" she has pronounced against herself. "Losing this cathedral is a tragedy," I say. "It is heartbreaking. Why are you stupid to feel so sad?"

"I will never see her again in the flesh," Claudine responds. I am confused about whether she is referring to the cathedral with the female pronoun as one would in French—La Cathédrale—and I'm certainly confused about her speaking of a building "in the flesh." Then Claudine leads us down a deeper path of why she is so upset. Next month she will become an American citizen. She is estranged from her mother, who still lives in Paris, and wonders whether she will ever see her mother again "in the flesh." To Claudine, getting her citizenship feels like another nail in the coffin distancing her and her mother even more, which is something she has chosen but also regrets at the same time. This cathedral represents Notre Dame, Our Lady, Claudine's mother. I say to her, "Our mothers are our first cathedrals."

Then Claudine continues telling me about the history of Notre Dame, how many generations of fathers and sons worked on it, that it is 900 years old and millions of hands have touched and built and crafted the stones. Claudine's love for this cathedral is heartfelt, and she expresses herself with poetry and deep feeling. At the end of the session, we both shed tears about the beauty of flying buttresses and how much they look like wings.

Despite society's common assertion "don't feel sorry for yourself," the capacity to cry and feel sorry for oneself can be a healthy place for many eating disorder sufferers. When a person develops this capacity, they embrace tenderness for themselves.

The Messiness of Tears. Clients' use of Kleenex in my office when they cry also reveals interesting patterns related to their eating disorder. Denise, an anorexic woman, brings her own tissues to session and, when she uses them, does not throw them away in my wastepaper basket but packs them in her pocketbook to take with her. "You can throw them out here," I point to the basket. "No, it's OK," Denise says, "I don't want to make you have to work harder by emptying my trash." Denise's implication is that my being her therapist is hard enough, and she does not want to impose on me any more than that. This interaction gives me an opportunity to point out how she believes she needs to spare me—even for something as minor as throwing out her tissues. It is a direct translation from her life growing up when she was the oldest child of eight siblings, and she concluded her needs were an unwanted burden on her mother. Her lovability was determined by not making demands. Not needing food and becoming anorexic felt like her badge of success in denying her needs.

Stella, a compulsive eater, "binges" on my tissues, and I need to replace them and empty the overflowing basket when she leaves. Stella is actually not depressed but angry and frustrated and vents this through copious tears. This is good for her in that she grew up in a house where her twin brother was the special one, and she had to make do with the smaller portion of everything and stifle her tears and anger. She grabs wads of tissues, and I enjoy her taking that abundance for herself.

Crying and Attachment, Hope, and Healing. In "The Meaning of Crying Based on Attachment Theory," social work psychotherapist Judith Kay Nelson (1998) posits that crying can be an expression of varied emotions—sadness, anger, joy, or fear. But, in adults, crying is triggered predominantly by emotions of loss. Crying is an attempt to undo the loss and bring about a reunion, just like the child will cry for the return of his absent mother. John Bowlby (1988), father of attachment theory, describes three stages of grief when a child is left alone: protest, then despair, and finally detachment. Dr. Nelson states that crying also has three types, and each type expresses an aspect of the grieving process: angry cries of protest, sad cries of despair, and detached noncrying, which is "the defeat of hope."

Nelson (1998) describes that the absence of tears in

> detached noncrying is symptomatic of a depression accompanying unresolved grief and is symbolic of it as well; tears do not flow just like the grief is not being worked through. Some people, stuck in this kind of response to loss, fear they would drown in never-ending tears if it were unleashed, while others openly long for the ability to weep. Detached noncrying represents a chronically denied or blocked grieving process. (p. 18)

She adds, "One tear is worth a thousand words" (p. 18).

My experience is that binge eaters are most able to cry, bulimics often use vomiting as an avoidance of crying, and the anorexic is the most detached and frozen and the least able to cry.

When clients become able to cry in session, tears represent relief, hope, and healing; they are an antidote to emotional eating.

Laughter

Laughing at one's foibles makes the trials and tribulations of life a lot easier. As I approached my birthday recently, I began to think about how many decades I have spent treating eating disorder clients. I think back to when my interest in food and eating first began. Then a memory from when I was a little girl comes leaping into my consciousness. I am six years old, and I get a new doll. I name her RoastBeef. How funny this is to me now. Fortunately, my parents never made fun of me even when all my little girl friends were playing with their dolls Barbie, Bitsy, and Betsy-Wetsy.

When Client and Therapist Laugh Together. Sometimes laughter is the best medicine and one of the best devices for handling stress. To laugh at our quirks provides relief, a temporary escape from ourselves, and a reprieve from our problems. Where there is humor, there is hope.

Therapist and client laughing together in the session provides a shared moment of affection and bonding. Therapy is not all hard work, grit, and determination. Humor offers moments of playful connection and a sense of partnership; it is the antidote to the perfection, rigidity, and depression so often experienced by eating disordered people.

Melissa comes bursting into my office both laughing and crying. She is caring for her disabled and dependent mother, and Melissa is at her wit's end with the constant onslaught of demands. She has made strides with her compulsive overeating, and we are working hard to help her not backpedal as she navigates this stress. "You can't believe what happened. My mother woke me up at 7 a.m. to say she needed my help because she is constipated! Who does she think I am—The Shit-Whisperer!?"

We both start laughing at Melissa's new identity of the Shit-Whisperer, and tears are also streaming down Melissa's face—tears of laughter, anger, frustration, and powerlessness. "Well," I observe, "that would explain why you are so 'pooped' all the time!"

Tears and laughter meld together as Melissa expresses her stress. She reminds me of Charlie Chaplin's quote, "To truly laugh, you must be able to take your pain and play with it."

I am surprised how many eating disorder clients identify with vampires—that craving inner beast who wakens at night to binge in a frenzy of biting and sucking.* Stacey, struggling to recover from severe bulimia, discussed how she connected with the ravenous, unquenchable appetite of the vampire and how when she binged her "fangs" came out to devour everything in sight. In one of her sessions, Stacey described the latest vampire romance novel she was reading. Caught up in the story, I ask, "So what finally happened to this vampire couple?" A mischievous smile crossed her face and Stacey replied, "They lived *capillary* ever after!" We laugh uproariously. Stacey had added a playful note to a very tough struggle. This moment of shared laughter declared, "We're in this together, we are a team, and we'll fight this bulimia together!"

Joe, an anorexic young man, described the impact of his father's death on his eating struggles. "And how did your dad die?" I asked. Joe answered with a rueful half smile, "My father was an alcoholic. He died of *neurosis* of the liver!" In the midst of a sorrowful time, Joe had found a shred of playfulness that lightened his grief and brought us together in our work.

Moira, a binge eater, poked fun at herself: "The most stable men in my life have always been Ben and Jerry!" I responded that one of my

---

*In the article "Psychological Perspectives on Vampire Mythology," author Margaret Shanahan (n.d.) likens the ways in which narcissistic mothers may prey on their children like vampires. She references psychoanalyst Alice Miller who described how an emotionally immature mother can reverse the appropriate flow of nurturing, creating a relationship in which the child is "sucked" by the mother to provide for her own needs. In the article "Dracula on the Couch: The Psychiatry of Vampires," Pierre (2015) references two articles by a social worker to help clinicians understand the meaning of vampires in psychotherapy: "Social Work, BDSM and Vampires: Toward Understanding and Empowering People with Non-Traditional Identities" by Williams and "Do We Always Practice What We Preach? Real Vampires' Fears of Coming out of the Coffin to Social Workers and Helping Professionals" by Williams and Prior.

best girlfriends used to be Sara Lee. We joined together in an affectionate, laughing connection.

"You're the same old boring therapist always trying to psychoanalyze me," complains Grace, not wanting to speak further about a topic I'm encouraging her to discuss. Knowing Grace for a long time, I reply, "And you're the same old boring resistant patient always trying to make me feel like a pain-in-the-neck shrink." We both laugh, let off steam at how we are annoying each other, clear the air, and then go back to business.

Isabella, a Hispanic compulsive overeater, described her childhood in which her mother forced her to clean their apartment every day. Isabella was not allowed to go out and play unless she first scoured the house, which was never quite clean enough for her mother's approval. Reflecting on her mother's obsession with cleanliness, Isabella laughed, although with some regret: "We may have been 'Spics,' but at least we were Spic 'n' Span!"

We can laugh together because Isabella knows I am a Spanish speaker and an aficionada of all things Hispanic. She feels free to make this jibe with me.

Rachelle, a bulimic woman, describes her enjoyment of sexual bondage with ropes. Although she has made some connection between her bulimia and bondage, she is uncertain how much more detail she wants to disclose to me. Unaware of what I am saying, I comment, "By not discussing this further, *you are tying my hands* in my trying to understand you better." Rachelle looks at me in astonishment, I catch my Freudian slip, and we begin to laugh heartily. This smooths the way for further communication.

Sometimes eating disorder clients will mention a favorite joke. Often the joke is about food and eating and gives us an insight into their particular conflicts. As a young girl, my favorite joke involved a mother cannibal who is cooking up a captured hostage in a big cauldron in the jungle. Her little cannibal son is poking the man with a fork. The mother scolds the boy, "How many times have I told you not to play with your food!"

Only years later did I consider the possible connection between my enjoyment of this joke and my own childhood compulsive eating. I realized I felt sorry for the young cannibal whose eating was criticized by his mother, because my own eating was often criticized by my mother. But I was also gleeful the cannibal boy was getting reprimanded by his mother because it made me happy that I wasn't the only one getting scolded over my eating.

Much has been written on the role of humor, laughter, and jokes in psychotherapy. Clinicians are often directed to wait for the client to initiate something humorous rather than generate it themselves; clinicians are also directed to make sure their humor is empathic not to offend the client. I don't always agree with those warnings.

Eating disorder clients are very stuck in their habits and live a diminished life because of preoccupations with food and weight, and a judicious barb—and sometimes aggressively tinged—can animate and challenge a client and help break through their resistance. Bruce, a successful business owner, was compulsively driven to keep building his company despite the toll on his health; he would rather do anything than develop a lifestyle and eating style that supported his well-being. We have been trying to disentangle his stumbling blocks. Bruce announced in one session, "I'm going to Estonia to explore the market there for my product." I rolled my eyes and responded, "Boy, some people are sure driven to leave no 'Estonia' unturned to expand their business even at the expense of their health!" Bruce laughs, and I am able to make my point about how much he was overextending himself in a way that opened the conversation in a less defensive, more relaxed manner.

When the Client Laughs at Us. Clients also enjoy zinging me at times with their barbs. I make what I consider an inspired interpretation to Greg, who rolls his eyes and responds, "Duh. No shit, Sherlock." Better a "biting" comment to me than biting into unwanted food!

The spirit in which the barb is expressed makes all the difference as to whether it deepens the therapeutic partnership. It was not initially possible to have a therapeutic partnership, let alone deepen one, with Stan, a bulimic man, who enjoyed putting me down more than working on himself. He could not permit much partnership with me. Every comment, question, observation, even my silence was pronounced by him as "lame." It's hard to make traction in therapy when everything the therapist says or even doesn't say is met with such a round dismissal.

I understand why Stan needed to spit out my help. At times, it felt he was spitting on me with contempt. He had been ridiculed all his life by a tyrannical father who made Stan feel small and inadequate. His father controlled all the power, and it did not help Stan's self-esteem that he was also dyslexic. Stan could not allow me the satisfaction of helping him even if it also meant he was cheating himself of help. This is what we call shooting oneself in the foot or, in therapy parlance, "the negative therapeutic reaction." Theodore Reik describes this as "victory through self-defeat."

At the end of one of Stan's session, I hobbled dramatically to open my office door for him. "What's the matter with you?" he grunted. "I'm lame just like you said," I quipped finally hoping to find a connection with him through humor. Stan did find this highly amusing and responded with, "See? I told you so! I was right!" He then added, "To prove that you accept your lame status, you should bow to me before each session. Then I'll know for real that you know your place." To Stan's great delight, I bowed before each session, which expressed my willingness to get off what he perceived as my high and mighty perch—the perch his father had inhabited all his life. Traction in treatment followed as Stan saw I was not in competition to one-up him but really trying to join him on equal footing. Stan developed an enjoyable sense of humor, learned to communicate his aggression more directly rather than turn it against himself through bulimia, and did not need to spit up his food or spit up on me to nearly the same degree.

As I lent myself to Stan's need to equalize the power balance between us, I am reminded of a lecture by clinical social worker Dr. Herb Strean, "The Patient as Supervisor to the Therapist." Dr. Strean speaks to the value of the therapist being flexible and appreciating that clients often have the wisdom about what they need and can prescribe aspects of their own treatment. Stan's negative transference to me as an authoritarian father figure was lessened when I "submitted" to his request; this enhanced the development of the therapeutic alliance.

Of course, therapists need to be comfortable with the patients' requests, and it must be done wholly with an eye to deepening the treatment and not out of a sadomasochistic enactment. Clearly not all requests are appropriate to accommodate—such as the patient who asked me whether I wore brassieres with underwires. These questions need not be gratified but used as a springboard to help the client bring their preoccupations to the light of day. Understanding Jill's interest about whether I wore underwire bras had meaning. Jill explained that she had read underwire bras may cause breast cancer, and because her mother had died from breast cancer when she was 12, she was trying to determine whether I was in danger and whether she could rely on me to be there for her.

Companions on the Journey

All the formal therapy techniques in the world are not sufficient to help someone relinquish their pain and their eating disorder. In *Maybe You Should Talk to Someone*, therapist Lori Gottlieb (2019) says, "Therapy isn't a paint-by-numbers business, and sometimes the only way to move patients beyond their stuckness is by taking a risk in the room, by going out of the therapist's own comfort zone" (p. 405)

When the client experiences the therapist as an emotional companion on the journey toward healing, then the process becomes vivid and alive. The root of the word *companion* derives from Latin and means "to break bread" (com = with, pan = bread). To break bread is an act of sharing, of togetherness, of comfort, of being present in the moment—the recipe for wonderful therapy. In discussing the death of his wife, Robert reached for a tissue to wipe his tears. And, to my surprise, he handed me a tissue as well. Although I was not crying, I understood his gesture to mean he wanted a partner to join him in his sorrow. He did not want to cry alone.

Fortified with curiosity, empathy, resilience, tears, and humor, patients continue their journey to declare peace with emotional eating (Cohen, 2013).

6. Eating Disorders Mirror Our Relationships

Eating is a relationship that can be either nurturing or abusive, responsive or judgmental, nourishing or punishing. As described in attachment theory, early experiences with our family teach us about love, trust, comfort, security, deprivation, and abundance. These experiences then translate to our relationship with food, money, self-care, and how we relate to other people. The eating styles of the anorexic, the compulsive eater, and the bulimic parallel the kind of relationships they develop with the people in their lives—rejecting, embracing, or the push and pull of closeness and distance.

Clients are surprised (as are therapists) to see how the relationship they have with food often begins to parallel the relationship with their therapist. This connection with the therapist then becomes a mirror to better understand their inner world of emotional eating, providing a rich avenue of exploration and healing.

The Therapy Relationship and the Bulimic

The bulimic wavers back and forth between secret gorging rampages and violent purges of the food she has consumed. She purges to "repent" her neediness in the hope of proclaiming, "I really can manage with very little. I'm able to give it back. I didn't mean to take it anyway." This oscillation between gorging and purging parallels her ambivalence about whether she deserves to take in nurturance and keep it. Her pattern of taking in and getting rid of food and people will often extend to frequent, short-term romances as well as multiple therapists.

In my initial evaluation with Zoe, she informed me that she had been bingeing and vomiting for the past 13 years.

From the first session, Zoe disliked me. She said I looked like her last therapist, Ms. T., who had closed her practice to join a cult religion. Ms. T. had written Zoe a letter saying her job on the commune was to scrub toilets, and she felt fulfilled in a way she never had as a therapist. Zoe had decided on first viewing that I could not be trusted—just like her bulimic self had decided many years before that food could not be trusted. Reassuring her that I would not leave abruptly nor would I ever prefer scrubbing toilets would have fallen on deaf ears.

Zoe told me that I resembled Ms. T., and so she could not trust me, nor did she want to work with me. I was her fifth therapist, and I remarked to Zoe that she seemed as bulimic in her relationships with people and therapists as with food—always trying to get rid of us. "You don't have to trust me," I said. Some of her previous therapists had tried to convince her they were indeed trustworthy, whereas I recognized that Zoe's "not trusting" position was exactly where she needed to be in this beginning relationship of ours.

So we began on this rocky road, and as Zoe's therapy unfolded, she confided what life had been like when she was growing up. She had adored her handsome father and always turned to him for comfort when she was little even though he drank too much. But when she was six, as she lay cuddled in his arms, he began to fondle her sexually, stroking and rubbing her body all over.

Zoe's world shattered to pieces. Her father's betrayal had destroyed forever her innocence and trust. He had turned on her and became poison, just like later in life, food—the comforting nurturer—had become poison in her mind as well. This shattered trust of her father not only spilled over to food but to all her relationships. Now her suspiciousness was reflected in her relationship with me as her therapist.

For this reason, our relationship became the avenue to discover and explore Zoe's inner world. Every time she wanted to leave therapy and "throw me up," we worked to trace back what I had done to trigger this new episode of mistrust. She began to express more openly her wariness about me without worrying that I would become angry or retaliate. With time, she began to understand the parallels between the trauma in her early life, her food, and her anxieties about trust. This gave Zoe a sense of relief that she was not just "crazy" but that her behavior had rhyme and reason.

The Therapy Relationship and the Compulsive Eater

For the overeater, the world never seems to offer enough sustenance. She is convinced her needs can never be satisfied. She does not trust in the abundance of food, just as she does not trust in the abundance of loving kindness. She believes it is safer to depend on food than on people. After all, food never leaves you, never rejects you, never laughs at you, never dies. And so she attempts to take care of herself all by herself—just her and the food. A colleague of mine discovered that a compulsive overeater client of hers was secretly seeing another therapist at the same time as if she were trying to spread her needs between two "mothers" because she believed one mother could not satisfy her.

Compulsive eaters relate to their therapists in a variety of ways. Many feel they cannot "get enough" from the therapist. They demand, "Tell me what to do. Give me advice. Talk to me. Can I text you between sessions?" Feeling deprived, they turn to the therapist as they do to food, trying to fill up the empty place inside. Some complain that their previous therapists did not talk enough, leaving them feeling cheated and hungry for more. Obviously, my role as therapist in this case is not to fill my patient up with words and chatter but to tune in to when she is feeling deprived and try to understand what is bringing about her feelings of emptiness at that moment.

Often, clients pull their chair closer to the therapist; one client sits on the floor near my chair. They are hungry for connection.

Other compulsive overeater clients work hard to guard against their hungry inner self not to burden the therapist. I know I am sitting with this kind of "defensive" overeater when I start feeling bored, sleepy, or hungry but have no reason to feel that. My own emotional state alerts me that my patient is struggling to keep her distance from her emotions and from me. She relates intellectually as if reciting an essay, "My Life Problems." This is her way of protecting us both from what she believes is her awful, repulsive neediness.

Lorraine, an obese 33-year-old gay woman, had been a binge eater since childhood. Shortly after she was born, her mother became ill, and she was sent to live with her grandmother for an extended time. By the time she was five and had returned home, her mother began having outbursts of rage, pulling Lorraine's hair and hitting her with a wooden spoon.

Through her therapy and her relationship with me, Lorraine realized she felt bad for needing and wanting too much. She was convinced her voracious appetite for care and attention had made her mother angry and had driven her away. Overeating became an effective way to comfort herself and divert her need for love and sustenance from others.

In session, Lorraine would pull her chair up close to mine in my office and scrutinize my face. As we got to know each other better, we learned that one meaning of her searching my face was to determine whether I was angry at her. Just as she had feared her mother's startling explosions, she now feared mine. And even though we kept working on Lorraine's overeating and bingeing, she found no relief.

Then, after my summer vacation, which came at a difficult time because Lorraine's grandmother was dying, I began to have a strange impression she wanted to bite me, both to extract more emotional milk or nourishment and also to express her anger that I had gone away at a time she needed me. My vacation brought up feelings of abandonment and old bruises about being left alone, but Lorraine was too afraid to reveal this. So she continued biting into food instead of "biting" me.

Following a particularly needy session in which she was upset about her grandmother's illness, she asked, "When will you be taking your next vacation? I think you should take one soon."

"What makes you think I should take a vacation soon?" I asked.

"You look tired and probably need some more time away from your patients," she said.

I said, "You feel that your neediness drains me, and you are sucking me dry—"

Lorraine interrupted, "I feel I want so much from you that you should go away and restore yourself."

"You believe I only have a finite amount to give you and that you may use it up," I continued. "You are scared of wanting too much from me—that I will get angry with you and pull away."

Although she continued to be scared of her voracious feelings, a gradual shift occurred in our work together after this session. She became more reflective about her fear of using people up and taking too much, just like in her relationship with food. Instead of constantly asking, "Is our time over yet?" which meant "I am afraid I have been a bad girl and taken too much from you," she began asking, "Do we have some more time left?" I understood her rephrasing the question to mean, "I am able to admit that I have hungry needs and I want more from you. Maybe I'm not so bad to admit that I want more."

As Lorraine was gradually able to take in my soothing presence and to know that I accepted her even when she was upset and wanting contact, she was able to interrupt her own binge with newfound coping methods. She began turning more to me and to her girlfriends rather than gorging on food.

The Therapy Relationship and the Anorexic

The anorexic abhors her emotional neediness and starves herself as a way of proclaiming, "Look how strong I am. I have no needs. I don't need food. I have triumphed over my body and I am in control!" And her eating style of subsisting on as little as possible will also mirror her dislike of having close relationships with people. In fact, the anorexic has been described as being lactose intolerant to the milk of human kindness. Karen, an anorexic girl of 18, has been forced by her parents to come to see me. She moves her chair as far away from me as possible. "If I could sit outside the window on the fire escape, I'd be more comfortable," she says.

The root of the anorexic disorder, in which the person prides herself on avoiding food and denying hunger, is directly related to the person's early family relationships.

Another client, Sally, was a tiny sparrow-girl who had been anorexic since age 12. She described how her father held court at the dinner table each night, lecturing his children, lecturing his wife, raising his voice, and intimidating the family. Sally's stomach would close up with tension at these times, but her father forbade anyone to leave the table until they cleaned their plate. Usually, she forced herself to finish by choking down her food.

This was only one of many painful memories Sally had of her father's domination over the family. Now in her early 20s, she led an isolated life with few close friends and also greatly feared her boss at work. Although she appeared emaciated, Sally came to therapy not for help with anorexia but for the deep loneliness and emptiness she felt inside.

Whenever I offered support and understanding to her in our sessions, Sally withdrew from me. My words made her wince. Then I realized she experienced my words, like her father's, as being forced down her throat. She felt obligated to "swallow" my "food for thought." But how could I help her if I couldn't speak and communicate?

I began experimenting with becoming quieter, not asking questions, and I discovered the less I talked, the more Sally slowly came out of her shell. Her experience had been that her body, mind, and soul were the possessions of her father, so to receive an interpretation from me confirmed her sense of inadequacy, as if I, too, were telling her what to think and feel. But when I became more passive, Sally took the reins of the sessions rather than feeling "force-fed" by me. Gradually, Sally became more trusting of me as a nurturing person in her life who did not want to dominate her, and she came to feel more in control of the therapy space we shared. Sally became more comfortable eating more, and she became more expressive in her relationships. She emerged from her need to fend off food and other people.*

The Therapy Session as a Meal

The therapy session is a meal we share with our clients—a time for digesting emotions, chewing the fat, metabolizing insights. We model

*There are many ingredients that go into successful therapy. In Sally's case, as well as our understanding the parallels between her eating and her relationship with me, her therapy included the use of behavioral techniques, anti-anxiety medication, and nutritional intervention.

how both a session and a meal have a beginning, a middle, and an end. I have been surprised how many therapists allow sessions to go over the scheduled time; for the eating disordered client this sends the message that you can always make it up to yourself and there is no structure to adhere to. Because many clients graze and snack all day long, when clinicians end the session on time, they are demonstrating the principle of "we have to stop." Of course, there are occasions for flexibility and bending the frame but not as a regular rule.

This is important for the compulsive overeater whose meal has a beginning and a middle, but she can never get to the end of feeding herself.

The bulimic has a beginning, then an end (when she throws up), and never a middle where she takes in food and keeps it. In contrast, the anorexic—with her enforced self-starvation—never even gets to the beginning of the meal in the first place.

Bodies Come Alive in Session

In the therapy session, we are more than just two minds and two voices. The intimacy between patient and therapist extends beyond verbal communication. We are also two bodies. I observe how the patients who sit before me speak to me in body language. I have had many nursing mothers proudly uncover their breasts to feed their babies in my office; a vegetarian patient who was oblivious that her chronic garlic breath smelled up the whole room; a teenager who hiked up her skirt in sessions; a patient whose little daughter climbed on my lap to cuddle in session and gave me a case of head lice; a man who tracked mud into my bathroom, leaving it for me to clean up; and the anorexic girl who blockades herself behind my couch cushions with only her toe sticking out.

Patients also have emotional reactions to the therapist's body, which, when deciphered, can help illuminate issues of body image, envy, hate, and sexuality. Especially in the therapy of eating disorders, where concerns about size, shape, weight, and appearance are so paramount, reactions to the therapist's body are often a valuable topic to be discussed and understood. My hairstyle, my gray hair, my breasts, my weight, my eyes, my jewelry, my clothes, my sexual orientation, and my hay fever–induced sneezing have all been commented on by patients at different times.

In session, tears spill, noses are runny, sweaty bodies exude their odor, farts occasionally ring out, perfume may sweeten the office, as does the aura of cigarette or cigar smoked before session—these are the earthy components of the therapy relationship. The patient who may feel inadequate, like a nobody (she has "no body" that she loves), is witnessed in her bodily humanity and accepted without judgment by the therapist.

As we work together as patient and therapist, patients often send me nonverbal messages, a body language message that needs to be translated into words. Blushing, yawning, burping—they all go with the territory. All of these nonverbal communications are intimate expressions of attachment. The therapist's body and the patient's body speak. The connection is deepened; attachment comes alive; hope takes root.

Justine comes to sessions always displaying her ample cleavage. She is a binge eater, and I know she always feels physically and emotionally hungry. What is her cleavage trying to tell me? Is she trying to seduce me? Or compete with me? Is she really looking for mothering from me and using her breasts as an invitation to be baby and mommy together? I do not know the answer, so I wait and watch and listen and try to make meaning out of Justine's nonverbal expression. No digital session on a computer screen could capture the energy of these moments with her.

Thawing Frozen Emotions

Just as the disappointments our clients experienced with the people they love became the original reason they turned to emotional eating, so human relationships can be the path toward recovery. We all grow in connection to others. The courage to turn to a therapist to unravel one's problems is a crucial beginning step in undoing the bond with food and replacing it with human nurturing.

As Shakespeare writes, "Give sorrow words. The grief that does not speak whispers the o'er-fraught heart, and bids it break" (*Macbeth*, Act 4, Scene 3). Emotional eating has frozen our clients' feelings and pains. Their relationship with us can help them thaw.

Part 2

Multicultural Perspectives, Gender Competency, and the Impact of Social Media in Eating Disorder Treatment

7

A Multicultural Perspective on Eating Disorders

They tried to bury us; they didn't know we were seeds.

Mexican proverb

Bingeing, purging, starving, and chronic dieting do not discriminate on the basis of race, gender, socioeconomic status, or sexual identity. Despite the stereotype of eating disorders mainly befalling skinny, rich white girls, increasing numbers of African Americans; Hispanics; Asians; Muslims; and lesbian, gay, bisexual, transgender, queer, and questioning (LGBTQ) people are presenting for eating disorder therapy.

Eating disorders are not color-blind, and the social work clinician needs to be aware of the unique and special issues relating to culture, socioeconomic status, immigration, assimilation, and discrimination that affect each individual client. We also need to appreciate the sense of isolation and alienation that many blacks, Latinos, Asians, Muslims, and Native Americans feel from mainstream American culture (Bardone-Cone, Higgins Neyland, & Lin, 2017, p. 279).*

Risk Factors for Minority Groups

For an informed and supportive treatment, let's consider the four risk factors that can provoke and trigger eating disorders among ethnic minorities.

Acculturation

The stronger the identification with one's own ethnicity, the more protected the person will be from body image distress and related eating

*Most of the research on minorities is focused on women. Similar to white men, men of different ethnic groups have lower rates of eating disorders as well.

disorders. Self-acceptance in having a higher body weight, as well as appreciating and liking one's ethnic features, is an inoculation against the American cultural mandate to be thin at all costs (Bardone-Cone et al., 2017).

However, the more a person identifies with mainstream American culture with its relentless pursuit of thinness and Anglo physical characteristics, the higher the risk for body dissatisfaction. Hispanic and African American cultures have traditionally been more accepting and appreciative of a wide range of body sizes. But as a woman becomes more ambitious to succeed in white America, dieting and achieving thinness become equated with her aspirations for more upward mobility. This can set the stage for the development of an eating disorder.

Acculturative Stress

People often experience conflict when there is a discrepancy between the ideals and expectations of the two cultures in which they live. The traditional role of the Hispanic woman, for example, was to be a homemaker with many children. This contradicts the current American ideal for a woman to be more independent, work outside the home, and earn money. Straddling both worlds can cause anxiety and stress especially for a first-generation woman as issues of loyalty to the values of her family of origin may compete and clash with her hopes for enhanced self-determination.

Turning to food—the cheapest, most available, anti-anxiety drug on the market—becomes a soothing comfort for the binge eater. Purging becomes a relief from stress for the bulimic. Self-starvation becomes a way to exert control over a situation that does not feel safe for the anorexic.

Discrimination

In spite of the gains made in recent decades, American society continues to discriminate against ethnic minorities. When a person internalizes the racist perspective that only white and thin bodies hold value, this negatively affects body esteem. Body shame can lead to the wish to "fix" one's body. Fixing, altering, and manipulating body size and appearance through unhealthy behaviors, attempts at weight loss, and plastic surgery can be the gateway to developing an eating disorder. In an effort to assimilate, many women believe, "If I can't have lighter skin, then at least I can make myself thinner." For many, thinness equates with access to power and the ticket to upward socioeconomic status.

Microaggressions

Microaggressions are verbal or behavioral slights that are brief, unexpected, and subtle acts of discrimination (Sue, 2010). People of color and different ethnic groups are continually exposed to microaggressions that indirectly communicate the message that the person is considered inferior. These effects are cumulative and take a psychological toll leading to the person's self-doubt, confusion, hurt, and pent-up anger. Uncertainty about whether to react and respond to a perceived insult—whether intentional or unintentional—leaves the person exhausted because of the catch-22: "You're damned if you do, and damned if you don't." The following are examples of microaggressions:

- A distinguished African American social work colleague of mine speaks of the numerous times the police pulled him over in his car for no reason or how he was looked at suspiciously in stores for no provocation beyond having black skin.
- A dark woman with her light-skinned baby is often asked if she is the nanny.
- The Asian American author R. O. Kwon (2019) demands, "Stop calling Asian women adorable" and recounts how many times in a professional setting she has been called cute, a pixie, or adorable and received intrusive comments on her "alabaster" skin and "silky" hair.
- A Mexican client tells me she had complained to her previous therapist about deep fatigue. The therapist responded, "Well, what you really need is a long 'siesta.'" My client did not know whether to be offended by the possible caricature that Mexicans are lazy or whether the therapist was trying to be empathic. She had a difficult time sorting this out because she had experienced previous racial slurs in her life that felt contemptuous. It left her feeling confused and on guard with the therapist.

Eating Disorders in Latinos and African Americans

Researchers have valiantly tried to analyze and quantify eating disorders in minority groups and have arrived at statistics like the following: "Latino males have significantly higher rates of bulimia than their Caucasians peers"; and "2.36% of black females have binge eating disorder [BED] while only 2.31% Latina females and 1.91% non-Latina Caucasians have BED" (Bardone-Cone et al., 2017, pp. 277, 279).

In truth, statistics are misleading because those who seek help for eating problems are only the tip of the iceberg compared with the number of people who actually suffer from eating disorders. Many also suffer from subclinical disordered eating behaviors that do not warrant a diagnosis from the DSM-5. Shame, stigma, fear, family resistance, inadequate health insurance or financial resources, and lack of awareness of treatment options are obstacles standing in the way of seeking treatment.

To understand eating disorders in the Hispanic population, we need to appreciate that "one size does not fit all." Latinos are not a homogenous group. In the United States, we have an extensive range of people identifying themselves as Latinos from the Mexican Chicano in Los Angeles, to the first-generation Puerto Rican in New York, to the white affluent Cuban in Miami. Some Latinos do not speak English, some are bilingual, some do not speak Spanish. Some are white, others are black, brown, or have Caribbean Indian heritage. They are all Latinos, to be sure, but with a variety of cultural experiences, ethnic differences, and geographic variations that defy easy generalization.*

As a Spanish-speaking therapist, I am interested to hear what language a bilingual person decides to use to discuss their eating problems—English or their "mother tongue." A bulimic Puerto Rican man I worked with spoke English in sessions, but he cursed in Spanish. He puked out his feelings in his native language. That choice has meaning—unique for each person—and is worthy of discussion.

African Americans in the United States are not a homogenous group either. Some live in the rural south, some in big cities, some speak Spanish, some speak French, some Creole, and others Portuguese. Some are from the Caribbean, others from Africa. They vary in skin color, hair texture, and ethnic features. As with Latinos, generalizations cannot be made about African Americans.

The important variable in understanding eating disorders among minority groups, I believe, relates to the level of education and socioeconomic class. People who are better off economically and more educated about mental health issues will often seek out therapy to directly address their eating disorder. For over 10 years, I worked at a community mental health clinic serving low-income Hispanic patients who presented problems that included depression, anxiety, concerns about children, and domestic strife. Although many of these patients did suffer

*I am fluent in Spanish and have had the pleasure of working with women and men from Argentina, Colombia, Cuba, Dominican Republic, Ecuador, Guatemala, Mexico, Puerto Rico, Spain, and Venezuela.

from eating disorders, the initial intakes screened only for alcoholism and drug use.

In the book *A Hunger So Wide and So Deep: A Multiracial View of Women's Eating Problems*, author Becky Thompson (1994) explains that for marginalized people,

> eating disorders can begin as survival strategies and self-preservation in response to a myriad of injustices including racism, sexism, homophobia, classism, the stress of acculturation, and emotional, physical, and sexual abuse. . . . Discomfort with weight, bodies, and appetite are often the metaphors girls and women use to speak of atrocities. To hear only concerns about appearance or gender inequality is to miss the complex origins of eating problems. . . . People who have suffered discrimination may not feel in control or safe in their culture, their families, or their bodies and may feel exiled from their bodies, appetites, hungers. (pp. 2, 12, 16)

Of course, minority women and men are not the only ones exiled from their bodies. No matter what your color or ethnic background, sexual, physical, and emotional abuse will cause dissociation and disruption with one's body-self. For all people, trauma disrupts an intact sense of one's body. However, the clinician needs to be especially mindful of the unique stressors of minority clients to develop an empathic and sensitive connection.

The Story of Alicia

Alicia, a young black Dominican woman struggling with a binge-eating disorder, describes how she experienced racism not just in the world at large but also as a young child at home with her parents. Parents may often absorb and internalize racism and may pass on their low self-image to their children:

> My first experience of racism began at home. My parents are light-skinned, and I was born with much darker skin. My mother was horrified as if my dark skin was a criticism and an assault on her. Starting when I was a child, Mom verbally attacked me by instructing me to pinch my nose and to purse my lips to make them smaller. She straightened my nappy hair when I was very young. I became divided from myself, and sneaking food became my only comfort. I absorbed her racism and hated myself and my body. I didn't feel like a fully formed self—just a collection of despised body parts.

> When I was 13, my cousin molested me. I didn't think I deserved any better, and I continued to bury myself in the anesthesia of food until I began a long-term therapy where my issues of rage and grief came bounding up to the surface.

In her therapy, Alicia confided that she would never marry a man with lighter skin than her. "I couldn't risk marrying someone who would wind up being as disappointed in my darker skin as my mother was and use it as a weapon against me."*

Alicia's story is reminiscent of the poignant description of the little black girl in Toni Morrison's (1999) *The Bluest Eye*:

> Every night, Pecola Breedlove prays for a miracle: she wants blue eyes. If she had blue eyes, she believes, then everything would be different. She would be beautiful. She would finally be worthy of her parents' love, deserving of the local grocer's respect, and visible to all those who do not see her. (p. 46)

Asian Americans and Eating Disorders: A Silent Struggle

Other ethnic groups struggle with eating disorders through their unique cultural lens. In the book published by NASW Press *Multicultural Perspectives on Race, Ethnicity, and Identity*, social workers Kim-Ju and Akutsu (2015) describe how Asian Americans are a diverse group in the United States consisting of over 25 distinct ethnic groups from East and Southeast Asia and therefore defy easy generalizations. Because Asians and Asian Americans tend to have small, slender bodies, they are often overlooked as a group that could suffer from eating disorders. But there is actually great size diversity, including plus-size Asian women. "All Asians aren't the stereotype of being small and petite. Being Asian is not one look. Being Asian is not one culture" (Wong, 2019, para. 9). Clearly, body size is not an indicator of whether an Asian American struggles with food issues.

Eating disorders and body dissatisfaction have grown significantly in the past few decades among Asians and Asian Americans. In fact, South Korea has become the world's leading plastic surgery capital.

Dr. Hiroyuki Suematsu, professor of clinical psychology at Nagoya University, says Japan's rate of bulimia is 10 times higher than it was 30 years ago (Hendricks, 2016). Whereas there were no reported cases

*Although Alicia's case demonstrates many themes in the black and Latino culture, this is her own unique story.

of bulimia 40 years ago, today it is now the country's biggest eating disorder problem.

Asians and Asian Americans are at increased risk for an eating disorder because of the pernicious effect of Anglo beauty standards. Girls and women seek out skin-lightening procedures and eyelid surgery to make their eyes larger with a more Western appearance.*

In the United States, Asian American immigrant children are often torn emotionally between the desire for autonomy, independence, and free expression versus the traditional Asian mandate to be conforming, deferent to parents' decisions, obedient, and honoring family wishes.

Sam Louie (2013), Chinese psychotherapist and author of *Asian Shame and Addiction: Suffering in Silence*, explains:

> The desire for autonomy and independence among immigrant Asian children in America is oftentimes drowned out by centuries-old Confucius views of hierarchy and patriarchy. In other words, to go against parental or family wishes can be deemed culturally shameful and damning. One way to suppress these feelings of shame, desire, and authenticity is to engage in an eating disorder. (p. 45)

Asians who suffer in silence experience a double bind:

> They may want help but how can they obtain it if it is viewed as being culturally reprehensible? . . . Needing help is unacceptable to most Asians. But if they don't get help, they risk drowning in a sea of hopelessness that traps addicts and keeps them tumbling endlessly down the spiral of shame. (Louie, 2013, p. 45)

The clash between the family-oriented traditional Asian household and the individualism encouraged in Western culture may cause parents—fearful of losing their children to what they consider an overly permissive world—to tighten their grip on their children. This environment leaves many girls trapped and wanting to take control of something—anything. Dieting, bingeing, purging, or starving can become the one thing over which they can grasp control (C. I. Hall, 1995; Kim, 2003).

The Story of Li Hua (Helen)

Li Hua, who calls herself "Helen" in English, a 38-year-old married professional Chinese woman, was born in Hong Kong. She weighed

---

*Blepharoplasty, also known as "double eyelid surgery," is a popular type of cosmetic surgery elected by many Asians, in which the skin around the eye is reshaped to create an upper eyelid with a crease (that is, "double eyelid"), which is more Western looking.

80 pounds and arrived at my office seeking help for anorexia after having been to many previous therapists.*

She referred to her eating disorder as "ED" and described ED as someone who criticized her incessantly, demanding long exercise routines that were "payment" for whatever food she ate. ED bullied her, dictated to her, and Helen felt frightened of his power but also believed the truth of what he demanded.

Helen spent our early sessions explaining her relationship with ED and admitted that only a small part of her wanted to get better because, in some ways, ED provided companionship for her. Although he was a dictator, ED gave her guidance when she was unsure of herself by demanding what she should do. ED bellowed that she should leave her son crying in his crib until she completed her full hour of exercise.

My early position was to listen empathically and comment about how hard her life sounded. I decided initially not to intervene between her and ED so as to better understand and appreciate his function in her life.

In their eagerness to be helpful, I believe clinicians often intervene too soon and underestimate the healing role of simply listening. The anorexic especially, like Helen, often experiences the therapist's words—like food—to be intrusive. Giving clients the time and space they need to sort out their feelings while we witness them quietly can be a compassionate act.

When Helen began talking about her mother, I learned that Mom was the predecessor for ED. Mom starved Helen emotionally, refusing to give her daughter any acknowledgment or validation for Helen's very real accomplishments. When Helen achieved professional success, her mother would say, "No big deal. This is what we expect of you

---

*Sometimes the universe has uncanny ways of introducing us to our clients. A month before Helen even called for her first appointment, an odd moment of serendipity occurred. I began getting glossy magazines in the mail entitled *Chinese Woman*. They were high-quality bilingual magazines featuring articles about successful Chinese women. I have no idea why I began receiving them or why they continue to this day.

When Helen came for her first appointment, I had to get accustomed to her accent; her English is thickly accented. After our first session, I wound up ordering Chinese food for lunch that day. My fortune cookie said, "Chinese Patient: Learn English!" I laughed out loud at the serendipity of this experience. When I mentioned this strange occurrence to a colleague, she quipped, "I wonder if your Chinese patient got a fortune cookie that said, 'American Therapist: Learn Chinese!'"

In the article "Uncanny Communication and the Porous Mind," Janine de Peyer (2016) speaks of the uncanny synchronicity that can occur between therapist and patients.

anyway." As Helen described it, "If I do something well, my mother shrugs it off as if this is what's expected of me, and there is never any praise. If I do something 'wrong,' then my mother is the first to berate me with how imperfect and disappointing I am. Even if I broke through the 'bamboo ceiling'—that's the glass ceiling for Chinese girls—that still wouldn't be enough for her."

In discussing her family in therapy, Helen felt disloyal, disobedient, and guilty. "Chinese children must always be good and respectful," she explained.

Anorexia became Helen's way of managing her hurt, her helplessness, and her resentment at being dominated by her mother. Self-starvation became her means to gain control and dominance over her food and the needs of her body. By not eating, she felt in charge, defiant, and less at the mercy of her deep hurt and sadness.

Helen had three selves lodged inside her: her eating disorder ED, her harsh internalized mother, and also a nascent tendril of her own authentic self. Helen was observant, smart, and yearning to be heard. She was hungry for connection, hungry to be witnessed, hungry to be liked.

She confessed that she never had a doll or a friend, and sometimes she played with her daughter's doll. Helen was ashamed and embarrassed by this childish behavior. I confided, "Well, I have a stuffed lamb named Charlotte. I love her and play with her, and I'm a lot older than you!" Helen asked if she could meet Charlotte. I brought my lamb into my office, and Helen held her close and murmured how much she liked her soft furriness. Helen said, "I never, ever had a girlfriend. Would you agree to be my BFF during our sessions?" I answered that I would be happy to be her best friend forever in our sessions. I was struck by how much emotional nurturing Helen wanted but how fearful of nourishment she was at the same time.

In another session, Helen told me that the tires on her car had been slashed in the middle of the night by a random vandal. Her mother blamed Helen for parking her car in the wrong place even though she had parked in front of her house.

Helen was unclear how to process this incident and said, "I don't know what I should feel about my tires being slashed, so I decided to just forgive the guy who did it." Her comment told me volumes about her inner life: that she was quite unaware of her internal emotions, she was not in touch with any appropriate anger, and, most of all, she was willing to short-circuit discussing her feelings so as to "forgive and forget." Emotionally, she was unable to "flesh out" her mixture of feelings, "chew the fat" about this experience, "digest" her reactions, and "metabolize" the experience. And she seemed light years away from feeling angry at her mother's accusatory comment, although she did acknowledge that it hurt her feelings. My role as her therapist was to help her focus and reflect on what she was feeling rather than dismiss it so quickly with "forgive and forget." Helen's need to keep conflicted feelings out paralleled her need to keep food out of her system as well.

At this point, I realized we never seemed to have enough time to discuss her eating behaviors because her need to put her life experiences into words was so pressing. I decided to refer her to a nutritionist who could concretely address Helen's issues about food while I continued exploring her emotional landscape.

Lindsay Krasna was the nutritionist I chose. Whereas I was old enough to be Helen's mother, Lindsay was closer to Helen's age. Now Helen was going to have another BFF, a young woman who could serve as a peer role model. With Lindsay's nutritional guidance and encouragement, Helen allowed a bit more food into her life and got her menstrual period back. Lindsay* shared with me her experience working with Helen:

> When I first met Helen, I was struck by the contrast between her personality and her approach to eating. Her demeanor was warm, sweet and charming, while her eating patterns were rigid, flavorless, and tyrannical. Helen had numerous "rules" to which ED held her hostage and fears of what would happen should she disobey those rules. She minimized the role of pleasure in eating and held fast to "healthiness" as the only priority in her food choices. Ironically, Helen's obsession with health ultimately distracted her from actually being healthy. She would often fill up on "high volume" items like vegetables and water to suppress her inner hunger. This allowed Helen to feel "full" temporarily but never truly satisfied or well nourished. Helen measured most of her food and only ate foods that ED "approved"—namely low-calorie fare. She ate in secrecy most of the time—due to the shame she had about feeding herself—which only deepened her sense of isolation.
>
> Helen and I quickly formed a sister-like bond which, along with her connection to Mary Anne, laid the groundwork for healing. Together, we worked to chip away at ED's stronghold on Helen. We challenged some of ED's strict food rules, debunked ED's irrational beliefs about weight control, and expanded Helen's food repertoire by eating "risky" foods in sessions together, such as unmeasured peanut butter and a chocolate dessert treat. Helen also learned new tools and strategies to help her combat ED on her

*Lindsay Krasna, RD, CEDRD-S, CDN, http://lknutrition.com.

> own, including better identifying and responding to her hunger and fullness cues, and strengthening her authentic voice around food, exercise, and body issues. Helen summed up the benefits she was experiencing from our work when she said at the end of one of our meetings: "our sessions are like training for my 'healthy' mind."
>
> Over time, it became obvious Helen was "absorbing" more nourishment in the form of food and in the form of these satisfying "new"tricious connections with Mary Anne and me.

Helen reflected on being a Chinese woman with the ongoing pressure to make her parents proud, honor their sacrifice of bringing her to America, "suck up her feelings," and not feel "too full of herself." She battled with the searing shame at her neediness for craving her mother's love and approval.* Taking in nourishment from me and Lindsay became a turning point in her sense of owning her body and her emotions for the first time in her life.

Muslim Americans and Eating Disorders: Under Cover

Islam is the second largest religion in the world today, and the number of followers is expected to exceed that of Christianity during this century. Because the U.S. Census Bureau does not track religious affiliation, the number of Muslims in the country today is unknown and is estimated to range anywhere from 2 million to 7 million. Some are orthodox, and others are secular; some are American born, and others emigrated from other countries; some are white, and some are black.

For Muslim women, there are four factors that create a perfect storm for the development of an eating disorder.

Patriarchy

Islam is more than a religion; it is also a culture that can be patriarchal.† The tradition is that fathers are the head of the home, and mothers do not always have an equal say. If a girl does not see her mother having an equal voice in her marriage, she may believe that women's opinions are not sufficiently valued. This will diminish the girl's own self-esteem (Cooper, n.d.).

---

*Although Helen's case demonstrates many themes in the Asian American culture, this is her own unique story.

†The chief executive of Apple is facing mounting criticism for offering an app created by the Saudi interior ministry that enables Saudi men to restrict the movements of women in their family. The app also notifies users if a woman tries to use her passport to flee the country (Vega, 2019).

Hostility

Muslim women and girls often feel hostility and criticism coming from Americans because some Americans associate Muslims with terrorism. Even though the girl and her family have nothing to do with violence, they are often targeted with antagonism. This can make Muslim females insecure and uneasy.

Clothing

Muslim women who wear the hijab, the distinctive head scarf to cover a woman's hair, may feel especially vulnerable to discrimination. Several countries have banned the hijab, and several states in the United States have tried to restrict its wearing.

Many Americans mistakenly believe that women who wear the hijab and especially the full-length burka are being forced into this by oppression from the family and the Muslim culture. In fact, many women enjoy wearing the hijab and claim,

> It's strange to be living in a world where if a woman decides to wear a bikini to the beach, it's a sign of her liberty and personal choice but if she decides to wear a burkini [modest swimwear that covers the body from head to toe], it automatically becomes associated with oppression. (Gahnem, 2017, para. 2)

A woman who does not feel in charge of her body becomes vulnerable to eating disorders as an attempt to help herself feel more in control (Islam and Eating Disorders, n.d.).

In addition, because Muslim women often wear modest clothes that are not form-fitting, many Americans erroneously assume that Muslims do not experience social pressure to be a certain weight because they are so covered up.

Marriage

To make a good marriage, girls are especially prized if they are thin. This pressure to be thin will create anxiety in females (Khimji, n.d.).

These four stressors of suppression within the family coupled with the pressures of American society can cause girls to feel alienated and not comfortable living in their own skin. Eating disorders, with their numbing comfort and distraction from inner anxiety, are prevalent in many Muslim communities.

Ramadan

Eating disorders flourish especially during Ramadan. Ramadan is a month in which Muslims devote themselves to religious study and self-discipline. Fasting is considered the most important aspect of this religious observance, and Muslims are required to fast every morning before sunrise, for up to 15 hours each day. At night, the fast is broken with large and lavish meals, and the cycle repeats the next day for the full month.

For those with an eating disorder, Ramadan can be a dangerous trigger. The cycle of starving and then feasting can mirror a person's ongoing eating struggle. In the essay "What It's Like to Have an Eating Disorder during Ramadan," author Adeline Hocine (2018) writes,

> Living with a secret eating disorder can feel like a daily battle—but as a Muslim woman, Ramadan in particular resembles something closer to war. In fifth grade, I saw an opportunity to mask my eating disorder with the veil of dedication to my faith. Suddenly, I felt inclined to participate for the first time; my Muslim parents never pressured me to observe Ramadan growing up. While mental illness [such as an eating disorder] is stigmatized, fasting for religious purposes is encouraged. By fasting to prove my faith, I have an entire community of people behind me validating my commitment. (para. 3)

"Ramadan was anorexia's way of justifying my starvation—the more I restricted, the more spiritually strong I was for being able to resist the temptation of food" (Haidrani, 2016, para. 2).

Exemptions from fasting are allowed for health reasons and would probably be granted if someone with an eating disorder requested dispensation for that year. But often Muslims with eating disorders will not ask because they now have religious justification to engage in starving—which may often lead to bingeing and purging—and many happily consider this time "an amazing opportunity to lose weight" (Haidrani, 2016, para. 6).

Muslims who are already in recovery will accept and appreciate the exemption from fasting to avoid setting up the starve–purge–binge cycle, but they are often looked at critically by those in their community who do not understand that an eating disorder is a legitimate reason to avoid fasting. Those in recovery explain that there are many ways to connect with God during that month and that you are not any less of a Muslim if you cannot fast (Kesvani, 2015).

Muslims Getting Help

Maryum Khwaja, a Muslim psychotherapist, says imams who grew up in Muslim countries tend to be less understanding of mental health struggles than their American-born colleagues (as cited in Chapin, 2016). These imams believe, "if you were to pray more you wouldn't have these eating disorders or mental-health issues" (para. 12). "If you covered your hair and dressed a certain way you would not have body-image issues" (Khwaja, as cited in Chapin, 2016, para. 12).

However, awareness is growing that eating disorders are not related to vanity but are genuine medical and psychological problems that require help. Parents are coming together with the following message:

> It is imperative to impart to our daughters and young girls of the community that there is no connection whatsoever between a female's intellect and character to her outwards appearance and size. When we see Muslim girls depressed and suffering from eating disorders in order to reach such unrealistic standards of beauty, it is a clear indication that we have neglected the divine solution of Hijab, which would have prevented us from ending up in such a scenario to begin with. (Syed, n.d., para. 11)

It should be noted that Muslim boys and men also develop eating disorders, although they often manage to fly under the radar. Because eating disorders are considered women's problems, Muslim men work hard to hide their distress. In "Islam and Eating Disorders" (Islam Eating Disorders, 2015), a YouTube video features a Muslim man encouraging other Muslim men to seek help. He states, "Allah said in the Quran 'There is a cure for every disease except death.'"

Clinicians who are culturally competent with this community will understand the enormous antagonism that Muslims are subjected to in this country. Learning how this effects each client and empathically appreciating how eating disorders can become a "solution" to feeling alienated will help deepen the alliance between therapist and client.

Muslim Women Speak Out

In 2017, the first Muslim Women's Day was celebrated and now takes place each year on March 27 to honor "real, diverse, and fierce Muslim women with the intention of amplifying the voices of Muslim women." MuslimGirl.com is the world's number-one English-language platform for Muslim women: "Our platform and social media presence became a defiant tool through which we talked back to the issues facing Muslim women on a daily basis. We are here, and have always been at the ready, to elevate the authentic and diverse narratives of our Muslimah sisters" (MuslimGirl.com, n.d., para. 2).

Muslim women are emerging from more traditional roles, have even become fashion models, and are celebrated in entertainment (Bacha, 2018; Sidhu, 2019).

The Story of Zulema

Zulema is a 30-year-old married Muslim woman with four children. Unlike her mother and six sisters, Zulema does not wear the hijab hair covering but comes to session in jeans and a tee shirt. Although she looks modern, she tells me anxiously that she did not tell her husband she was coming to therapy for her bulimia for fear of his reaction—to the knowledge both that she is bulimic and that she is seeking outside help. Instead, she tells him she is going for weekly treatment of her varicose veins. She is also worried that he will discover she took a taxi to my office and was alone with the male driver.

Zulema has been married since age 16 to her first cousin. Three of her sisters have married his three brothers. Her aunt is her mother-in-law, and her brothers-in-law are her first cousins. Zulema has been bulimic since age 13.

At age 13, with the onset of puberty, Zulema's anxiety, depression, and PTSD reached an upsurge. She describes a frantic worry that her family would begin priming her for marriage. Zulema is one of 10 children. She describes the physical abuse her father committed against her mother, including his pulling her mother up the stairs by her long hair. Zulema did not want to get married but was afraid to say anything. She discovered the "solution" of bulimia—a form of self-medication that comforts her, quells her anxiety, and gives her an outlet to discharge tremendous resentment. She turned her focus away from her emotional problems to the rhythmic soothing of gorging followed by the forceful spasms of purging.

Zulema came to therapy with me for two years. In her sessions, Zulema spoke of her sadness at never having gotten an education and of having to get married so young. She began antidepressant medication, which helped improve her mood and bulimia. We spoke of her being Muslim and me Jewish, and we prided ourselves on how well we got along and how the Middle East should take a lesson from us. Zulema discontinued therapy when her family moved out of state, but I still hear from her every few years.

We developed a very affectionate relationship in which Zulema felt understood, but I always wished she could have stayed longer. I think one of the most helpful parts of her therapy was my pointing out that bulimia is a language. Every time she threw up, I asked her to translate what her vomit wanted to say in words and in emotional feelings. This idea of linking her behavior to emotions was very new to her, and she found it an intriguing way to get to know herself better. Mostly, it seemed that Zulema's bulimia was a silent protest of rage against the strictures of her life. And it was also a way of crying for the little girl inside who felt frightened and lost.*

Orthodox Jews and Eating Disorders

The majority of Jews are assimilated into mainstream American life, but Orthodox Jews stand apart—living in communities with their own culture and traditions and their own unique struggles with eating disorders. Observant Jews range from Modern Orthodox to Sephardic Jews to Chasidim to Ultraorthodox (Haredi), with many shades of religious expression in between.

In the stricter communities, women do not have jobs outside the home, and men devote much of their time to studying the holy book of the Torah. Secular education is limited, and teenagers are set up by matchmakers and do not date casually.

A cheeky, maybe disrespectful Jewish motto declares what every religious holiday celebrates: "They tried to persecute us. We survived. Now let's eat!" And, indeed, abundant food plays an integral role in every Jewish holiday and the weekly Sabbath (Shabbos) from Friday night sundown through Saturday sundown. Throughout the Jewish calendar, many days of fasting are also required so, inadvertently, this can feed into the feast-or-famine pattern of so many eating disordered people.

Eating disorders have been increasing among Orthodox Jews and are a major concern; in one study of Ultraorthodox and Syrian Jewish communities in Brooklyn, one out of 19 girls was diagnosed with an eating disorder, a rate about 50 percent higher than that of the general population in the United States (Berg, Levinson, & Wollner, n.d.).

Parents are often reluctant to seek help because of the strong stigma that mental illness has in this community. For this reason, adolescents and young adults may not get eating disorder treatment at an early stage, when therapy could have averted a more serious situation. When

*Although Zulema's case demonstrates many themes in Muslim culture, this is her own unique story.

families wait too long to seek help, there may be no other choice but hospitalization.

Sari, an 18-year-old Orthodox girl, was brought to me by her parents. She had advanced anorexia, and it was clear she needed hospitalization to stabilize her weight and eating. Her mother was alarmed at this idea:

> But what would happen if the community finds out? It would be a disgrace, and maybe ruin her chances to get married into a good family. I also have three younger daughters who I will need to marry off, and I don't want to jeopardize their chances.

I sympathized with her about the community being so judgmental but added, "What would happen if you didn't get Sari the treatment she needs, and she dies?" This brought home to her the severity of her daughter's illness, and the family arranged for Sari to go to an out-of-town inpatient eating disorder rehabilitation facility. They hoped that by sending her out of town, they could keep her hospitalization a secret, and this would protect the family from shame and stigma. The mother did not fully grasp that anyone looking at Sari could tell she was severely anorexic.

Unique aspects of religious Jewish life contribute to religious girls' and boys' vulnerability to eating disorders, as summarized below.

Religiosity versus Secularism

Living in the 21st century with America's outspoken, sexualized, irreverent lifestyle flies in the face of observant people trying to lead a pious, traditional way of life. They are living in a modern, secular world while trying to obey the tenets of their religion. As described with other minority groups, the frustration and turmoil of straddling both worlds can make the numbing solution of an eating disorder a way to escape and retreat from confusion, conflict, and guilt.

Matchmaking

Most young people are set up by matchmakers. Boys often request that girls be between dress size 0 and size 4. Making a good match is paramount to the young girl's life, and she will go to any lengths to become the prized thin bride that boys demand. "The pressure to make a good *shidduch* [match], and overvaluing a thin bride, can objectify young women and foster body dissatisfaction which may further the development of an eating disorder" (Gorden, 2015, para. 12). What this often means is that girls with bulimia, anorexia, and binge eating (which can be a reaction to stringent dieting) go underground to achieve this thinness, striving to keep their eating disorder a secret.

Age of Marriage and Childbirth

Girls are expected to marry young and begin having many children. Birth control is not acceptable for the most part. In religious circles, the couple meet for only a few dates before making the decision to get married. Because boys and girls are segregated in schools, teens have no experience developing a friendship with someone of the opposite sex, let alone being ready for marriage and a sexual relationship. It is terrifying for many girls and boys to be so sheltered and then expected to leave their parents' home to have an adult relationship with a partner. Eating disorders—especially anorexia with its loss of menses—will help a girl "solve" her fears by regressing to a younger age. Her eating disorder is an attempt—albeit unconsciously—to take herself out of this pressure to get married so early. Anorexia provides a way to stall adult responsibilities by literally stopping the biological clock.

Religious Rigidity

Orthodox Judaism contains 613 commandments that dictate a wide range of behaviors. People with obsessive–compulsive tendencies often misuse religious regulations for their own psychological need for rigidity and control. This rigidity can also create a breeding ground for an eating disorder.

Fasting

There are two major fasting days required in Judaism as well as five minor fasts. It is also customary for a bride and groom to fast on the day of their wedding as a form of spiritual preparation. Rabbi Dovid Goldwasser, an international expert on eating disorders in the Orthodox world, is often consulted at Yom Kippur—the most holy day of fasting for Jews—about what families should do when their child is in recovery from anorexia and expected to fast on this holy day. With great wisdom and humanity, Rabbi Goldwasser advises, "I try to answer their spiritual conflict and say God wants you to eat. Because you want to heal your anorexia, your eating on that day is considered as if you fasted" (Rabin, 2011, para. 28).

Holocaust Trauma

The trauma of the Holocaust gets passed down in families, resulting in the intergenerational transmission of trauma. In my practice, I have seen three generations with eating disorders, from Holocaust survivors to their children and grandchildren. Shattering stories about the atrocities that survivors endured cause deep, soulful pain and trauma across the generations. Strong survivor guilt leads to conflicts about living, thriving, deserving, eating, feeling safe, and being happy.

The Story of Malka

Malka had gone to college and was on a pre-medical education track. She was a bright, educated 21-year-old girl with bulimia. She dropped out of school to get married and kept her bulimia a secret from her husband. During Shabbos, you are not allowed to use electricity and turn on lights. Malka had thrown up in the bathroom after the Sabbath dinner and desperately wanted to make sure she had cleaned up everything to protect her secret. She wanted to turn on the bathroom light to check. But she remembered the Rabbi's wife during the premarriage classes saying, "Anyone who turns on electricity during Shabbos will have mentally defective children." Although Malka had an extensive science background, she was fearful of turning on the lights and, instead, crawled around on the floor in the dark to clean up. In sharing this suffering and shame with me, we built an alliance to help her speak about her inner worries about being a married and sexual woman as well as working on reducing and eliminating her purging behavior.*

Psychotherapy with Orthodox Jews

Judaism is a complex blend of culture, beliefs, and traditions. Some women cover their hair for modesty and wear wigs once they are married, but some women, like those in the Syrian community, are free to wear slacks. Some ultrareligious men spend their days studying the Torah, but others work in the secular world. The culturally competent clinician will ask about the specific religious values and practices of each client to better understand the role of ritual, observance, food, dieting, and weight for each person.

Many women in Orthodox Judaism are speaking out about the pressures and expectations on Orthodox women (Braun, 2006; Schischa,

*Although Malka's case demonstrates many themes in Orthodox Jewish culture, this is her own unique story.

2011). Aviva Braun, a clinical social work psychotherapist specializing in eating disorders, is featured in the documentary about Orthodox women with eating disorders, *Hungry to Be Heard*. As a therapist, a modern Orthodox woman, and someone who has also recovered from an eating disorder, Ms. Braun observes,

> When I have worked with Orthodox clients, the challenge is often to help them identify their innermost desires and hungers which have not really been acknowledged very much in their lives. And when women get married young, there's often no time to think about their needs. The only way to start the process of recovery is to help my clients acknowledge their hunger for anything in their lives that isn't about food as well as their inner hunger to be heard. (OUCommunityServices, 2013)

"Women assume the role of nurturer within the Orthodox family," Ms. Braun continues. "They are under tremendous pressures to be superwomen—they are expected to work and cook and clean the house and be everything. And a lot of times, this leads to eating disorders because of this pressure to be perfect. Even during pregnancy, Orthodox women experience a pressure to continue to be thin!"

The *Mi Shebairach*, a healing prayer in Judaism, speaks of the goal of life and perhaps can be applied to the eating disordered person: "Help us find the courage to make our lives a blessing."

Native Americans and Eating Disorders

Over 500 Native American tribes are recognized within the United States. There is little research on Native Americans with eating disorders and, because there is such diversity of indigenous people, observations about eating disorders may not apply to all the various, unique tribes (Striegel-Moore, Rosselli, Holtzman, Dierker, & Swaney, 2011).

Although prevalence of alcohol and drug abuse as well as the incidence of obesity is well known in many indigenous communities, eating disorders often go unnoticed. Dr. Jami Bartgis, director of research at the National Council of Urban Indian Health, explains that there are many more pervasive problems among the Native American population and that eating disorders have not made the radar yet. Dr. Bartgis adds,

> We've got the highest suicide rate of any ethnic group in the country; we've got incredible trauma problems. There's depression. There's traumatic stress. There's behavioral-health issues like diabetes and obesity. And of course, diabetes and obesity can result

> from binge eating and can be life-threatening. But I'm guessing the reason we haven't addressed eating disorders is because we're trying to put out all these other fires. (Whitefield, 2011, p. 7; see also Lynch, Heil, Wagner, & Havens, 2007)

Sheena Roetman (2015), a journalist who is part Lakota and specializes in Indian affairs, states,

> We need to acknowledge and confront the lack of resources for people suffering from eating disorders in our communities. We have vastly improved upon programs for suicide prevention, alcohol and drug addiction, diabetes, and domestic and sexual abuse, but we have yet to address this growing problem in Indian country. (para. 7)

Many Native Americans experience the unique cultural impact regarding feelings of loss and dislocation related to oppression throughout their history and by forced assimilation. Most mental health problems in the Native community, it is believed, are the result of generational trauma. When people cannot process their trauma, they pass it on to their children, and the cycle continues. Slavery, genocide, abuse, and extreme poverty have historically disproportionately affected Native Americans; these are all examples of generational trauma. We need to break the cycle with culturally appropriate treatment. Along with culturally informed psychotherapy and medication, traditional medicine and ceremonies need to be incorporated into treatment (Oberg, 2016).

In "Recommendations for the Treatment of American Indian Populations," Dr. Carolyn Barcus, member of the Society of Indian Psychologists, writes,

> The problems of an individual in some tightly knit Native communities become the problems of the community as well. Treatment therefore would need to include family and friends rather than just the healer and the client. The goal is not to strengthen the client's ego but to enhance the client's connectedness to the community, which also strengthens the community. Mental health providers are advised to be well grounded in this systems approach to treatment. (Council of National Psychological Associations for the Advancement of Ethnic Minority Interests, 2003, p. 26)

The Role of the Social Work Clinician

As we saw in the stories of Alicia, Helen, Zulema, and Malka, we must recognize the tremendous differences in our clients' backgrounds. Each racial and ethnic group needs to be treated with care, sensitivity, and cultural competence.

Identify Differences . . . and Similarities

Despite these differences, all of these clients share a similar common denominator—an attempt to detour, distract, and deflect their pain through emotional eating. The language of pain comes in many dialects, and our role as clinician is to reach the shared humanity of each unique client and to help them value and articulate their experiences.

"It happened again yesterday," says Nadia, a compulsive overeater, as she walks into my office. Nadia is an adopted African American and Asian woman, and her looks may be called exotic.

"Oh, no," I say. "Not again!"

We both know what she means. Another person on the street or in a store or on the bus or in the bank has said to Nadia, "Where are you from?" or Where were you born?" or "What are you really?" or "You speak English really well." Nadia was born in New York City, but because she is mixed race and adopted, her concerns about belonging, the meaning of home and identity, and fitting in are always close to the surface.

"What's really been helpful in these situations is your telling me to just inwardly roll my eyes," she says. "I've done a lot of eye rolling since we discussed this. But the funniest thing is I don't feel so alone since I just read an article about the first deaf-Asian-Jewish-transgender male model!"*

"Oh my goodness," I exclaim, "he has more hyphens in his identity than you do!"

Nadia laughs, and we settle into her session. Nadia's trust in me as someone who is interested in learning what it means to be her unique self was very hard-won, with many accusations about what she felt was my insensitivity. I welcomed those accusations as they gave us a chance to examine and repair her experiences of my failures in empathic attunement. And, as I eventually pointed out to Nadia, expressing herself directly to me is the opposite of running to binge on food when she is uncomfortable, unhappy, or feeling insulted. "Bravo for direct communication!" I would encourage her. Now she is using her mouth more for talking, complaining, and expressing rather than stuffing her feelings.

Becoming Culturally Competent

The authors of "Racial Microaggressions in Everyday Life: Implications for Clinical Practice" point out that although the task of establishing

*See Azoulay (2018).

an effective therapeutic relationship applies to all therapy relationships, working with clients who differ from the therapist in race, ethnicity, culture, and sexual orientation poses special challenges (Sue et al., 2007). White therapists who are products of their cultural conditioning may be prone to engage in racial microaggressions. In clinical practice, microaggressions are likely to go unrecognized by white clinicians who are unintentionally and unconsciously expressing bias. As a result, therapists must make a concerted effort to identify and monitor microaggressions within the therapeutic context. This process is reminiscent of the importance of becoming aware of potential transference and countertransference issues between therapist and client and how they may unintentionally interfere with effective therapy. A therapist's willingness to discuss racial matters is of central importance in creating a therapeutic alliance with clients of color (Sue, 2010).

I would add that being a minority therapist does not automatically confer perfect attunement regarding multicultural competency especially if the patient is of a different background or social class. In other words, all therapists need to challenge themselves about their own racial identities and their feelings and biases toward others.

The National Association of Social Workers (NASW) Code of Ethics charges social workers with the ethical responsibility to be culturally competent. Cultural competence refers to the process by which individuals and systems respond respectfully and effectively to people of all cultures, languages, classes, races, ethnic backgrounds, religions, spiritual traditions, immigration statuses, and other diversity factors in a manner that recognizes, affirms, and values the worth of individuals, families, and communities and protects and preserves the dignity of each.

In 2015, the NASW Committee on Racial and Ethnic Diversity published *Standards and Indicators for Cultural Competence in Social Work Practice*. Recommendations include the following:

- "Social workers shall demonstrate an appreciation of their own cultural identities and those of others" (p. 4).
- "Social workers must also be aware of their own privilege and power and must acknowledge the impact of this privilege and power in their work with and on behalf of clients" (p. 4).
- "Social workers will also demonstrate cultural humility and sensitivity to the dynamics of power and privilege in all areas of social work" (p. 4).
- "Social workers shall possess and continue to develop specialized knowledge and understanding that is inclusive of, but not limited to, the history, traditions, values, family systems, and artistic expressions such as race and ethnicity; immigration and

refugee status; tribal groups; religion and spirituality; sexual orientation; gender identity or expression; social class; and mental or physical abilities of various cultural groups" (p. 4).

- "Social workers shall be change agents who demonstrate the leadership skills to work effectively with multicultural groups in agencies, organizational settings, and communities. Social workers should also demonstrate responsibility for advancing cultural competence within and beyond their organizations, helping to challenge structural and institutional oppression and build and sustain diverse and inclusive institutions and communities" (p. 5).

Furthermore, in 2019, the *Position on Racism and Oppressive Practices within Social Work* stated that

> the National Association of Social Workers is the largest professional member organization of Social Workers in the world. As a body, we too must ensure that in word and in deed, we remain committed to calling out and working to address oppression, racism, and marginalization in ourselves, our profession, our educational systems, communities, and places of employment. As an organization, we shall continue to address social disparities, advocate for justice, and value the dignity and worth of all individuals. (NASW, New York City chapter, 2019, paras. 1–2)*

Examining Our Biases

Though great strides have been made, one of the elements missing in the NASW position paper and other guidelines is the directive for clinicians to improve their sensitivity to patients of extreme sizes—both obese and emaciated anorexics. Clinicians—as do most members of society at large—will often have unexamined biases toward fat people that provoke anger and revulsion. And anorexics provoke horror and maybe even envy in many people.

A recent research study from Harvard University (Goldberg, 2019) demonstrated that people's biases have dropped dramatically for sexual

*Clinicians will welcome the increasing research on minorities and eating disorders. A special edition has been published in 2019 of *Eating Disorders: The Journal of Treatment and Prevention* on the "State of the Art Research on Treatment and Prevention of Eating Disorders on Ethnic Minorities," which includes the articles "Cultural, Ethnic and Racially Diverse Differences in Disordered Eating Correlates," "Prevention Research with Ethnic and Racially Diverse Individuals," and "Treatment and Treatment Experiences with Ethnic and Racially Diverse Individuals." The articles have also been translated into Spanish (Perez, Ramirez, & Trujillo-ChiVacuán, 2019).

orientation and race—but not weight. The study showed that body weight attitudes are even showing a slight tendency of becoming worse over time.

I believe cultural competency should extend to this population who often feel discriminated against and alien in society (Goldberg, 2019; Hobbes, 2018).

Understanding the Unique Challenges of the Poor

The social worker is often the first point of contact for those not familiar with the value of mental health treatment. It is critical that the therapist understands the pervasiveness of eating disorders in poor communities and the possible treatment options.

Unfortunately, poor and working-class women and men may not have the insurance, resources, time, support, or even the hope that their problems can be improved. If they do seek help at a mental health clinic or hospital, it is important that social work clinicians screen not only for depression, anxiety, domestic violence, PTSD, and alcohol and drug use but also for destructive eating behaviors and full-fledged eating disorders.

Rather than blaming those who are financially insecure for their food choices, we need to acknowledge that fresh and healthy foods are more expensive than junk food and that this is an impediment to improving the nutrition of the poor.

Conclusion

> *We cannot hold a torch to light another's path without brightening our own.*
>
> Martin Luther King, Jr.

Helping our clients embrace and appreciate the diverse heritages they embody enriches an inner sense of belonging—to one's culture, to one's body, to one's self. A patient of mine, a gay actress from the Middle East, quips that she is a "Lebanese Lesbian Thespian."

One of my favorite musicians, Arturo O'Farrill, the Afro-Cuban jazz pianist, lovingly describes his Mexican, Cuban, German, and Irish heritage. When he was honored at the Irish America Hall of Fame, he played the Irish ballad "Danny Boy" with a charming Afro-Cuban jazz arrangement.

The Israeli poet Yehuda Amichai believes that no matter where our parents come from, no matter how many years ago, no matter how assimilated we are, we carry their roots inside us. He writes, "And the migration of my parents / Has not subsided in me" (Amichai, 2015, p. 58).

In appreciation of Dr. Maria Root's (1993) unapologetic "Bill of Rights for Racially Mixed People," I have written a version to extend to all people—minority, mainstream, fat, and skinny.

I have the right

- not to justify my existence in this world.
- not to be responsible for people's discomfort with me.
- to be comfortable in my body no matter what my size, color, religion, or ethnicity.
- to be unapologetic about my need for respect at all times.

I have the responsibility

- to seek help when I realize my eating behaviors have become hurtful to my health and well-being.
- to create a life that is a full and vibrant expression of my heart and soul.

8

Gender, Sexual Identity, and Eating Disorders: What's the Connection?

Unconditional love is life's most powerful medicine.

Robert Ivker, DO

As a young, newly minted social worker just starting out in the early 1970s, I thought sexual expression described three orientations: heterosexuality, homosexuality, and bisexuality. Then one day, the psychiatric director of the mental health center where I worked called me into his office and said, "We are beginning a hormone program for transsexuals, and we would like you to run a therapy group for them."

"What are transsexuals?" I asked. From there, very quickly, my education broadened about the varieties of sexual identity. I studied everything I could on the topic, but I was astonished when my first group members arrived.

This was a group of preoperative men transitioning to become women, and all had begun female hormone injections to decrease their masculine traits and increase breast development. But, even within that gathering, a wide variety of different people appeared. They ranged from men dressed as women who could definitely pass as female, to flamboyant drag queens, to men who wanted to have the surgery to fully transition to female, to men who just wanted breasts and no sex reassignment surgery, to men dressed as traditional males with breasts, to the transsexual who expressed his desire for surgery to become the lesbian lover of his girlfriend.

What I learned—just as with eating disorders—was that everybody's sexual expression is unique as a fingerprint. What I also learned—just as with eating disorders—was that these men were at odds with their bodies and were searching for ways to live more comfortably in their own skin.

More Visibility, Less Stigma, and Yet . . .

Fast forward 40 years and, with less stigma and a somewhat more open climate, people are identifying, defining, and claiming their own personal and unique expressions of sexual identity. But challenges remain.

Gender Expression, Terminology, and the DSM-5

The Gay & Lesbian Alliance Against Defamation (GLAAD, n.d.) has published a dictionary of terms to define the wide range of diverse sexual and gender expression within the LGBTQ community (see also Mlotek, 2019). Terms that clinicians will need to know include cisgender, nonbinary, transgender, queer, polyamory, intersex, BDSM (bondage, domination, and sadomasochism), and sex reassignment surgery.

New terms emerge all the time, such as heteroflexible (straight-ish), homoflexible (gay-ish), skoliosexual (attraction to nonbinary people), and, as one of my clients, who formerly identified as a lesbian and now decided she is straight, quipped, "I am a 'wasbian.'" Her description also suggests that sexual identity may not be static throughout one's life but may shift and evolve over time.

In 2013, the American Psychiatric Association's (APA's) fifth edition of the DSM (DSM-5) replaced the outdated diagnosis "gender identity disorder" with "gender dysphoria" to highlight that gender issues are no longer considered disorders. Gender dysphoria (sometimes referred to as "gender dysmorphia") describes a feeling of dissatisfaction or discomfort between the gender you were assigned at birth and the gender you now claim (APA, n.d.).

But controversy exists in the field about whether transgender issues should even be listed as a psychiatric illness in the first place. In the article "Being Trans Is Not a Mental Disorder," Grinker (2018) argues against including a psychiatric diagnosis in the DSM and claims that being trans should be a personal or social identity, not a psychiatric one.

Conversely, some transgender advocates argue that the inclusion of gender dysphoria in the DSM is necessary to help advocate for health insurance to cover medical treatment for transgender people, including insurance coverage for hormone therapy and gender-affirming surgeries.

Gender and Politics

Gender fluidity has now come to the awareness and political landscape of mainstream America. Between 2014 and 2019, 15 states and Puerto Rico passed laws prohibiting mental health professionals from practicing "conversion therapy" for minors. Conversion therapy has been used for the purpose of attempting to change someone's sexual orientation or gender identity to become exclusively heterosexual—sometimes by even resorting to electroshock therapy. Nearly 700,000 LGBT adults in the United States have received conversion therapy at some point in their lives (Brinton, 2018).

In 2019, New York lawmakers passed the Gender Expression Non-Discriminating Act, which will add gender identity as a protected class under New York's discrimination and hate crime laws.

Several states have also added a gender-neutral option to birth certificates to now include male, female, or a nonbinary option. This also makes it easier for nonbinary and transgender people to change their birth certificates to affirm their gender identity (Fitzsimons, 2019).

In 2016, a landmark policy decreed by President Barack Obama allowed transgender people for the first time to serve openly in the armed forces and receive medical care for gender transition.

Yet in 2019 under the Trump administration, the U.S. Department of Defense sought to enforce limitations on transgender people serving in the military, a policy that has been the subject of court challenges. The policy will bar most transgender individuals from serving if they require hormone treatments or transition surgery. This will affect approximately 2,500 active service members (Beech & Ali, 2019). A Pentagon official has said, "Any service member with gender dysphoria, a serious mental condition, has a potential negative impact on force readiness. All service members must meet established readiness standards to maintain the effectiveness and lethality of the force" (Philipps, 2019, para. 12).

NASW has been actively involved in promoting wellness, safety, and equality for all LGBTQ people; the National Committee on Lesbian, Gay, Bisexual, and Transgender Issues was originally created in 1976 and became an authorized committee in 1979 (NASW, n.d.-c). The NASW (n.d.-a) Web site states, "Social workers have a shared commitment to promoting laws, policies and programming that affirm, support, and value LGBT individuals, families, and communities" (para. 1). NASW also maintains a list of professional conferences throughout the United States for therapists working with this community (NASW, n.d.-b).

NASW Press has published several books to help social work clinicians deepen their knowledge of the LGBTQ community, including

Affirmative Practice: Understanding and Working with Lesbian, Gay, Bisexual, and Transgender Persons by Ski Hunter and Jane C. Hickerson (2003) and *Prejudice to Pride: Moving from Homophobia to Acceptance* by Ann Marie Petrocelli (2012).

Increased Visibility

Media coverage of LGBTQ people has become increasingly multidimensional, reflecting both the diversity of this community and the growing visibility of LGBTQ families and relationships.

Advances have been made to bring more visibility and dignity to the community, including the annual LGBTQ History Month begun in 1994, Gay & Lesbian Pride Month established in 2000, and the Lesbian, Gay, Bisexual, and Transgender Pride Month in 2009. In 2019, the New York Fashion Week show featured 34 trans, nonbinary models, and *T: The New York Times' Style Magazine* devoted its fashion issue to "The New Androgyny."

The American entertainment industry increasingly presents movies, theater, and television programs with gay and transgender actors and story lines with nonbinary characters. More actors have declared themselves gay, and programs such as *Queer as Folk, Queer Eye, Tales of the City,* and *The L Word* have centered on gay and trans characters. A 2019 series *Interested In* explores people's experiences the first year after coming out of the closet.

Continued Conflict and Struggle

Despite strides made toward acceptance, the struggles of the transgender person can involve a painful and complicated mixture of dealing with the person's own internal judgments, family judgments, and society's judgments. The home page of the National Center for Transgender Equality Web site states that half of all people who identified as transgender while still in school (K–12) report being verbally harassed, and nearly a quarter report being physically assaulted because they were transgender. These experiences of assault and bullying and the ongoing threat of violence can lead to PTSD, which sharply increases vulnerability to substance abuse and eating disorders. More than a third of all transgender individuals have attempted suicide at least once.

Internal struggles often emerge when a person experiences the growing realization that they do not feel congruent with the sex they were born into. This inner awakening can be fraught with doubt, confusion, fear, the wish for secrecy, and tremendous inner upheaval as he or she wonders, "Who am I really? Is there something wrong with me? Who can I tell? Can I make myself change? Should I just stay underground? What should I do next?" Many nonbinary people have internalized the hatred our culture holds for any sexual expression different from heteronormative "plain vanilla." This makes the process of coming out even more difficult.

The psychodynamic issues of coming out even to oneself can often be addressed fruitfully in psychotherapy as client and therapist work to uncover the transgender person's layers of confusion to arrive at that individual's most authentic core self.

This early struggle can become intensified when the transgender person reveals their identity to their family. Families are often scared, enraged, or rejecting of their child's disclosure. I worked with a bulimic girl whose parents forced her to move out when they discovered she was in a lesbian relationship; I worked with a young Jewish man whose parents sat *shiva* for him (the Jewish ritual for the dead) on learning he was gay. But I also worked with a compulsive overeater bisexual woman whose mother was openly gay, her brother was gay, and her father was closeted gay, so for her to declare she was "bi" in this family was just business as usual as everyone had openly claimed their unique identity without any issues.

Lesbian comedian Hannah Gadsby unwittingly followed the social work tenet of "partializing the problem" when she came out to her mother. In her 2018 Netflix comedy special, *Hannah Gadsby: Nanette*, she laughs about gingerly testing the waters when she tentatively said, "Mom, I think I'm a little bit lesbian."

Eating Disorders in the LGBTQ Community

The Trevor Project, an organization focused on suicide prevention efforts among LGBTQ youths, has partnered with the National Eating Disorders Association. According to a Trevor Project (n.d.) assessment, more than half of LGBTQ youths surveyed in 2018 reported that they had been diagnosed with an eating disorder, and many others were suspected of having an underlying eating disorder. Similarly, a 2017 report from the Human Rights Campaign Foundation found that the vast majority of LGBTQ youths surveyed reported some type of disordered eating (Malina, 2019).

The connection between eating disorders in the LGBTQ community and suicidal ideation is also significant. A majority of LGBTQ youths (58 percent) diagnosed with an eating disorder revealed that they had considered suicide, and 34 percent of those who have attempted suicide in the past 12 months have been diagnosed with an eating disorder (Trevor Project, n.d.).

Although research remains limited on eating disorders among LGBTQ populations, the National Eating Disorders Association reports the following statistics:

- Gay males are thought to represent only 5 percent of the total male population but, among males who have eating disorders, 42 percent identify as gay.
- In one study, gay and bisexual boys were significantly more likely to have fasted, vomited, or taken laxatives or diet pills to control their weight in the past 30 days.
- Gay males were seven times more likely to report bingeing and 12 times more likely to report purging than heterosexual males.
- Compared with heterosexual men, gay and bisexual men had a significantly higher prevalence of bulimia and any subclinical eating disorder.
- Females identified as lesbian, bisexual, or mostly heterosexual were about twice as likely to report binge eating at least once per month in the past year.
- Elevated rates of binge eating and purging by vomiting or laxative abuse were found in gay, lesbian, and bisexual people in comparison with their heterosexual peers.
- A sense of belonging and connectedness to a gay community group was related to fewer current eating disorders. This suggests that belonging to a supportive community, which can help people feel less alone, may have a protective effect against eating disorders. (National Eating Disorders Association, n.d.)

The roots of eating disorders within the gay community can be similar to those for hetero men and women, but there can also be unique stressors. Stressors for LGBTQ people involve struggles around self-disclosure, harassment, discrimination in school or the workplace, and fears about being rejected by family and loved ones. Shame, confusion about one's sexual identity, or uncertainty about the next step can create high levels of anxiety, depression, low self-esteem, and unhealthy coping strategies, such as abusing alcohol or drugs, promiscuous sex, and eating disorders.

Eating disorders and body dysphoria are often interrelated. Nonbinary individuals grapple with their body's perceived flaws because of gender mismatch. To live in a body that is not experienced as having the right genitals, the right shape, the right weight, the right muscularity, or the right hair becomes a stressful daily experience of feeling persecuted by one's own body. This experience of feeling persecuted by one's own self leads to attempts to alter and manipulate the offending body parts, often leading to devastating results. Diet pills, laxatives, anabolic steroids, cutting and other forms of self-harm, and repeated plastic surgeries take a toll on physical and emotional health. Drugs and alcohol, as well as bingeing, purging, and starving, can be numbing agents and an escape valve from the stress of living in a body you dislike and maybe even hate (National LGBT Health Education Center, 2018).

Research has shown that gay and bisexual men as well as lesbian women are more likely than heterosexuals to have experienced abuse and victimization in childhood. Sexual and physical abuse often provoke higher rates of eating disorders and body dissatisfaction in both men and women as they grapple with betrayal, pain, and vulnerability. Therefore, gay and bisexual people may suffer a higher rate of both sexual abuse history and eating disorders (Feldman & Meyer, 2007; Fries, 2017; Hospers & Jansen, 2005).

Psychotherapy of the Transgender Eating Disorder Client: Do Ask, Do Tell!

The National Eating Disorders Association began a Marginalized Voices Project, and in an excerpt from an article, "This Gendered Body: Living with an Eating Disorder and Finding My Voice as a Queer Nonbinary Person," the author paints a picture of growing up in a shape that felt alien and describes how their eating disorder temporarily relieved their discomfort. The anonymous author realized,

> I felt there was something deeply wrong with my body. I didn't just want to be smaller. I wanted to rid myself of my femaleness. . . . My eating disorder has always been closely tied to my non binary gender identity. The disconnect that a queer child or adolescent feels when they realize they are different is so uncomfortable that it causes many of us to retreat into ourselves and hide who we really are for the sake of protecting our safety. . . . When you don't feel comfortable in the body in which you were born, and you have no support from society or your peers to express your true inner self, it can make sense to turn on yourself, to do drastic and harmful things to your own body. (Anonymous, n.d.)

This is a poignant example of the author's struggle to verbalize and share their struggle of reconciling gender dysphoria, eating disorders, and secrecy.

Treatment

Gender-affirming treatment for body image dysphoria and eating disorders in transgender adolescents should focus on early intervention. By addressing these issues during high school or even earlier, clinicians can help prevent depression, anxiety, self-harm behaviors, substance abuse as well as eating disorders.

Some clients with gender dysphoria are not able to learn to love and accept their bodies even after recovering from an eating disorder. They need to change their bodies, and full recovery from an eating disorder may not be possible until they have access to hormones or surgery.

Gender-affirming therapy includes

- recognizing that everyone's experiences with their LGBTQ identity are unique as a fingerprint.
- consistently using the names, labels, and pronouns that the client prefers (he, she, they).
- providing gender-neutral bathrooms at agencies.
- understanding the unique stressors of each client in relation to their family, friends, love relationships, work, or school.
- exploring emotional issues such as depression, sexual and physical abuse, and trauma.
- investigating substance abuse history as well as an eating disorder history.
- addressing the negative beliefs or concerns relating to clients' bodies, sexuality, and gender identity.
- reducing internalized homophobia.
- understanding that a client's gender identity (what sex they feel congruent with) is different from their sexuality (who they are attracted to).
- encouraging the client to seek support systems within the gay community, as feeling connected to the gay community may have a protective effect against eating disorders.

One hopes that all gender-nonconforming people will find their own fulfilling path to open sexual self-expression with the support of friends, family, the workplace, and legal protection. The freedom to contact their inner authentic self will bring great relief and joy as they synchronize their inner selves with their outer sexual identity. Many will then say, "I now feel whole for the first time in my life."

In a blog post for Adios, Barbie, titled "Gay Women Don't Get Eating Disorders. Or Do They?" Rose Barcklow (2017) writes, "I've learned that the only way to stay in recovery is to recklessly and wholeheartedly love myself and to feel no shame in doing that" (para. 10).

The clinician's goal with gender-nonconforming eating disorder clients is to help them become unapologetically authentic.

The Case of Megan

At times, therapists must confront their countertransference. Megan is an obese, compulsive overeater woman who identifies herself as a lesbian and uses the pronoun "she." She is married to Alex, born a woman, who identifies by the pronoun "they." Alex is taking testosterone and developing secondary male traits, whereas Megan, who dresses in male clothing, has no plan for further transition. Both women have had "top surgery" to remove their breasts.

Countertransference reactions by therapists may arise when treating gender-nonconforming people, and a clear awareness of one's reactions will help the clinician avoid responding with fear, disapproval, or even anger. When Megan told me about her and Alex's elective mastectomies, I had a flash of anger and then sadness as a friend of mine lay dying from breast cancer. I had the irrational fantasy of wishing I could bring Megan's healthy breasts to my friend to save her life.

But I reminded myself that Megan's, Alex's, and my friend's breasts all have separate lives and histories and were not interchangeable. Recognizing this helped me return to my spirit of inquiry as I strove to understand the meaningfulness of Megan's relationship to her breasts, her body, her food, and her weight.

The Case of Vickie

Vickie is a bisexual bulimic woman who is obese. In her therapy, she addressed the triggers to her purging and with consistent focus and effort, she was able to put an end to that form of self-harm. Vickie is in a BDSM relationship with her partner Jeff, and together they enjoy a full range of sadomasochistic sex play, including beatings, caning, and the use of "funishment" toys. Vickie has helped me understand how she rewove her early traumatic history of her mother's hateful physical abuse into loving, measured, and attentive physical pain through Jeff's caring and devotion; she has woven together an intricate mixture of pleasure and pain both into her sexual life and her bulimic life. She still craves the abuse—she tells me it is hardwired in her—but it now takes place in the context of a mutual consenting relationship where she gets to choose what happens and how much.

One morning Vickie came for her session and regaled me with a great sexual encounter she had with Jeff over the weekend in which they explored breath work. She described how he strangled her and how exciting it felt to have her breath almost stop and have her life in his hands. On hearing this, I pictured Jeff, who was a foot taller and about 75 pounds heavier than Vickie.

I shrieked out loud without any filter reining me in: "Don't do that! You could die!"

Vickie carefully explained all the precautions they took, but I remained frightened for her. The wonderful part of being a clinical social worker is that you can always find a colleague with the experience you need, and I reached out to several therapists in the field who have experience with BDSM clients for help in handling this. I understood that shrieking might not be considered the most effective therapeutic technique.

Social work clinician Sari Cooper, sex therapist certified by the Association of American Sexual Educators and director of the Center for Love and Sex, validated my concerns that Vickie is putting herself at risk. Cooper explained that this is considered "edge play" and that some in the BDSM community agree not to practice it. She helped me formulate what I needed to discuss with Vickie, such as asking what her safe word is and her safe signal (in case she can't speak) as well as the need for her to learn techniques to press safer parts of her neck to lessen the risk. Cooper also advised that I warn Vickie that some people have died as a result of this practice.

Social work clinician Paula Marchese confirmed that obesity and diabetes add to the risk factors, as does the method of pressing on one's windpipe. Marchese encouraged me to step back and ask Vickie what she understands about breath play and this type of choking. Does she think there are risks? If so, what are they? Marchese added,

> The challenge is to share your concern in a way that helps her to question her knowledge and beliefs, her understanding of what she is doing, and hopefully experience some beginning doubt or anxiety of her own about the possible devastating consequences of this particular type of play. I would try to check in with how Vickie is feeling about my questions so the second I become the enemy who is judging or trying to take something away, we can talk about it. Similar to working with someone struggling with anorexia, you might want to get them to eat, convince them what will happen if

they don't eat, but finding a way to help them want to eat is a different story. (Personal communication, March 19, 2019)*

Conclusion

Although the case of Vickie may not be something we specifically grapple with every day, it illuminates three principles that clinicians need to consider in working with gender-nonconforming clients as well as any client who is racially, ethnically, religiously, or politically different from us: (1) The therapist needs to always be involved in enhancing their own self-awareness about personal bias and prejudice. Self-awareness is enriched by personal psychotherapy, conferences, and professional reading and study groups. (2) The therapist needs to be committed to a spirit of inquiry, curiosity, and developing a nonjudgmental stance to help clients achieve open communication about their needs and fears. At times, we judiciously use our own countertransference reactions to deepen the treatment relationship. (3) Supervision and consultation with other professionals help shed light on our blind spots and propel the therapy forward.

Many therapists will ask about a client's gender and sexual identity at intake. I do not. I may ask a general, open-ended question: "Anything about your sexual self or relationships that is relevant to mention?" But I keep in mind that for many people, sexual identity is a delicate subject. Only when a trustful relationship is established are clients more likely to share a topic that could promote shame or confusion. I do not want clients to feel obliged to reveal more than they are prepared to discuss. In trusting the process of therapy and its gentle unfolding, we believe "all in due time."

---

*Special thanks to Sari Cooper, who forwarded some instructional articles to me: "To Choke or Not" (Murrell, 2015), "Take Your Breath Away" (Norische, 2014), and "Legal Dangers of Rough Sex" (Marborough, 2009). Special thanks also to social work clinician Paula Marchese, who validated my concern for this type of "breath play" and encouraged me to step back and formulate questions to enhance our discussions.

9

The World of Social Media, Eating Disorders, and "Selfie-Esteem"

Around 2007, the world changed. Apple released the first iPhone, Facebook became widely available, Twitter was launched, and the Internet reached over a billion users worldwide. By 2019, Internet users in the United States reached 345,660,847—over 94 percent of our country's population (Internet World Stats, 2019; Taffel, 2018).

The burgeoning of social media has become a double-edged sword for those with eating disorders and the therapists who treat them. Online communities can be part of the problem or part of the solution.

The growing availability of helpful and healing online information on eating disorders has blossomed; this has served to reduce the stigma and shame for those seeking therapy. But everyday use of social media exacerbates feelings of loneliness and isolation as users tend to "compare and despair," concluding that others have more fulfilling lives. Further, there are damaging and dangerous online communities promoting eating disorder behaviors, toxic comparisons with others, and low self-esteem.

In "The Lonely Burden of Today's Teenage Girls," psychotherapist Mary Pipher and Sara Pipher Gilliam (2019) state,

> Adolescent girls describe themselves as particularly vulnerable to the banes of our increasingly digital culture, with many of them struggling to manage the constant connectedness of social media, their rising levels of anxiety and the intense emotions that have always been central to adolescence. (para. 2)

The American Association of Pediatrics now warns that too much social media use can lead to depression and anxiety. Social media works against basic developmental goals—physical, cognitive, relational, sexual, and maturational. Girls sleep with their phones and react to every notification. As they create more interesting, supposedly happier virtual personas for themselves, their real selves diminish. Girls collect "likes" instead of making friends. They can be devastated by a cruel text or a tepid reaction to a selfie. Long before they hold hands with a date, they are exposed to online pornography and misogynistic messages.

Social Media, Eating Disorders, and Body Dysphoria

Social media has become the centerpiece of many young people's lives—the way they gather information about the world, the way they interact with others, and how they form their sense of self. For our clients, the digital world can be alluring, enthralling, captivating, and maybe even addicting.

The relationship between social media and the development of eating disorders and body dysphoria disorders (BDD) is significant. *BDD* refers to a preoccupation with one's perceived defects or flaws in appearance—flaws that are generally minor or imagined. People with this disorder often feel so ashamed and anxious about their looks that they spend a great deal of time checking the mirror, avoiding social situations, and experiencing considerable inner distress.

BDD typically starts in the early teenage years and affects both males and females. Males can suffer from a variation—muscle dysphoria—in which they believe their bodies are not muscular enough no matter how much they engage in vigorous workouts and body building. Females worry about not being thin enough (even if they are anorexic) or pretty enough (Mayo Clinic, n.d.).*

In a cyber world that bombards women and girls constantly with images of beauty and perfection, females become convinced that their lovability depends on how they look. The tyranny of thinness reigns in these images, and airbrushed cyber images of models with perfect bodies, perfect skin, and perfect hair leads girls and women to feel they are not measuring up and need to improve their looks as soon as possible.

Saturated with online images, Fernanda, an 18-year-old girl with café au lait skin and large brown eyes who is recovering from a binge-eating disorder, was upset when a boy she was dating stopped calling with no explanation. She immediately concluded she was not pretty enough and decided to get lip fillers and remove an insignificant

***Body dysmorphia* refers to the conviction that the person has a flaw or defect in their appearance, rendering them ugly or deformed. This often affects their functioning in social, school, or work-related situations.

mole from her chin. She began stalking Luis on his social media sites, looking for clues as to whether he had another girlfriend and whether she might be more attractive than Fernanda.

"Look how quickly you jump to the conclusion that your looks were the reason for the breakup," I point out.

"Well, what else could it be?" she demands.

"I can't read Luis's mind, but you could ask him what happened. You are entitled to an explanation. From what you've told me, I can think of 10 reasons for the breakup that have nothing to do with you or your appearance and have more to do with Luis's confusion about his own life."

Many people conclude "I'm fat and ugly" to explain a myriad of disappointments that actually have nothing to do with looks. It is sad that appearance often becomes the default explanation they give themselves for why they have been hurt. I point out to Fernanda that (a) she could ask Luis for an explanation, (b) she may have to accept the uncertainty of never finding out, and (c) instead of directly facing her resentment toward Luis, she turns her anger about the breakup against herself and her looks. I try to help Fernanda interrupt her default position of targeting her appearance and hope to expand her thinking to include other explanations that are not about her looks.

The Dark Side of Social Media

The dark side of social media includes cyberbullying and cyberstalking, which has subjected many teens to humiliation about their weight, appearance, and popularity. The destructive aspects of the Internet include Web sites that

- promote Snapchat dysphoria.
- extoll the "virtues" of emaciation through pro-eating disorder sites (pro-ana or pro-mia).
- endorse harmful images and information on Facebook and Instagram.
- publicize pornography.

Snapchat Dysphoria

The *Journal of the American Medical Association* has identified a new disorder: Snapchat dysphoria. This syndrome describes how people—particularly young women or men—use apps (applications) on Snapchat and Instagram to "enhance" their own appearance. With these apps and filters, they can make their eyes look wider, their lips plumper, their skin smoother, eyebrows more arching, and bodies more toned. They then seek out plastic surgery to turn themselves into this enhanced version and strive to match their real-life self to their idealized image. So prevalent is this surreal practice of photo editing and plastic surgery that this new term *Snapchat dysphoria* has been coined and has caught on.

British photographer Rankin explored these apps and their potentially harmful effects in a photo series entitled *Selfie Harm* (Brucculieri, 2019). He argues that rather than celebrating true individuality, these apps perpetuate a homogenized expression of beauty as people strive to be "social media ready."

With Snapchat dysphoria, "We're at a new level when we actually lose touch with our own face or look surprised when we look in the mirror," observes Renee Engeln, author of *Beauty Sick* (Brucculieri, 2018b, para. 32; see also Brucculieri, 2018a; Hosie, 2018).

An increasing number of people with Snapchat dysphoria seek plastic surgery to look like an idealized version of themselves. Even more astounding are the increasing numbers of people all over the world who are sinking massive amounts of money into repetitive plastic surgery to look like identical versions of Barbie and Ken dolls (Fuller, 2015; Lisi, 2017; *People* staff, 2015; Plastic Surgery Fact, n.d.).

Pro-Ana and Pro-Mia

The pro-anorexia and pro-bulimia movement consists of blogs, Web sites, and chat forums in which people with anorexia, bulimia, and other eating disorders support each other to achieve extreme weight loss no matter how unhealthy the methods may be. The following quotes come from pro-ana and pro-mia Web sites:

- "i need an ana buddy!! im about 94 lbs (i was a little bit thinner but i fucked it up)."
- "Hello i am 13 and I am looking for an ana buddy so I can be motivated and so I can also motivate you. I know it is hard not being able to look like a model so let's help each other."
- "Bones are clean and pure. Fat is dirty and hangs on you like a parasite. Starve off the parts you don't need. They're ugly and they drag you down."

For people devoted to these sites, weight loss is considered the holy grail and the true meaning of life. They believe anorexia and bulimia are lifestyle choices and not mental illnesses. Members share tips on how to suppress hunger, how to best induce vomiting, and how to use laxatives and emetics, and the sites include photographs of emaciated people for further encouragement. Eating disordered individuals encourage others to maintain unhealthy behaviors and provide "thin-spiration." Unwittingly, Kate Moss created the rallying cry for this movement with her popular thinspirational motto: "Nothing tastes as good as skinny feels."

Starving to Perfection, Anorexic Nation, My Skinny Dream, and House of Bones are names of different chat rooms where teenagers and adults discuss disliking their body features, competing with friends to lose weight, and obsessing about how to achieve weight goals. People are not welcome on these sites if they are merely a "wannarexic," a casual dieter who is not dedicated to an eating disordered lifestyle (Dretzin & Maggio, 2008; Helton, 2014; "Pro-Ana," n.d.).

Psychotherapists and other health care professionals are concerned about the proliferation of these sites, which promote self-harming eating behaviors. Strong efforts have been made to eradicate these pro-eating disorder sites although they keep sprouting up. Clinical social worker and eating disorder expert Karen Koenig warns,

> Pro-ana/pro-mia groups work very much like a cult religion luring in girls in their teens and early 20s with misperceptions about their weight and body image that make them vulnerable to pro-ana/pro-mia messages. Individuals with eating disorders have an underlying need for reinforcement of their beliefs which they find on these Web sites. (As cited in Van Pelt, 2009, para. 8)

The Web site Skinnygossip invites its members to post critiques of models' and actresses' bodies and weight: "Slice and dice to your heart's content!" Members must verify that their body mass index is under 18.5, which is the "underweight" category.

ANAD (n.d.-b) states that these sites

> can pose a serious threat to some individuals, not simply because they promote eating disorder behaviors, but because they build a sense of community that is unhealthy. They lure the impressionable and persuade them that the Pro-Ana community is providing caring and nurturing advice. (para. 2)

The Academy for Eating Disorders (n.d.) states that

> websites that glorify anorexia as a lifestyle choice play directly to the psychology of its victims, provide support and encouragement to engage in health threatening behaviors, and neglect the serious consequences of starvation. (para. 6)

Instagram and Facebook

Instagram has also been implicated in promoting eating disorders. Launched in 2010, Instagram has grown into an enormous social network. By 2016, Instagram had 500 million registered users worldwide, making it the third largest social media platform after Facebook and Tumblr. Currently, 53 percent of young adults between the ages of 18 and 29 in the United States use this social media platform. Some Instagram posters encourage anorexia as well as orthorexia, a pathological obsession with only eating foods one considers healthy. This focus on only eating "clean, pure, and virtuous" can go to such an extreme that people actually damage their health by cutting down on even nutritious food. Adherents to these posts, with their rigid and unhealthy advice, can wind up suffering from nutrition deficiencies and eating disorders as well.

Facebook has also been tied to an increase in negative body image feelings among users, which can lead to a higher risk of eating disorders as well. In the article "Do You 'Like' My Photo? Facebook Use Maintains Eating Disorder Risk," Dr. Pamela K. Keel is quoted as saying, "Now your friends are posting carefully curated photos of themselves on their Facebook page that you're being exposed to constantly" (Mabe, Forney, & Keel, 2014, p. 517). When the photos clients are viewing are of a friend, rather than some unknown actress, looking beautiful and popular, this can hit closer to home and create more anxiety. Comparing themselves to real-life friends who display their pictures when they are looking their best can create competition, negative self-judgment, and envy around body image and popularity. It has been said that "comparison is the thief of happiness," and vulnerable people—especially those with eating disorders and body image insecurity—are hungry for "likes" on their Facebook page and jealous of friends who have more traffic to their site. And the more time on Facebook, say the researchers, the more time to compare oneself unfavorably to people you know.

This anxiety about not measuring up may then lead to the question, "What can I do to fix myself, lose weight quickly, and change my looks?" Those questions are the gateway to body image dysphoria as well as unhealthy eating behaviors (Nauert, 2014, 2015).

Pornography

Pornographic images and videos are alive and well on the Internet, and often they are the first glimpse of sexuality that a young person has. No longer just a furtive magazine hid under the mattress, pornography today allows us to watch people writhing and moaning and, sometimes, in real time.

Heterosexual, homosexual, multiple-partner, transsexual, and BDSM sex are all on the menu. Here's what a young person is apt to learn from watching porn: all men have six-pack abs and bulging biceps, and they get an erection at the drop of a hat. And all women have flat stomachs and huge breasts, and they get an orgasm in five seconds or less.

LaDonna tells me she learned when and how to moan during sex by watching porn stars online, not by when she herself is getting pleasure.

Ricky has endlessly compared himself to gay porn actors on the Internet. He tells me he's scared his body and his techniques won't measure up when he has his first gay experience, which he yearns for.

The pressure on young people to live up to these performances can cause great anxiety. Simple experimenting, fondling, and learning together with your partner about mutual pleasure seem to be quaint notions of the past, as are kissing and romance. Now it can feel like everyone has to be an expert right out of the gate.

Pornography can sometimes add spice to a sexual relationship, but when you are inexperienced, impressionable, and vulnerable to body image distress or eating disorders, this may not be the case.

When clinicians assess teenagers for eating disorders and other addictions, they need to inquire about their clients' online life and what kind of sites they like to visit.

One hopes that when at-risk individuals develop an empathic connection to a real live therapist, they will not be drawn down the rabbit hole of a toxic online world. The connection with a therapist can be energizing and enlivening and provide a warm atmosphere to counteract the pull of the damaging online world. We want our clients to absorb our genuine wish for their health, healing, and wholeness.

The Upside of Social Media

Despite toxic communities promoting anorexia and bulimia and body image dissatisfaction, social media also provides pro-recovery communities and support. Body positivity posts, the Health at Every Size movement, intuitive eating groups, online chat rooms, treatment referrals, as well as e-books, podcasts, self-monitoring apps, YouTube videos, Facebook groups devoted to recover communities, Instagram posts with hashtag communities like #edrecovery (with over 3 million posts), and other online recovery groups have increased people's access to helpful and healing resources for eating disorders. Celebrities have shared their personal struggles online, which may help break through the isolation felt by so many sufferers.

This is the positive side of social media, and directing our clients to these pro-recovery Web sites can enhance eating disorder healing and increase body positivity.

Social Work in the Digital World: Cyberspace and Psychotherapy

In the magazine *Social Work Today*, three articles address the new world of cyberspace for the social worker: "Evaluating Health Apps" (Sage & Eaton, 2019), "Web-Based Intervention Plays Preventive Role for Teen Depression" (Getz, 2019), and "Evaluating Technology Use in Client Assessment" (Jones & Hitchcock, 2019). The last article includes a new tool to help social workers understand their clients' relationship with technology as well as a component for social workers to self-assess their own digital literacy and evaluate how they use technology in their practices.

NASW has published a report on standards for technology in social work practice that says,

> Social workers' use of technology is proliferating. Technology has transformed the nature of social work practice and greatly expanded social workers' ability to assist people in need. Contemporary social workers can provide services to individual clients by using online counseling, telephone counseling, videoconferencing, self-guided Web-based interventions, electronic social networks, mobile apps, automated tutorials, e-mail, text messages, and a host of other services. Social workers' use of technology has created new ways to interact and communicate with clients, raising fundamentally new questions about the meaning of the social work–client relationship. (NASW, Association of Social Work Boards, Council on Social Work Education, & Clinical Social Work Association, 2017, p. 7)

The New York State Society for Clinical Social Work (2018) now includes a section in its Code of Ethics about how to navigate social media and telehealth. And the Clinical Social Work Association (Groshong & Aronson, 2019) has authored a cautionary article, "LCSWs and the Use of Texting in Mental Health Treatment."

Social work therapists are working hard to keep up with the ever-changing digital world.

Telementalhealth

Telementalhealth refers to conducting psychotherapy on a variety of digital platforms through the Internet using Skype, Facetime, Doxy, iCouch, Thera-link, Theranest, and other Web counseling sites. Not every site is compliant with the Health Insurance Portability and Accountability Act, which raises legal and ethical questions for practitioners about safeguarding client privacy so that online communication and information cannot be compromised. Telementalhealth is a boon for clients who may be disabled and cannot travel to see a therapist face to face and also for those who live in more isolated areas and cannot easily access mental health care.*

Telementalhealth is booming and seductive as one advertisement I recently came across declares how "efficient and flexible" it can be:

> With a lot on your plate and mind, the last thing you need to worry about is one more place to be and the barriers that can prevent you from getting there. Teletherapy allows for maximum flexibility for overworked and overcommitted clients.

My professional conviction is that online sessions, where we cannot see our patients in person, should not be considered best practices for the treatment of eating disorders. We need to observe and witness eating disorder patients "in the flesh" to monitor their physical appearance for signs and symptoms that may not be obvious on a computer screen. Puffy cheeks can be a symptom of throwing up, abrasions on the knuckles as people force their hands in their mouths to provoke vomiting can also be a sign of bulimia, and significant weight loss or weight gain can all be hidden from view of the therapist when online.

I recommend online therapy only for the occasional times when clients cannot come to the office due to illness or being out of town, and I would recommend this only with established clients the therapist already knows. Our clients have resorted to bingeing, purging, or starving to deal with anxiety and depression rather than turning to people for support. Our eating disordered clients need to have "full bodied" relationships with their therapists in the same room. All five senses are needed in the therapy room.

---

*In *The Digital Age on the Couch*, Alessandra Lemma (2017) argues that "There are occasions when Skype therapy is better than nothing. For some patients this may be the only way they can tolerate any engagement in a therapeutic process. And the therapy may be helpful. Sometimes it is a lifeline and this should not be underestimated. But it is also vital to recognize it is not equivalent to the in-person experience" (p. 138). However, she also states that online therapy is not suitable for patients with body image disturbances who need help to be rooted in their own bodies in the therapist's actual presence" (p. 112). The Web site https://personcenteredtech.com/ offers articles about digital ethics for therapists as well as telementalhealth.

In the article "Sleepwalking towards Artificial Intimacy: How Psychotherapy Is Failing the Future," Todd Essig (2018) argues that intimacy between people should involve person-to-person connection, and when we leave bodies out, intimacy is reduced to something artificial. He asserts that therapists may find it is easier and less stressful to substitute texting for talking, but when therapists become willing to take bodies out of the room, "they contribute to the fantasy that therapy without a human relationship is the same" (para. 18).

E-mails, Texts, and the Therapy Relationship

In the article "The Downside of the Digital World in Treatment" clinical social worker Valerie Frankfeldt (2019) discusses how

> dilemmas can arise in treatment through the use of texts and emails. Patients can cancel or terminate while evading their guilt or anger by substituting an email instead of a person-to-person conversation. This then leaves both the client and the therapist deprived of the opportunity to discuss and understand this together. We also see how clients or therapists "shooting" off texts or emails can threaten to convert a therapy interaction into something analogous to ordering and canceling on Amazon. It's just a click away! Being in the room together with the patient, on the other hand, helps us both slow down and reach deeper into ourselves and to the other. (p. 7)

Frankfeldt (2019) acknowledges that e-mails and texts may have a positive function:

> Certain patients can express things in writing that they might feel could not be said safely in person because it would make them feel too vulnerable. Perhaps they could say provocative, rageful things without fear of immediate in-person reprisal. We can then deal with these issues when we are face to face. (p. 18)

There are times I find e-mail to be helpful with the eating disorder client. Hungry for contact, the client often feels reassured by being able to e-mail the therapist between sessions. Sometimes clients send me a description of what they ate when they are trying to get back on track after a binge, sometimes they send an update on a parent in the hospital, and sometimes they share a great epiphany about themselves that they are afraid they will forget by the next time we meet. I generally respond with, "That's a great topic to discuss in our next session." And I will always inquire in the session why she worried about forgetting the biggest epiphany of her life before she saw me again.

In *Reclaiming Conversation: The Power of Talk in a Digital Age*, author Sherry Turkle (2015) describes how

> we live in a technological universe in which we are always communicating. And yet we have sacrificed conversation for mere connection. We find ways around conversation, tempted by the possibilities of a text or an email in which we don't have to look, listen, or reveal ourselves. The case for conversation begins with the necessary conversations of solitude and self-reflection. They are endangered: these days, always connected, we see loneliness as a problem that technology should solve. Afraid of being alone, we rely on other people to give us a sense of ourselves, and our capacity for empathy and relationship suffers. (p. 183)

The Cell Phone in the Therapy Room

An increasing number of my patients now walk into their sessions tapping away on their cell phones. Sometimes I feel in competition for attention with the rings, dings, and buzzes of their phones. Cyberspace has invaded the therapy space.

Hazel, a bulimic woman, brings her cell phone over to my chair in her session to show me the video she has made of spreading her deceased mother's ashes in a river in their hometown in Trinidad. As we watch the stream washing away her mother's ashes, Hazel begins to cry, and my eyes well up too. Hazel has always preferred throwing up rather than experiencing any hurtful emotions. Crying has always felt too out of control for her, and she would rather get rid of her feelings in one fell swoop through vomiting. I am glad Hazel has brought her cell phone to session to share this video with me; it is a raw and heartfelt experience to watch the ashes that were once her mother being swept away. Hazel cries in front of me and seems to realize we can be in this together. Vomiting, in contrast, has been so lonely and solitary.

Susan, recovering from a binge-eating disorder, is exhausted by the ongoing health problems of her mother and the latest crisis involving risky surgery. "Here is what my mother's stomach with the strangulated hernia and impacted bowels looked like before the operation," says Susan as she comes bounding over to my chair with her cell phone outstretched to show me the picture. But I don't want to see her mother's stomach, and I hold my hand up to say no. For a brief moment, I feel like a bad therapist turning down Susan's wish to share something with me that is so important to her. But I grant myself the permission to have limits and to say no. Susan rarely says no to herself when it comes to food or spending. I will listen to how she feels about being told no in our relationship—something she cannot do for herself.

Although I request that patients turn off their cell phones in sessions, I am also learning that some clients cannot easily relinquish attention to their phones, and I've begun to understand how that can relate to their eating disorder.

Lisa, who has struggled with binge eating, bulimia, and anorexia, holds her phone close to her in each session. It seems like her security blanket. She talks about the impending death of her mother. Tears come to her eyes, but she reaches for her cell phone and checks it.

"What just happened?" I ask. "Where did you go?"

She looks surprised because she does not think she went anywhere. "I guess I was just distracting myself from what we were talking about."

This moment enables me to point out to Lisa how she turns to her cell phone in the same way she resorts to bulimia to help distract herself from feelings that are painful. Rather than tolerate difficult emotions and sit with them, experience them, and speak about them, Lisa avoids and detours them. I bring her back to the session by observing and wondering how talking about her mother made her run away.

Clients with an attachment to their cell phone like Lisa represent a new challenge for therapists. When I was a young teenager, our one and only acronym when we signed our letters was SWAK (sealed with a kiss), but now there is new language for therapists to learn: Snapchat, Twitter, Tumblr, texting, sexting, Whatsapp, BFF, LOL, YOLO, JK, LMAO, catfishing, memes, selfies, trolls, hashtags, blogs, and an array of emoticons to represent one's feelings, including an emoticon that is throwing up.

Clients have shown me photographs on their cell phones, read me letters from boyfriends they want help deciphering, and shared pithy Instagram posts that have inspired them. They have revealed group chat e-mails to prove why they constantly suffer from FOMO (the fear of missing out). In these cases, the cell phone has enhanced our connection by proving that, indeed, a picture or text message can be worth 1,000 words.

Sometimes this can present unusual problems. In the recent past, three girls have shown me pictures of their mothers on their cell phones to demonstrate how much prettier the mother is than they are. And, yes, I study the mothers' photos and see that in each case the mothers are prettier than their daughters. Now what does a therapist do or say? My response has been, "Yes. Your mother is very attractive. But why can't there be room in your family for two attractive women?" It can be a brave new world in cyberspace and psychotherapy.

A social work colleague of mine describes needing to keep her cell phone on vibrate while in session because she is expecting an update on a family emergency. While her client is talking, Siri unwittingly gets activated and chirps, "Interesting! I didn't know that!" Client and therapist burst out laughing at the inclusion of this new persona, Apple's virtual personal assistant, in the therapy room.

We often discover that clients have searched social media to learn more about us. We are powerless against that beyond discussing the meaning; the best we can do is limit what we post. However, social work clinicians need to know it is considered a professional breach of ethics to look up their patients online. Therapists often "Google" or search for information before seeing new clients or may even follow them on social media. This is considered unethical because the therapist is willfully obtaining information about patients that they are not bringing into the treatment room. A new term has even been coined to describe this ethical breach: "Patient Targeted Googling" (Grohol, 2018).

Conclusion

In one month, I received e-mails encouraging me to buy "Too Hot to Handle" pocketbooks, "Eye Candy" jewelry, "Fever" blouses, "Get Noticed" handbags, "Flirty" mink false eyelashes, sweat pants with "Juicy" emblazoned in rhinestones on the backside, and offerings from an online fragrance company for Obsession and Opium perfumes. This frenzied and hyped-up advertising stimulates our cravings and our belief that if only we had more things, we would be happier.

Clinicians—like our clients—are also bombarded by digital stimulation and can appreciate living in a world flooded with online advertising. We also have to figure out for ourselves how to become mindful of the media we digest and how to regulate our intake of so much information. Then, in turn, we can help our clients regulate themselves.

Therapists are always seeking to enhance authentic communication with clients. We want to get to know this person sitting in our office and why they developed an eating disorder and what went wrong in their early attachments. We help them to travel their inner road, with its thoughtful and quiet pathways, to connect with their imagination, their desires, and their most genuine self.

If clients sharing their social media interests with us can deepen how we understand them, then it is a worthy tool. But if it causes distance and detachment, then we need to help clients see they are trying to push us away. And sometimes we just don't know.

My client Eddie comes for his appointment and loves how the setting sun is casting a golden glow on the walls of my office and curtains. He takes out his cell phone and starts taking pictures of my office without asking permission. I feel intruded on by his photographing my private space and yet pleased that he is stepping out of his obsessive anorexic thoughts and his dark depression into the light and colors of the sunset. I don't know what to say about this, so I decide to "marinate" on it for a while—just like I ask my clients to marinate when they are confused or uncertain. I file this away for possible discussion with Eddie once I can think of what, if anything, I want to say.

Both the therapist and the client need to tolerate marinating in confusion. For clients, this pauses the impulsive, automatic reach for bingeing or purging whenever an uncomfortable feeling assails them. It is okay to "stew" in one's confusion; it is part of the process of reflecting on what we feel, accepting the discomfort, and appreciating the complexity of our inner selves.

How clients, like Eddie, use smart phones and social media both in and out of sessions has become a brand-new challenge for therapists. We must stretch ourselves, our clinical judgment, and our imagination to handle therapy situations we never even imagined before.

Conclusion

One of my favorite sayings is, "It's never too late to have a happy childhood." In my definition, a happy childhood includes warm and loving relationships with abundant empathy for our emotions, safety, security, joyful play and laughter, and encouragement for our growth and development.

But all of us—clients and therapists alike—carry within us wounds, battle scars, and broken hearts. It's so hard to be a human! So we identify and smile at the cartoon that depicts a huge convention hall with a banner across the podium that states, "Convention for Adult Children of *Functional* Families" (emphasis added). And the convention hall is empty except for four lonely attendees.

Our clients come to us with the hope that we will cure them of their emotional eating misery—and also the fear that we will. Each treatment hovers between the client's wishes to live whole and peaceful in their body and intense worry about how to handle the pain of life without the soothing medicine of bingeing, purging, or starving.

This dilemma is healed through the therapist's empathic attunement and our coming to appreciate the multiple meanings that the eating disorder has served in the client's life. Our relationship will hopefully enliven our clients and stimulate curiosity so that they will develop an attachment with us that is filled with the richness of language and feelings. More than anything, it is this human and compassionate dimension that helps mend the wounds of the past. All true healing must begin with the human heart. No behavioral technique can reach the hurt heart and soul of the eating disordered person. What can is our understanding and our affection—and, yes, sometimes love—as we try to discover why the client has come to believe that trusting food is safer than trusting people.

The singer Leonard Cohen has observed that there is a crack in everything, and that's how the light gets in. And similarly, it is our imperfect humanity connecting with the client's imperfect humanity that will kindle hope and healing.

In the Japanese tradition of kintsugi, when a piece of pottery develops a crack it is repaired with gold filler. Rather than devaluing the bowl or hiding the crack, the gold filler illuminates where the crack is. Now this bowl becomes unique, with a scar unlike any other. There is no shame in its defect; rather its uniqueness is celebrated. The bowl has become stronger, more beautiful, and resilient in those broken places.

Therapy provides the gold filler of compassion, empathy, and love that helps fill in the cracks of the person's wholeness and well-being. With our help, our clients can sink their teeth into life, not into their relationship with food.

Ear Lobes in Five Generations

With giggles and nervous anticipation, we took my granddaughters Keira and Ravenna, ages eight and nine, to get their ears pierced on Thanksgiving weekend. My own grandmother had taken me to have my ears pierced when I was nine years old, so I was thrilled to pass on the tradition. I thought how much this was a female rite of passage.

As we left for the jewelry store, Keira asked if it would hurt, and I explained if you pinched your ear lobe hard for three seconds that would give you an idea. She pinched her lobe and decided she would be okay with that. I heard her instruct Ravenna to pinch her ear to get an idea. Ravenna wasn't sure she wanted to test it out, so she had Keira pinch her lobe for her and then decided she also would be OK.

We sallied forth to the jewelry store with their mother. I thought about how my own mother—born of an Eastern European Jewish mother—had her ears pierced at birth. It was the custom of the day. In my family, we started with small gold hoops and grew into larger ones at each milestone birthday.

When I had my ears pierced back then, the doctor inserted a needle with thick black thread, and only after a month could we put in the gold earrings. My father would clean those black threads every night, and it was a moment of wonderful intimacy as we both stood looking at my ears in the mirror as he carefully cleaned the threads.

The girls' mother and I decided to go to a neighborhood woman jeweler who let the girls pick out the studs they would wear after the piercing. They got to choose from a drawer filled with green, gold, and pink stones. Gone was the black thread and gone was the needle. Now we have "piercing guns"—an unfortunate name, I thought.

The jeweler first marked each girl's ears with a pen to determine the right place to "shoot" the gun. I thought she made the dot too high up on their ear lobes, and I requested she lower it just a little. She bit her lip, moved the mark down, and said nothing.

Watching these little girls comfort each other before the procedure was wonderful. Ravenna held both of Keira's hands and squeezed them reassuringly. When it was Ravenna's turn, Keira told her to say, "Puppies, puppies, puppies," over and over for reassurance. Since the girls had recently gotten puppies they had fallen in love with, this was a sweet comfort.

It was all over! The girls were ecstatic, prancing around the jewelry shop examining their ears with pride in the store's mirror.

I thanked the jeweler for lowering the holes, and she pointed to my ears and said in a critical tone, "Your problem is your holes are too low."

The fun of the day abruptly stopped. My breath stopped for a moment. My pleasure in the day was pierced. I looked at myself anxiously in the jewelry store mirror. Of all my body image concerns, my ear lobes were never on the list. Now they were. I could not stop hearing her comment as I went home and checked again in the mirror. And again each day for a while. Her comment reverberates. Although my earrings had always looked fine to me, maybe I was a fool, and the expert had discovered a flaw of mine that I didn't even know I had.

My mother had always criticized my weight, my feet, my hair, my breasts, and—did I mention—my weight? Until now, my ear lobes had been one of my body parts on the neutral, demilitarized list. This reminded me of Cindy, a patient who once came to me for eating and body image therapy who told me she hated every part of her body. "Every part?" I asked with surprise and consternation. "Well," replied Cindy, "my wrists are OK." How sad only a small, insignificant body part was acceptable to her.

A recent documentary, *The Illusionists*, portrayed women in Asia and Africa as obsessed with skin whitening products and procedures, whereas white Americans and Europeans are obsessed with spray tanning and tanning salons. Every woman wants to look different from who she really is.

How vulnerable we are as women. What power we give other women to hurt us. And how much power other women wield to criticize each other. Does it come from having been little girls once upon a time with critical mothers who maybe themselves were criticized by growing up in a culture that relentlessly examines and judges females and their appearance? How do I go back to all the days of my life from age nine to 70 when I was not self-conscious about my ear lobes?

We are all vulnerable to these body criticisms, internal and external, big and small, at any age. My hope is that this book serves as inspiration to develop wellsprings of resilience and to break the prison of old memories so we can reclaim contentment with our looks and ourselves.

Appendix A: The Diagnoses of Eating Disorders

In 2013, the APA revised the *Diagnostic and Statistical Manual of Mental Disorders* (DSM-5). In the 1994 edition of the DSM, eating disorders were divided into three categories: anorexia, bulimia, and eating disorders not otherwise specified (such as binge eating).

To reflect our current, more comprehensive understanding of these illnesses, there are now seven distinct categories of eating and feeding disorders. They are all characterized by a "persistent disturbance of eating or eating-related behavior that results in the altered consumption absorption of food and that significantly impairs physical health or psychosocial functioning" (APA, 2013, p. 103).

The more thorough and in-depth our understanding of eating disorders, the more improved the treatment.

Bulimia Nervosa

Criteria for bulimia nervosa include the following:

1. Recurrent episodes of binge eating (rapid consumption of a large amount of food in a short period of time).
2. A feeling of lack of control over eating behavior during the eating binges.
3. The binges are usually followed by efforts to compensate and undo the weight gain from overeating: self-induced vomiting; overuse of laxatives, diuretics, or enemas; strict dieting or fasting or vigorous exercise to prevent weight gain.
4. A minimum average of at least one binge-eating episode a week for three months.

5. One's self-evaluation is unduly influenced by body shape and weight.

Bulimia nervosa is diagnosed as mild (an average of 1–3 episodes of inappropriate compensatory behaviors per week in an attempt to undo weight gain), moderate (average of 4–7 episodes), severe (8–13 episodes), or extreme (14 or more).

Childhood physical or sexual abuse increases the likelihood of bulimia when the person enters their teenage years. Bulimics may have a heightened incidence of alcohol and substance abuse as well as frequent episodes of self-harming behavior such as cutting. They may suffer from increased depression and suicidal tendencies as well.

Bulimia nervosa is far less common in males than it is in females, with an approximately 10:1 female-to-male ratio. However, clinicians report that more bulimic men are seeking treatment than ever before.

Of the seven eating disorders, bulimia and binge-eating disorder are the most responsive to treatment with medication. Both depressed and nondepressed bulimics seem to improve with antidepressant medication, which can significantly reduce the number of bingeing episodes per week as well as reduce the urge to binge and purge.

Binge-Eating Disorder

Binge-eating disorder, also called compulsive overeating, is the most common eating disorder. It has been established in the DSM-5 as a bona fide diagnosis since 2013, and recent psychiatric literature confirms how extensive this disorder is. It is characterized by the following criteria:

1. Recurrent episodes of binge eating without the regular use of inappropriate compensatory behaviors characteristic of bulimia nervosa and anorexia nervosa. Unlike bulimia, where people "get rid" of the food they have eaten, individuals with this disorder "keep it."
2. Eating a much larger amount of food than what most people would eat in a certain period of time.
3. Feeling a loss of control during the binge episode over how much one is eating.

The binge eater feels extreme distress, shame, and guilt after the gorging episodes, which usually involve rapid eating, becoming overly full, and not eating out of feelings of hunger. The compulsive overeating occurs at least once a week for three months.

The DSM-5 rates the severity of binge-eating disorder by mild (1–3 binges a week), moderate (4–7), severe (8–13), and extreme (14 or more episodes).

Anorexia Nervosa

Anorexia nervosa is characterized by the following criteria:

1. Restriction of food leading to significantly low body weight (less than minimally normal).
2. Intense fear of gaining weight or becoming fat or behaviors that interfere with weight gain even though the person is underweight.
3. Disturbance in the way in which one's body weight, size, or shape is experienced, undue influence of body weight or shape on self-evaluation, or denial of the seriousness of the current low body weight.
4. Anorexia can be a restrictive type (self-starvation) or binge-eating and purging type during the last three months.

The degree of anorexia ranges from mild to moderate, severe, or extreme. There are more anorexic females than anorexic males with a ratio of 10 to 1.

Additional Diagnoses of Feeding or Eating Disorders

Pica

Eating nonnutritive, nonfood substances on a persistent basis over a period of at least one month that is severe enough to warrant clinical attention. Typical substances ingested might include paper, soap, cloth, hair, string, wool, soil, chalk, talcum powder, paint, gum, metal, pebbles, charcoal or coal, ash, clay, starch, or ice. The prevalence of pica is not known, and the onset of pica can occur in childhood, adolescence, or adulthood. Unlike anorexia, bulimia, or binge eating, pica is not an attempt to lose weight.

Rumination Disorder

Repeated regurgitation of food over a period of at least one month. Regurgitated food may be rechewed, reswallowed, or spit out.

Avoidant or Restrictive Food Intake Disorder

An eating or feeding disturbance where the person is phobic of food and often has extreme sensitivity to the appearance, color, smell, or temperature of food. It is also called "chronic food refusal." The person with this disorder has significant weight loss and nutritional deficiency, with marked impairment in functioning.

Other Specified Feeding or Eating Disorder

This diagnostic category includes eating disorders that are not severe enough to warrant inclusion in one of the above categories. They include atypical anorexia (in which a person practices self-starvation but is in a normal weight range), low-frequency bulimia nervosa or binge-eating disorder, and purging disorder without the binge component. Night eating syndrome describes awakening from sleep to overeat or excessive eating after the evening meal.

Orthorexia

Although not formally recognized in the DSM-5, orthorexia describes an obsession with healthy eating. People with orthorexia become so fixated on so-called healthy eating that they actually damage their own well-being. Symptoms include compulsive checking of nutritional labels, cutting out an increasing number of food groups (all sugar, all carbs, all dairy, all meat, all animal products), and an inability to eat anything but a narrow group of foods that are deemed "healthy" or "pure."

Body Dysphoria

Refers to the conviction that the person has a flaw or defect in their appearance, rendering them ugly or deformed. This often affects their functioning in social, school, or work-related situations. This can include

- being extremely preoccupied with a perceived flaw in appearance that to others can't be seen or appears minor.
- strong belief that you have a defect in your appearance that makes you ugly or deformed.
- belief that others take special notice of your appearance in a negative way or mock you.
- engaging in behaviors aimed at fixing or hiding the perceived flaw that are difficult to resist or control, such as frequently checking the mirror, grooming, or skin picking.
- attempting to hide perceived flaws with styling, makeup, or clothes.
- constantly comparing your appearance with others.
- always seeking reassurance about your appearance from others.
- having perfectionist tendencies.
- seeking frequent cosmetic procedures with little satisfaction.
- avoiding social situations.

- being so preoccupied with appearance that it causes major distress or problems in your social life, work, school, or other areas of functioning.

Clients with body dysphoria disorders especially obsess over one or more body parts:

- Face, such as nose, complexion, wrinkles, acne, and other blemishes
- Hair, such as appearance, thinning, and baldness
- Skin and vein appearance
- Breast size
- Muscle size and tone
- Genitalia

Appendix B: Resources

General Recovery Resources

AED: The Academy for Eating Disorders was founded in 1993 and is an international professional association committed to leadership in eating disorders research, education, treatment, and prevention. It includes a search engine to find an eating disorder therapist, blogs, and an annual international conference. http://www.aedweb.org

ANAD: The National Association of Anorexia Nervosa & Associated Disorders offers a helpline, treatment directory, conference, blogs, and YouTube Recovery Channel programming. http://www.anad.org

ANRED: Anorexia Nervosa and Related Eating Disorders describes eating disorders, treatment options, parent support tips, and self-help advice. http://www.anred.com

Body Positive offers support for people of every size to enhance their health and well-being. Includes activism alerts and help for larger women as well as children. http://www.bodypositive.com

Eating Disorder Hope, founded in 2005, offers online recovery tools and a wealth of information about eating disorders as well as online events. http://Eatingdisorderhope.com

Eating Disorders Resource Catalogue began in 1980 and offers podcasts, a free catalog of books and reviews, and treatment referrals. http://EDCatalogue.com

Eating Disorder Treatment and Information Center, founded in 1991, offers treatment referrals, comprehensive information on eating disorders and related issues, and a free monthly newsletter. The newsletter includes book reviews (Mary Anne Cohen is the professional book reviewer) and conference and workshop updates. http://EDReferral.com

EmotionalEating.Org: The New York Center for Eating Disorders offers articles, continuing education credits for social workers, and information on psychotherapy. http://emotionaleating.org

F.E.A.S.T. is a global community of parents and families affected by eating disorders. Founded in 2007. https://www.feast-ed.org/what-is-feast/

Food Addicts in Recovery Anonymous is a 12-step program modeled after the 12 steps of Alcoholics Anonymous and offers meetings, literature, and brochures for professionals. http://www.foodaddicts.org/

Health at Every Size is a community championing body diversity and the rights of fat people and challenging the conversation about weight stigma. Includes podcasts. http://www.haes.org

Healthy Place includes articles, blogs, and coping skills for eating disorder recovery. https://www.healthyplace.com/blogs/survivinged/

International Association of Eating Disorders Professionals offers conferences, webinars, courses, and the latest news in the field for professionals. http://www.iaedp.com

Movies to Stream: *The Illusionists* examines how global advertising firms, mass media conglomerates, and the beauty, fashion, and cosmetic surgery industries are changing the way people around the world define beauty and see themselves. The film explores how these industries saturate our lives with narrow, Westernized, consumer-driven images of beauty with little acknowledgment for biological realities or cultural differences. https://www.kanopy.com/product/illusionists-0

Slim Hopes: Advertising and the Obsession with Thinness and *Killing Us Softly: Advertising's Image of Women* by Jean Kilbourne, a pioneer activist and filmmaker. Dr. Kilbourne has explored the toxic portrayal of women in the media and how advertising has given rise to increased public health issues around eating disorders, body dissatisfaction, alcohol and tobacco abuse, and violence against women. http://www.jeankilbourne.com

National Association for Males with Eating Disorders provides support for males affected by eating disorders. Includes blogs, articles, books, and videos. http://www.namedinc.org

National Eating Disorders Association offers a screening tool for self-assessment, treatment referrals, information for parents, activism events, and blogs. https://www.nationaleatingdisorders.org/screening-tool

Only Healthy provides eating disorder forums as well as information on statistics and related Web sites. http://www.onlyhealthy.com/the-complete-list-of-eating-disorder-resources/

Recovery Warriors offers podcasts, inspirational articles, and treatment referrals. http://www.RecoveryWarriors.com

Something Fishy is a pro-recovery Web site founded in 1995 to raise awareness about eating disorders and provides treatment referrals and an online community to connect with others. http://www.something-fishy.org/

Multicultural Resources

Online Resources

Eating Disorder Hope identifies eating disorders in the Muslim community. https://www.eatingdisorderhope.com/blog/identifying-eating-disorder-issues-in-the-muslim-community

Eating Disorders among Native Americans describes the prevalence of eating disorders in Native American communities. http://www.thebellavita.com/exploring-eating-disorders-among-native-americans/

Islam Eating Disorders is a Facebook group that describes how Islam views eating disorders and offers inspirational insights. https://www.facebook.com/IslamEatingDisorders/

Marginalized Voices Project on Minorities of the National Eating Disorders Association offers information for the LBGQ community. https://www.nationaleatingdisorders.org/marginalized-voices

Mochi is a destination for Asian American women to share their stories, experiences, and passions. Its mission is to amplify Asian American voices and support the growth and inclusion of Asian American women. https://www.mochimag.com/about-mochi/

Muslim Anti-Racism Collaborative offers education and resources to promote racial justice. http://www.muslimarc.org/about

Muslim Girl provides personal articles from Muslim women about eating disorder recovery. http://muslimgirl.com/?s=eating+disorders

Muslims and Eating Disorders provides eating disorder support for the Muslim community. http://waragainsteatingdisorder.com/

Nalgona Positivity Pride for Chicana Women is a Chicana body positivity pride Web site. https://www.nalgonapositivitypride.com/

Orthodox Union provides professional and parent workshops, hosts a conference on eating disorders, and produced the documentary Hungry to Be Heard, focusing on the rising rates of anorexia, bulimia, and other eating disorders in the Jewish community. https://www.ou.org/community/eating-disorder-awareness/hungry-to-be-heard/

Relief Resources for Orthodox Jews is a mental health referral organization providing information and referrals to clinicians or programs experienced in treating Orthodox Jewish patients. https://reliefhelp.org/

Thick Dumpling Skin is a Web site for Asian and Asian American women to discuss body image. http://www.thickdumplingskin.com/

Publications

Brodey, D. (2005, Sept. 20). Blacks join the eating disorder mainstream. *New York Times*. Retrieved from https://www.nytimes.com/2005/09/20/health/psychology/blacks-join-the-eatingdisorder-mainstream.html

Cohen, M. A. (1997). *Tostadas y mermelada para el desayuno: Hacer las paces con la alimentacion emocional* [French toast for breakfast: Declaring peace with emotional eating]. Madrid: Ediciones Piramide, 1997.

Cohen, M. A. (2013). *Lasagna for lunch: Declaring peace with emotional eating*. New York: New Forge Press.

Cohen, M. A. (2016). *French toast for breakfast: Declaring peace with emotional eating*. New York: New Forge Press.

Eating Disorders: Every Body Is Beautiful. (n.d.). *New findings on eating disorders in Native Americans*. Retrieved from https://eatingdisorders.com/news/studies-and-research/new-study-reveals-findings-on

-eating-disorders-in-native-americans

Eng, D., & Han, S. (2018). *Racial melancholia, racial dissociation: On the social and psychic lives of Asian Americans*. Durham, NC: Duke University Press.

Latinas Unidas en Servicio Comunidades. (2014). *My family, my self: The Latino guide to emotional well-being (Mi familia y yo: Guía de bienestar emocional)*. Center City, MN: Hazelden.

Molinary, R. (2007). *Hijas americanas: Beauty, body image, and growing up*. Emeryville, CA: Seal Press.

Wiley-Blackwell. (2011, January 6). New study reveals impact of eating disorders on Native Americans. *ScienceDaily*. Retrieved from https://www.sciencedaily.com/releases/2011/01/110106191606.htm

Resources on Eating Disorders and Mental Health in the LGBTQ Population

Fenway Guide to Lesbian, Gay, Bisexual, and Transgender Health: https://store.acponline.org/ebizatpro/Default.aspx?TabID=251&ProductId=21572

National Eating Disorders Association: https://www.nationaleatingdisorders.org/identity-eating-disorders

The National LGBT Health Education Center/The Fenway Institute: https://www.lgbthealtheducation.org/

Trans Lifeline: https://www.translifeline.org/about

Trans Folx Fighting Eating Disorders offers support groups, healing intensive retreats, advocacy work, and a resource list of gender-sensitive health care providers. https://www.transfolxfightingeds.org/home

References

Academy for Eating Disorders. (n.d.). *AED position statement on pro-anorexia Web sites.* Retrieved from https://archive.is/20071014045846/http:/aedweb.org/policy/pro-anorexia_sites.cfm

Addiction Hope. (n.d.). *Signs that might indicate you have a food addiction.* Retrieved from https://www.addictionhope.com/blog/signs-indicate-food-addiction/

Ainsworth, M.D.S., Blehar, M. C., Waters, E., & Wall, S. N. (1978). *Patterns of attachment: A study of the strange situation.* Mahwah, NJ: Erlbaum.

Albert, E., & Block, J. (2019, March 24). It will take more than a $34,000 drug to stop postpartum depression. *New York Times.* Retrieved from http://www.nytimes.com

American Psychiatric Association. (2013). *Diagnostic and statistical manual of mental disorders* (5th ed.). Arlington, VA: Author.

American Psychiatric Association. (n.d.). *What is gender dysphoria?* Retrieved from https://www.psychiatry.org/patients-families/gender-dysphoria/what-is-gender-dysphoria

Amichai, Y., with Alter, R. (Ed.). (2015). *The poetry of Yehuda Amichai.* New York: Farrar, Straus, & Giroux.

Anonymous. (n.d.). *This gendered body: Living with an eating disorder and finding my voice as a queer nonbinary person.* Retrieved from https://www.nationaleatingdisorders.org/node/6825

Association for Size Diversity and Health. (n.d.-a). *HAES fact sheet.* Retrieved from https://www.sizediversityandhealth.org/content.asp?id=161

Association for Size Diversity and Health. (n.d.-b). *HAES principles.* Retrieved from https://www.sizediversityandhealth.org/content.asp?id=152

Azoulay, B. (2018, October 12). *This deaf Jewish-Asian transgender model just made history.* Retrieved from https://forward.com/schmooze/411898/happy-national-coming-out-day-meet-imgs-first-deaf-jewish-asian/

Bacha, C. (2018, March 27). Muslim models breaking barriers in the fashion industry. *Teen Vogue.* Retrieved from https://www.teenvogue.com

Bacon, L. (n.d.). *The HAES manifesto*. Retrieved from https://lindabacon.org/HAESbook/pdf_files/HAES_Manifesto.pdf.

Bacon, L., & Aphramor, L. (2011). Weight science: Evaluating the evidence for a paradigm shift. *Nutrition Journal*, Article 9. doi:10.1186/1475-2891-10-9

Barcklow, R. (2017, Nov. 6). Gay *women don't get eating disorders. Or do they?* Retrieved from http://www.adiosbarbie.com/2017/11/gay-women-dont-get-eating-disorders/

Bardone-Cone, A., Higgins Neyland, M. K., & Lin S. L. (2017). Eating disorders in racial/ethnic minorities. In J. Fries & V. Sullivan (Eds.), *Eating disorders in special populations* (pp. 277–312). Boca Raton, FL: CRC Press.

Barre, R. (2019, April 19). *Curiosity—The key that opens the door to the self.* Retrieved from https://theshiftlesswanderer.com/blog/2019/4/19/curiosity-the-key-that-opens-the-door-to-the-self

Bass, E., & Davis, L. (1994). *The courage to heal*. New York: HarperCollins.

Beech, E., & Ali, I. (2019, March 12). Pentagon sets limits on transgender troops. *Huffington Post*. Retrieved from https://www.huffpost.com/entry/pentagon-sets-limits-transgender-troops_n_5c88709be4b038892f488491?ncid5newsltushpmgnews__TheMorningEmail__031319

Berg, T., Levinson, D., & Wollner, E. (n.d.). *Eating disorders in the Jewish community*. Retrieved from https://www.nationaleatingdisorders.org/eating-disorders-jewish-community

Bill B. (Pseud.). (1981). *Compulsive overeater*. New York: CompCare.

Boskind-White, M., & White, W., Jr. (1991). *Bulimarexia: Binge/purge cycle*. New York: W. W. Norton.

Bowlby, J. (1988). *A secure base: Parent–child attachment*. New York: Basic Books.

Bowld, C. (2018). *What goes down: The end of an eating disorder*. Scotts Valley, CA: Create Space.

Braun, A. (2006, May 12). A problem that's hard to stomach. *Jewish Week*. Retrieved from https://www.scribd.com/doc/47936083/Jewish-Week-Article?secret_password=65bp0qn0wsydd2hpsfz

Brinton, S. (2018, January 24). I was tortured in gay conversion therapy. And it's still legal in 41 states. *New York Times*. Retrieved from http://www.nytimes.com

Brodesser-Akner, T. (2017, August 2). Losing it in the anti-dieting age. *New York Times*. Retrieved from http://www.nytimes.com

Bromberg, P. (1998). *Standing in the spaces*. Oxford, England: Psychology Press.

Brucculieri, J. (2018a, March 9). Instagram influencers are all starting to look the same. Here's why. *Huffington Post*. Retrieved from https://www.huffpost.com/entry/instagram-influencers-beauty_n_5aa13616e4b002df2c6163bc

Brucculieri, J. (2018b, February 22). "Snapchat dysmorphia" points to a troubling new trend in plastic surgery. *Huffington Post*. Retrieved from https://www.huffpost.com/entry/snapchat-dysmorphia_n_5a8d8168e4b0273053a680f6

Brucculieri, J. (2019, March 6). Teenage girls in this photo series show the scary effects of editing apps. *Huffington Post*. Retrieved from https://www.huffpost

.com/entry/rankin-selfie-harm-photo-series_l_5c7d35e0e4b0e5e313cd4a70?ncid=newsltushpmglifestyle__Lifestyle__03062019

Bruch, H. (1973). *Eating disorders: Obesity, anorexia nervosa, and the person within*. New York: Basic Books.

Carey, B. (2019a, March 5). Fast-acting depression drug, newly approved, could help millions. *New York Times*. Retrieved from http://www.nytimes.com

Carey, B. (2019b, March 5). How to quit antidepressants: Very slowly, doctors say. *New York Times*. Retrieved from http://www.nytimes.com

Carroll, D. (2014). *The importance of trust and curiosity in treatment*. Retrieved from https://www.nclap.org/importance-trust-curiosity-treatment/

Chapin, A. (2016, June 6). For Muslims with eating disorders, Ramadan can pose a dangerous choice. *The Cut*. Retrieved from https://www.thecut.com/2016/06/muslims-eating-disorders-ramadan.html

Chosen Bays, J. (2017). *Mindful eating: A guide to rediscovering a healthy and joyful relationship with food*. New York: Penguin Random House.

Cohen, M. A. (2013). *Lasagna for lunch: Declaring peace with emotional eating*. New York: New Forge Press.

Cohen, M. A. (2016). *French toast for breakfast: Declaring peace with emotional eating*. New York: New Forge Press.

Cooper, D. M. (n.d.). *Identifying eating disorder issues in the Muslim community*. Retrieved from https://www.eatingdisorderhope.com/blog/identifying-eating-disorder-issues-in-the-muslim-community

Council of National Psychological Associations for the Advancement of Ethnic Minority Interests. (2003). *Psychological treatment of ethnic minority populations*. Washington, DC: Association of Black Psychologists.

Cozolino, L. (2004). *The making of a therapist*. New York: W. W. Norton.

Cozolino, L. (2014). *The neuroscience of human relationships: Attachment and the developing social brain* (2nd ed.). New York: W. W. Norton.

Davis, H., & Attia, E. (2017). Pharmacotherapy of eating disorders. *Current Opinion in Psychiatry, 30*, 452–457. doi:10.1097/YCO.0000000000000358

Davis, W. N. (2009, Winter). Individual therapy for eating disorders: Getting a good start. *Perspectives*, 5–7.

Dayton, T. (2008). *Emotional sobriety*. Boca Raton, FL: Health Communications.

de Peyer, J. (2016). Uncanny communication and the porous mind. *Psychoanalytic Dialogues, 26*, 156–174.

Dretzin, R., & Maggio, J. (Producers). (2008, January 22). Growing up online [Television series episode]. *Frontline*. Retrieved from https://www.pbs.org/wgbh/frontline/film/kidsonline/

Eating Disorders. (n.d.). *Antidepressants for eating disorders*. Retrieved from https://eatingdisorders.com/blogs/s/antidepressants-for-eating-disorders

Edelman, H. (2006). *Motherless daughters*. Boston: Da Capo Press.

EDReferral.com. (n.d.). *What are the medications or drugs to treat eating disorders?* Retrieved from https://www.edreferral.com/ed-medications

Ensler, E. (2019). *Apology*. New York: Bloomsbury.

Essig, T. (2018, June 7). Sleepwalking towards artificial intimacy. How psychotherapy is failing the future. *Forbes*. Retrieved from https://www.forbes.com

Feldman, M. B., & Meyer, I. H. (2007). Childhood abuse and eating disorders in gay and bisexual men. *International Journal of Eating Disorders, 40*, 418–423. doi:10.1002/eat.20378

Fitzsimons, T. (2019, January 30). N.J. to become fourth state with gender-neutral birth certificate option. *New York Times*. Retrieved from http://www.nytimes.com

Flores, P. (2004). *Addiction as an attachment disorder.* New York: Jason Aronson.

Forester, D. (2019). EMDR. In A. Seubert & P. Virdi (Eds.), *Trauma-informed approaches to eating disorders* (pp. 165–177). New York: Springer.

Fradkin, H. (2012). *Joining forces: Empowering male survivors*. Carlsbad, CA: Hay House.

Frankfeldt, V. (2019, June 14). Digital communication in psychoanalysis: An oxymoron? *Psychoanalytic Social Work*. Retrieved from https://static1.squarespace.com/static/57ce11e5d482e9784e52f046/t/5d102cbc45897f00010ecf89/1561341116947/Digital1Comm.1PDF1post.pdf

Fries, J. (2017). Eating disorders in sexual and gender minorities. In J. Fries & V. Sullivan (Eds.), *Eating disorders in special populations*. Boca Raton, FL: CRC Press.

Fuller, B. (2015, March 19). Human Barbie: Lacy Wildd having 37th surgery to look like plastic doll. *Hollywood Life*. Retrieved from https://hollywoodlife.com/2015/03/19/human-barbie-lacey-wildd-plastic-surgery-pics/

Gahnem, S. (2017, October 30). *Liberated in fashion: How I can express myself in all modesty.* Retrieved from http://www.adiosbarbie.com/2017/10/liberated-fashion-can-express-modesty/

Gay & Lesbian Alliance Against Defamation. (n.d.). *Glossary of terms—Transgender*. Retrieved from https://www.glaad.org/reference/transgender

Gentile, K. (2007). *Creating bodies: Eating disorders as self-destructive survival.* Hillsdale, NJ: Analytic Press.

Getz, L. (2019). Web-based intervention plays preventive role for teen depression. *Social Work Today*. Retrieved from https://www.socialworktoday.com/news/enews_0319_1.shtml

Gillespie, C. W. (2018). *Putting together the puzzle pieces of full eating disorder recovery.* Seattle: Kindle Direct Publishing, Amazon.

Gillespie, C. (2019). Weighing in on eating disorder issues. *Eating Disorder Journal, 20*(5). Retrieved from https://www.edreferral.com/journal/the-eating-disorder-journal-may-2019-vol-20-no-5

Goldberg, C. (2019, January 11). *Study: Bias drops dramatically for sexual orientation and race—but not weight.* Retrieved from https://www.wbur.org/commonhealth/2019/01/11/implicit-bias-gay-black-weight?utm_sq=fzdyts98jd

Gorden, C. (2015, February 25). Eating disorders in the Orthodox Jewish community. *Contemporary Psychoanalysis in Action*. Retrieved from https://www.psychologytoday.com/us/blog/contemporary-psychoanalysis-in-action/201502/eating-disorders-in-the-orthodox-jewish-community

Gottlieb, L. (2019). *Maybe you should talk to someone.* Boston: Houghton Mifflin Harcourt.

Grinker, R. R. (2018, December 6). Being trans is not a mental disorder. *New York Times*. Retrieved from http://www.nytimes.com

Grohol, J. M. (2018, July 8). *Google and Facebook, therapists and clients*. Retrieved from https://psychcentral.com/blog/google-and-facebook-therapists-and-clients/

Groshong, L., & Aronson, M. (2019). *LCSWs and the use of texting in mental health treatment*. Retrieved from https://www.clinicalsocialworkassociation.org/resources/Documents/CSWA%20-%20Text%20Therapy%20-%205-22-19.pdf?utm_source=Copy+of+Copy+of+E-News+-+6-7-19&utm_campaign=E-News+-+2-24-17&utm_medium=email

Gunnars, K. (2018, February 6). *5 obesogens: Artificial chemicals that make you fat*. Retrieved from https://www.healthline.com/nutrition/5-chemicals-that-are-making-you-fat

Haidrani, S. (2016, June 10). The unspoken challenges of having an eating disorder during Ramadan. *Vice*. Retrieved from https://broadly.vice.com/en_us/article/4xkkdn/the-unspoken-challenges-of-having-an-eating-disorder-during-ramadan

Hall, C. I. (1995). Asian eyes: Body image and eating disorders of Asian and Asian American women. *Eating Disorders: The Journal of Treatment & Prevention, 3*, 8–19.

Hall, J. (2004). *Roadblocks on the journey of psychotherapy*. New York: Jason Aronson.

Harrison, C. (2018). *Debate: A conversation on weight management and health at every size*. Retrieved from https://convertkit.s3.amazonaws.com/landing_pages/incentives/000/448/070/original/Christy_Harrison_FNCE_Slides.pdf?1542161742

Harvard Health Publishing. (2019, June 24). *Why people become overweight*. Retrieved from https://www.health.harvard.edu/staying-healthy/why-people-become-overweight

Healthline. (n.d.). *Can antidepressants treat binge eating disorder?* Retrieved from https://www.healthline.com/health/eating-disorders/antidepressants-for-binge-eating#1

Helton, S. (2014, April 22). *Pro-Ana: "Thinspiration" and social media*. Retrieved from https://www.thefix.com/content/pro-ana-%E2%80%98thin%E2%80%99-inspiration-social-media

Hendricks, S. (2016, May 4). *Japan's healthcare system is failing thousands of women*. Retrieved from https://www.medelita.com/blog/japan-mental-health-women/

Hirschmann, J., & Munter, C. (2008). *Overcoming overeating*. New York: OO Publishing.

Hobbes, M. (2018, October 8). Weight stigma is one of the last socially acceptable forms of discrimination. *Huffington Post*. Retrieved from https://www.huffpost.com/entry/obesity-health-fat-shaming-stigma_n_5bbb93b9e4b028e1fe400979

Hocine, A. (2018, May 16). What it's like to have an eating disorder during Ramadan. *Teen Vogue*. Retrieved from https://www.teenvogue.com/

Hollis, J. (2003). *Fat is a family affair*. St. Paul, MN: Hazelden.

Hosie, R. (2018, February 6). More people want surgery to look like a filtered version of themselves rather than a celebrity, cosmetic doctor says. *Independent*. Retrieved from https://www.independent.co.uk/life-style/cosmetic-surgery-snapchat-instagram-filters-demand-celebrities-doctor-dr-esho-london-a8197001.html

Hospers, H. J., & Jansen, A. (2005). Why homosexuality is a risk factor for eating disorders in males. *Journal of Social and Clinical Psychology, 24*, 1188–1201.

Hunter, S., & Hickerson, J. (2003). *Affirmative practice: Understanding and working with lesbian, gay, bisexual, and transgender persons*. Washington, DC: NASW Press.

Internet World Stats. (2019). *Usage and population statistics*. Retrieved from https://www.internetworldstats.com/stats.htm

Irving, W. (1899). In J. Wood (Comp.), *Dictionary of quotations*. Retrieved from https://www.bartleby.com/345/authors/258.html

Islam and Eating Disorders. (n.d.). *Islam and eating disorders*. Retrieved from http://waragainsteatingdisorder.com/

Islam Eating Disorders. (2015, June 5). *Islam and eating disorders: Male eating disorders. Message from Turkey* [Video]. Retrieved from https://www.youtube.com/watch?v=Nxxc6VBS3ZU

Jasper, K. (1989). *Are eating disorders addictions?* Retrieved from https://nedic.ca/download-file/1540817018.14092-12/

Joelson, R. (2016). *Help me! A psychotherapist's tried-and-true techniques for a happier relationship with yourself and the people you love*. New York: Health Psychology Press.

Johnson, C. (1985). The initial consultation for patients with bulimia and anorexia nervosa. In D. Garner & P. Garfinkel (Eds.), *The handbook of psychotherapy of anorexia and bulimia* (pp. 9–51). New York: Guilford Press.

Jones, N. P., & Hitchcock, L. I. (2019). Evaluating technology use in client assessment: The BPD technology assessment checklist. *Social Work Today, 19*(2), 12–15. Retrieved from http://viewer.zmags.com/publication/73abbb6c#/73abbb6c/13

Karges, C. (n.d.). *How do antidepressants treat bulimia?* Retrieved from https://www.eatingdisorderhope.com/information/bulimia/how-do-antidepressants-treat-bulimia

Kaufman, G. (1985). *Shame: The power of caring*. Cambridge, MA: Schenkman Books.

Kesvani, H. (2015, June 26). This is what it's like to recover from an eating disorder during Ramadan. *Buzzfeed*. Retrieved from https://www.buzzfeed.com/husseinkesvani/this-is-what-its-like-to-recover-from-an-eating-disorder-dur

Khimji, Z. (n.d.). Eating disorders prevalent among Muslim girls. *Islamic Insights*. Retrieved from http://www.islamicinsights.com/news/community/eating-disorders-prevalent-among-muslim-girls.html

Kim, E. A. (2003, January 27). Asian Americans and eating disorders: A silent struggle. *Seattle Pi*. Retrieved from https://www.seattlepi.com/lifestyle/article/Asian-Americans-and-eating-disorders-A-silent-1106134.php

Kim-Ju, G., & Akutsu, P. (2015). Racial and ethnic identities of Asian Americans: Understanding unique and common experiences. In E. P. Salett & D. R. Koslow (Eds.), *Multicultural perspectives on race, ethnicity, and identity* (pp. 85–104). Washington, DC: NASW Press.

Knoll, J. (2019, June 8). Smash the wellness industry. *New York Times*. Retrieved from http://www.nytimes.com

Koenig, K. R. (2019, June 24). Three steps to challenge internalized weight stigma. *Social Work Today*. Retrieved from https://www.socialworktoday.com/archive/exc_0719.shtml

Kubler-Ross, E. (1969). *On death and dying*. New York: Scribner.

Kunst, J. (2012, August 8). Got curiosity? The drive that everyone is talking about. *Psychology Today*. Retrieved from https://www.psychologytoday.com/us/blog/headshrinkers-guide-the-galaxy/201208/got-curiosity

Kwon, R. O. (2019, March 23). Stop calling Asian women adorable. *New York Times*. Retrieved from http://www.nytimes.com

Lemma, A. (2017). *The digital age on the couch*. London: Routledge.

Linehan, M. (2014). *DBT skills training manual* (2nd ed.). New York: Guilford Press.

Lisi, B. (2017, February 6). See it: "Human Ken doll" Rodrigo Alves can't breathe properly after having 50 plastic surgeries. *New York Daily News*. Retrieved from https://www.nydailynews.com/entertainment/tv/human-ken-doll-breathe-properly-due-plastic-surgery-article-1.2965595

Louie, S. (2013). *Asian shame and addiction: Suffering in silence*. Bellevue, WA: Author.

Lynch, W. C., Heil, D. P., Wagner, E., & Havens, M. D. (2007). Ethnic differences in BMI, weight concerns, and eating behaviors: Comparison of Native American, White, and Hispanic adolescents. *Body Image, 4*, 179–190. doi:10.1016/j.bodyim.2007.01.001

Mabe, A. G., Forney, K. J., & Keel, P. K. (2014). Do you "like" my photo? Facebook use maintains eating disorder risk. *International Journal of Eating Disorders, 47*, 516–523. doi:10.1002/eat.22254

Malina, S. (2019, Feb. 25). *Four ways to support LGBTQ youth during National Eating Disorder Awareness Week*. Retrieved from https://www.hrc.org/blog/four-ways-to-support-lgbtq-youth-during-national-eating-disorder-awareness

Marborough, L. (2009, December 13). The legal dangers of rough sex. *Daily Beast*. Retrieved from https://www.thedailybeast.com/the-legal-dangers-of-rough-sex

Markowicz, K. (2018, February 4). It's not anti-feminist to want to look good. *New York Times*. Retrieved from http://www.nytimes.com

Mayo Clinic. (n.d.). Body dysmorphic disorder. Retrieved from https://www.mayoclinic.org/diseases-conditions/body-dysmorphic-disorder/symptoms-causes/syc-20353938

Metro Health. (n.d.). Antidepressant medicines for eating disorders. *Metro Health*. Retrieved from https://metrohealth.net/healthwise/antidepressant-medicines-for-eating-disorders/

Mlotek, H. (2019, March 20). A dating app for three, plus. *New York Times*. Retrieved from http://www.nytimes.com

Montecatini. (n.d.). *Antidepressants and eating disorders*. Retrieved from https://www.montecatinieatingdisorder.com/eating-disorders/articles/antidepressants-and-ed/

Morrison, T. (1999). *The bluest eye*. New York: Vintage Books.

Muhlheim, L. (2019, June 20). *Medications used to treat eating disorders*. Retrieved from https://www.verywellmind.com/medications-used-to-treat-eating-disorders-4153046

Murrell, S. (2015, July 2). *To choke or not*. Retrieved from https://www.nuvo.net/voices/ask_the_sex_doc/to-choke-or-not/article_0f895d2d-690c-576d-8b3e-48e393170708.html

MuslimGirl.com. (n.d.). *10 years of MuslimGirl.com: Our top 8 video highlights*. Retrieved from http://muslimgirl.com/53737/10-years-of-muslim-girl-com-8-milestone-vids/

National Association of Anorexia Nervosa and Associated Disorders. (n.d.-a). *Eating disorder statistics*. Retrieved from https://anad.org/education-and-awareness/about-eating-disorders/eating-disorders-statistics/The Illusionists

National Association of Anorexia Nervosa and Associated Disorders. (n.d.-b). *Eating disorders and the Internet*. Retrieved from https://web.archive.org/web/20101019032231/http://www.anad.org/get-information/eating-disorders-and-the-internet/

National Association of Social Workers. (2015). *Standards and indicators for cultural competence in social work practice*. Washington, DC: Author.

National Association of Social Workers. (n.d.-a). *Lesbian, gay, bisexual & transgender (LGBT)*. Retrieved from https://www.socialworkers.org/practice/LGBT

National Association of Social Workers. (n.d.-b). *LGBTQIA conferences*. Retrieved from https://www.socialworkers.org/practice/LGBT

National Association of Social Workers. (n.d.-c). *National Committee on Lesbian, Gay, Bisexual & Transgender Issues (NCLGBTI)*. Retrieved from https://www.socialworkers.org/About/Governance/National-Appointments/National-Committees/Committee-on-LGBT-Issues

National Association of Social Workers, Association of Social Work Boards, Council on Social Work Education, & Clinical Social Work Association. (2017). *NASW, ASWB, CSWE, & CSWA standards for technology in social work practice*. Washington, DC: National Association of Social Workers.

National Association of Social Workers, New York City chapter. (2019). *Position on racism and oppressive practices within social work*. Retrieved from https://cdn.ymaws.com/www.naswnyc.org/resource/resmgr/statements_and_important_news/2019/final_statement_on_racism_03.pdf

National Eating Disorders Association. (n.d.). *Eating disorders in LGBTQ+ populations*. Retrieved from https://www.nationaleatingdisorders.org/learn/general-information/lgbtq

National LGBT Health Education Center. (2018, February). *Addressing eating disorders, body dissatisfaction, and obesity among sexual and gender minority youth*. Boston: Author.

Nauert, R. (2014, March 6). Facebook tied to higher risk of eating disorders. *PsychCentral*. Retrieved from https://psychcentral.com/news/2014/03/06/facebook-tied-to-higher-risk-of-eating-disorders/66756.html

Nauert, R. (2015, April 20). Young women compare themselves on social media. *PsychCentral*. Retrieved from https://psychcentral.com/news/2015/04/20/young-women-compare-themselves-on-social-media/83713.html

Nelson, J. (1998). The meaning of crying based on attachment theory. *Clinical Social Work Journal, 26*, 15–18.

New York State Society for Clinical Social Work. (2018, November). *Code of ethics*. Retrieved from https://nysscsw.memberclicks.net/assets/code%20of%20ethics%202018%20final.pdf

Norische. (2014, March 21). *Take your breath away: Basics of breath play*. Retrieved from https://dominantguide.com/176/take-your-breath-away-basics-of-breath-play/

Nusbaum, G. (2006). Interest or intrusion? Navigating the thin line and what is in between in a psychoanalytic group for women with incest traumas and eating disorders. *GROUP, 30*, 359–374.

Oberg, B. (2016, April 11). *Mental health needs of the Native American community*. Retrieved from https://www.healthyplace.com/blogs/recoveringfrommentalillness/2016/04/mental-health-needs-of-the-native-american-community

Ofer, G., & Durban, J. (1999). Curiosity: Reflections on its nature and functions. *American Journal of Psychotherapy, 53*, 35–51. doi:10.1176/appi.psychotherapy.1999.53.1.35

OUCommunityServices. (2013, June 5). *Hungry to be heard* [Documentary]. Retrieved from https://www.youtube.com/watch?v=KaCCAx04H8M

Peeke, P. (2014, April 24). What's the difference between white fat and brown fat? *Women's Health*. Retrieved from https://www.womenshealthmag.com/health/a19896462/fat-facts/

People staff. (2015, October 15). French couple spends more than $300,000 on plastic surgery to look like Barbie and Ken. *People*. Retrieved from https://people.com/bodies/couple-gets-plastic-surgery-to-look-like-barbie-and-ken/

Perez, M., Ramirez, A. L., & Trujillo-ChiVacuán, E. (Eds.). (2019). Special issue on the state of the art research on treatment and prevention of eating disorders on ethnic minorities [Special issue]. *Eating Disorders, 27*(2).

Petrocelli, A. M. (2012). *Prejudice to pride: Moving from homophobia to acceptance*. Washington, DC: NASW Press.

Philipps, D. (2019, March 13). New rule for transgender troops: Stick to your birth sex, or leave. *New York Times*. Retrieved from http://www.nytimes.com

Pierre, J. (2015, October 29). Dracula on the couch: The psychiatry of vampires. *Psychology Today*. Retrieved from https://www.psychologytoday.com/intl/blog/psych-unseen/201510/dracula-the-couch-the-psychiatry-vampires

Pipher, M., & Gilliam, S. P. (2019, August 15). The lonely burden of today's teenage girls. *Wall Street Journal*. Retrieved from https://www.wsj.com

Plastic Surgery Fact. (n.d.). *Barbie woman plastic surgery before and after photos*. Retrieved from https://plasticsurgeryfact.com/barbie-woman-plastic-surgery-before-and-after-photos/

Pro-ana. (n.d.). *Wikipedia*. Retrieved from https://en.wikipedia.org/wiki/Pro-ana

Prochaska, J., Norcross, J., & DiClemente, C. (1994). *Changing for good*. New York: William Morrow.

Rabin, R. C. (2011, April 11). Rabbis sound an alarm over eating disorders. *New York Times*. Retrieved from http://www.nytimes.com

RAINN Organization. (n.d.). *Statistics*. Retrieved from https://www.rainn.org/statistics

Raymond, A. (2019, May 3). *Disordered eating to intuitive eating: Supporting your clients in repairing their relationship with food*. Retrieved from https://empoweredeatingrd.com/ditching-diet-culture/disordered-eating-to-intuitive-eating-supporting-your-clients-in-repairing-their-relationship-with-food/

Redefining Wellness. (2019). *Redefining wellness: The ultimate diet-free guide for teens & families*. New York: Author.

Richardson, T. (2012). *The power of ONE*. Retrieved from http://www.eatingdisordersrecoverytoday.com/the-power-of-one

Roetman, S. (2015, November 12). *Decolonizing eating disorder treatments*. Retrieved from http://www.adiosbarbie.com/2015/11/decolonizing-eating-disorder-treatments/

Root, M.P.P. (1993). *Bill of rights for racially mixed people*. Retrieved from https://www.safehousealliance.org/wp-content/uploads/2012/10/A-Bill-of-Rights-for-Racially-Mixed-People.pdf

Ross, C. C. (2012). Eight surprising parallels between food and drug addiction. *Psychology Today*. Retrieved from https://www.psychologytoday.com/us/blog/real-healing/201209/eight-surprising-parallels-between-food-and-drug-addictions

Ross, C. C. (2017). *The food addiction recovery workbook*. Oakland, CA: New Harbinger.

Rossini, E. (Producer and director). (2015). *The illusionists* [Motion picture]. Italy. Retrieved from https://theillusionists.org/watch/

Roth, G. (1993). *Breaking free from compulsive eating*. Indianapolis, IN: Bobbs Merrill.

Rothschild, B. (2000). *The body remembers: The psychophysiology of trauma and trauma treatment*. New York: W. W. Norton.

Safer, D. L., Telch, C. F., & Chen, E. Y. (2009). *Dialectical behavior therapy for binge eating and bulimia*. New York: Guilford Press.

Sage, M., & Eaton, M. (2019). Evaluating health apps. *Social Work Today, 19*(2), 8–9. Retrieved from http://viewer.zmags.com/publication/73abbb6c#/73abbb6c/9

Scheel, J. (n.d.). *PTSD and eating disorders: A clinical understanding of symptoms representing victim and abuser.* Retrieved from https://www.nationaleatingdisorders.org/blog/ptsd-and-eating-disorders-clinical-understanding-symptoms-representing-victim-and-abuser

Schischa, R. (2011, March 9). Rabba, therapist team up to fight eating disorders. *Forward.* Retrieved from https://forward.com/sisterhood/135977/rabba-therapist-team-up-to-fight-eating-disorders/

Seubert, A. (2018). Becoming known: A relational model utilizing gestalt and ego state-assisted EMDR in treating eating disorders. *Journal of EMDR Practice and Research, 12*(2), 71–86. doi:10.1891/1933-3196.12.2.71

Shanahan, M. (n.d.). *Psychological perspectives on vampire mythology.* Retrieved from https://thewebofnarcissism.blogspot.com/2010/12/psychological-perspective-on-vampire.html

Shapiro, F., & Forrest, M. S. (2004). *EMDR: The breakthrough therapy for anxiety, stress and trauma.* New York: Basic Books.

Sheppard, K. (1993). *Food addiction.* Boca Raton, FL: Health Communications.

Sidhu, H. (2019, March 27). 8 Muslim woman characters challenging stereotypes in entertainment. *Teen Vogue.* Retrieved from https://www.teenvogue.com

Smith-Theodore, D. (2018, September 4). The eating disorder trap: Dancers and the illusion of perfectionism. *Pointe.* Retrieved from https://www.pointemagazine.com

Smolar, L. (n.d.). *Fitbit's new device for kids is extremely problematic—Here's why.* Retrieved from https://www.nationaleatingdisorders.org/blog/fitbits-new-device-kids-extremely-problematic-heres-why

Strean, H. (1992). *Why people fail.* Tarrytown, NY: Wynwood Press.

Striegel-Moore, R. H., Rosselli, F., Holtzman, N., Dierker, L., & Swaney, G. (2011). Behavioral symptoms of eating disorders in Native Americans: Results from the ADD Health Survey Wave III. *International Journal of Eating Disorders, 44,* 561–566. doi:10.1002.eat.20894

Sue, D. W. (2010). *Microaggressions in everyday life: Race, gender, and sexual orientation.* New York: Wiley.

Sue, D. W., Capodilupo, C. M., Torino, G. C., Bucceri, J. M., Holder, A. M., Nadal, K. L., & Esquilin, M. (2007). Racial microaggressions in everyday life: Implications for clinical practice. *American Psychologist, 62,* 271–286. doi:10.1037/0003-066X.62.4.271

Syed, Z. (n.d.). Photoshopped reality. *Islamic Insights.* Retrieved from http://www.islamicinsights.com/news/community/photoshopped-reality.html

Taffel, R. (2018, November/December). The "millennial effect": How young clients are leading therapists to new places. *Psychotherapy Networker.* Retrieved from https://www.psychotherapynetworker.org/magazine/article/2321/no-more-same-old

Tarman, V. (2019). *Food junkies: Recovery from food addiction.* Toronto: Dundurn.

Thich, N. H., & Cheung, L. (2010). *Savor: Mindful eating, mindful life.* New York: HarperCollins.

Thompson, B. (1994). *A hunger so wide and so deep: A multiracial view of women's eating problems.* Minneapolis: University of Minnesota Press.

Trevor Project. (n.d.). *Eating disorders among LGBTQ youth: A 2018 national assessment.* Retrieved from https://www.nationaleatingdisorders.org/sites/default/files/nedaw18/NEDA%20-Trevor%20Project%202018%20Survey%20-%20Full%20Results.pdf

Tribole, E., & Resch, E. (2012). *Intuitive eating.* New York: St. Martin's Press.

Turkle, S. (2015). *Reclaiming conversation: The power of talk in a digital age.* New York: Penguin Press.

Van Pelt, J. (2009). Eating disorders on the Web—The pro-ana/pro-mia movement. *Social Work Today, 9*(5), 20. Retrieved from https://www.socialworktoday.com/

Vega, N. (2019, February 13). Apple pressured to remove Saudi app that allows oppression of women. *New York Post.* Retrieved from https://nypost.com

Walsh, B. T. (2013). The enigmatic persistence of anorexia nervosa. *American Journal of Psychiatry, 170,* 477–484.

Warner, S. (1966). *Self-realization and self-defeat.* New York: Grove Press.

WebMD. (n.d.). *Types of depression.* Retrieved from https://www.webmd.com/depression/guide/depression-types#1

Whitefield, A. (2011, October 5). Turning a blind eye to eating disorders. *Indian Country Today.* Retrieved from https://newsmaven.io/indiancountrytoday/archive/turning-a-blind-eye-to-eating-disorders-NRUCjmXKCkO_zJB8Nd8Xmg/

Whitfield, C. (1987). *Healing the child within.* Boca Raton, FL: Health Communications.

Wilson, B. (2015). *Alcoholics anonymous.* New York: AA World Services.

Winnicott, D. W. (1953). Transitional objects and transitional phenomena: A study of the first not-me possession. *International Journal of Psychoanalysis, 34,* 89–97.

Wong, B. (2019, July 31). This photo shoot featuring Asian women is stunningly diverse. *Huffington Post.* Retrieved from https://www.huffpost.com/entry/asian-plus-size-curve-models_l_5d41c6c0e4b0db8affb25177?ncid=newsltushpmgnews__TheMorningEmail__080219

Index

In this index, *f* stands for figure and *n* stands for footnote.

About the Author

Mary Anne Cohen, LCSW, BCD, is a social work therapist and has been a member of the National Association of Social Workers (NASW) since 1972. She has served as the director of the New York Center for Eating Disorders since founding the center in 1982. She has treated hundreds of people with a wide range of eating disorders, supervises social work therapists, and has written two internationally acclaimed books on this topic: *French Toast for Breakfast: Declaring Peace with Emotional Eating* and *Lasagna for Lunch: Declaring Peace with Emotional Eating.*

Cohen offers professional training workshops to social workers on eating disorders and body image at the NASW Addictions Institute, the New York State Society for Clinical Social Work (Metropolitan, Staten Island, and Rockland County chapters), and the New York University School of Social Work and provides trainings for social workers in hospitals, eating disorder treatment centers, and alcoholism facilities.

She has been the professional book reviewer for EDReferral.com (Eating Disorder Referral and Information Center) since 2014. She created a continuing education training webinar for social workers and mental health professionals, "Declaring Peace with Emotional Eating," for Gurze.com, and both her books have been turned into continuing education courses for mental health professionals (see https://secure.ce-credit.com). Cohen also broadcast a weekly radio show for three years on the topic of eating disorders on AM and FM radio stations to New York City and the tristate area, interviewing experts in the field throughout the United States.

About the Author

[illegible]